W9-BBO-530

d20.
PSk

WITHDRAWN
FROM
COLLECTION

FORDHAM
UNIVERSITY
LIBRARIES

METAPHYSICS

METAPHYSICS

D. W. HAMLYN

Professor of Philosophy, Birkbeck College,
University of London

Fordham University
New York, N. Y.

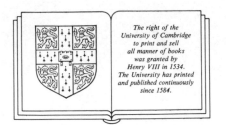

The right of the
University of Cambridge
to print and sell
all manner of books
was granted by
Henry VIII in 1534.
The University has printed
and published continuously
since 1584.

CAMBRIDGE UNIVERSITY PRESS

CAMBRIDGE
LONDON NEW YORK NEW ROCHELLE
MELBOURNE SYDNEY

BD
111
.H25
1984
COP.

Published by the Press Syndicate of the University of Cambridge
The Pitt Building, Trumpington Street, Cambridge CB2 1RP
32 East 57th Street, New York, NY 10022, USA
296 Beaconsfield Parade, Middle Park, Melbourne 3206, Australia

© Cambridge University Press 1984

First published 1984

Printed in Great Britain by
The Pitman Press, Bath

Library of Congress catalogue card number: 84 – 1881

British Library Cataloguing in Publication Data
Hamlyn, D.W.
Metaphysics
1. Metaphysics
I. Title
100   BD11

ISBN 0 521 24449 8 hard covers
ISBN 0 521 28690 5 paperback

Fordham University
LIBRARY
AT
LINCOLN CENTER
New York, N. Y.

BO

Contents

Preface

I am indebted to Jonathan Sinclair-Wilson of Cambridge University Press for suggesting that I write this book and for encouraging it on its way. I hope that it may prove something of a companion piece to my *The Theory of Knowledge* (Macmillan, 1971). At all events, the thanks that I expressed in that book to Birkbeck College students are due again here. I have lectured on metaphysics at the College for more years than I care to remember, and successive generations of students have criticized, probed and commented on the views that I have expressed, in the way that Birkbeck students are ever willing to do. My debt to them is vast and I shall always be grateful.

Parts of a draft of the book were also read at a seminar which I, together with Mrs Dorothy Edgington, gave at the College. I am grateful for many comments made by her and others at the seminar.

I owe a very special debt to Mr Ian McFetridge who kindly read the first draft of the book and who made comments and criticisms which have been invaluable. He has saved me from many mistakes. Apart from the criticisms which he made, I am very grateful to him for the encouragement that his remarks afforded.

Thanks are due to other colleagues and students for points which are too numerous to mention. I am grateful, finally, to Mrs Georgia Wyver and Miss Maureen Cartwright for secretarial assistance of many kinds and for general help with the book.

1. Introduction

What is metaphysics?

It is not easy to set out exactly what metaphysics is, and the whole question of what it is has often been thought problematic. From time to time it has even been doubted whether it really exists or is possible. The origins of the *term* 'metaphysics' are, however, clear enough. The word is the title of one of Aristotle's works, or rather it is the title that was given to a certain compilation of Aristotelian writings in the ancient world, probably in the library at Alexandria. The compilation was so called because it seemed to those responsible for it to consist of works coming after those on physics (*meta ta phusika*). The title was in that sense a library classification. The correctness of the library classification would imply that there was at least a similarity of theme in those writings. It would not necessarily suggest that Aristotle himself had any conception of a distinct discipline, an autonomous branch of philosophy, the exposition of which was to be found there. Indeed, in the work that we now have under the title *Metaphysics* Aristotle discusses matters which have, to say the least, a considerable overlap with those discussed in the *Physics* and in other works of his.

It would be a mistake nevertheless to suggest that there is not in the *Metaphysics* discussion of issues which have a definite similarity to and continuity with those discussed by later philosophers under the same heading. One of the questions that Aristotle raises in his work is about the possibility of a science of being-*qua*-being. There are problems about the interpretation of that conception, especially about the sense of 'being' that is involved, but one can say roughly that what Aristotle had in mind was a form of knowledge of what is, simply in respect of its being such and not in respect of its being a thing of a certain kind. In Aristotle's view the aim of the special sciences is to make clear the nature of specific kinds of thing – of natural bodies, of living things, and so on. The question now raised is whether it is possible to inquire fruitfully about what it is simply to be, without reference to specific kinds of thing. It is equivalent to the question whether a general ontology is possible, whether, that is, it is possible and useful to say anything about what

1

there is at a more abstract and general level than is provided by inquiries into the existence and nature of specific kinds of thing, such as physical or biological things.

Plato had tried in his *Sophist* to provide an account of 'being' and of the connexion of that notion with other very general notions such as 'sameness' and 'difference'. In that context, however, it was implied that those terms were the names of certain abstract entities which he called 'Forms'; and Aristotle would have no truck with such entities. Scholars have tried to set out Aristotle's own answers to his question – answers which may have varied from time to time; but these need not concern us in detail. What is important for present purposes is the conception of an inquiry into being in general – general ontology, or what mediaeval philosophers called *metaphysica generalis*, as opposed to *metaphysica specialis*.

In the popular mind the term 'metaphysical' has come to signify any form of reasoning (and for that matter other things too) which is excessively general, abstract and subtle. Among philosophers, from Descartes onwards, it has come to have the distinct sense of having to do with what lies beyond what is available to the senses – with what is not merely abstract but in some sense transcendent also. When Kant came to put forward his criticisms of contemporary metaphysics – speculative metaphysics as he called it – in his *Critique of Pure Reason* in the eighteenth century, he characterized metaphysics in two ways: first, in terms of its subject-matter, saying that the main concerns of metaphysics were God, freedom and immortality; second, in terms of the form of the judgments that it involved, saying that it was a necessary condition of metaphysics that it should involve judgments which are synthetic *a priori*, i.e. judgments which purport to be informative and not true merely because of the relations between the concepts presupposed in them (synthetic) and which also purport to provide knowledge the validation of claims to which is possible without reference to sense-experience (*a priori*).[1] Whether or not the latter is true of all metaphysical judgments, the characterization does not do much to make clear what metaphysics is. Moreover, Kant's own substitution for metaphysics, his so-called 'critical philosophy', the aim of which is to establish the bounds of pure reason, relied equally upon synthetic *a priori* judgments.

Kant's specification of metaphysics in terms of its subject-matter is,

---

[1]   For further accounts of these terms see my *Theory of Knowledge* (London and Basingstoke: Macmillan, 1971), ch. 9, or articles on them in P. Edwards (ed.), *Encyclopaedia of Philosophy* (New York and London: Collier-Macmillan, 1967).

although often quoted, idiosyncratic even in relation to the metaphys-icians of his time. A great many philosophers have, of course, had things to say about God and about the problem of the freedom of the will, although rather fewer have had any real concern with immortality. It cannot be denied that many of those philosophers whom we have come to think of as metaphysicians have discussed issues which relate to these ideas. Nevertheless, such issues do not seem to be the central concern of, say, Spinoza and Leibniz, let alone Berkeley and Hume. (Such a judg-ment might be disputed, particularly perhaps in the light of Spinoza's concern with God and freedom, but there is a sense in which it remains true all the same. I shall not myself be concerned with the issues in ques-tion, although I shall return in the last chapter to the reason why.) Yet a basic issue between Spinoza and Leibniz is the nature of the underlying reality which reason tells us must be so, whatever the senses tell us. In other words: What is the nature of substance(s)? Must there be only one of these or many, and if the latter how many? These are metaphysical issues indeed.

It is impossible to give a proper sense of the arguments over these issues without a detailed account of the views of these philosophers. Indeed, one of the difficulties in trying to give an account of the nature of metaphysics by abstracting it from its practitioners is that one is liable to get bogged down in history. It is in any case possible to see lines of continuity between Kant's 'critical philosophy', considered as an attempt to set out the necessary presuppositions of the human understanding, and some of the matters which are raised in Aristotle's *Metaphysics*. Hence what Kant saw as speculative metaphysics (con-sidered as an attempt to use pure reason to arrive at an account of a reality which transcends those presuppositions of human understanding) cannot be all that there is to metaphysics.

Moreover, metaphysics went on after Kant, even if sometimes in a slightly different dress – in, for example, Hegel and other nineteenth-century metaphysicians – most of whom thought that it was possible in one way or another to go beyond the limits which Kant thought he had shown as holding good for pure reason. There are also the anti-rationalist reactions to this in the various forms of existentialism, and a variety of returns to a pre-Kantian spirit in philosophy. The history of metaphysics, like history in general, is untidy.

In what follows, although I shall often illustrate the claims made by reference to figures in the history of philosophy, I shall simply present *one* view of metaphysics and of the forms that it can take. I do not wish, however, to imply that this is the only possible view or that this is all there is to be found in the history of the subject; but neither do I wish to suggest that what I have to say is without historical foundation. I think, indeed, that it is possible to detect in the history of thought two main conceptions of metaphysics, two trends in metaphysical thinking. They are not unconnected with each other and it may fairly be argued that under certain conditions one may lead to the other, and that this has been the case in the thinking of some philosophers. There is, however, no necessity that this should happen, and it is important to be clear about the considerations which suggest a distinction between the two conceptions.

Two concepts of metaphysics

The distinction which I have in mind is in a way implicit in what I have already said. It corresponds to a certain extent to a distinction between two kinds of metaphysics which is set out by P. F. Strawson at the beginning of his book *Individuals*, although, in my opinion, in a very misleading way. The distinction which he makes is one between, in his terms, descriptive and revisionary metaphysics. He characterizes his own book as an essay in descriptive metaphysics, and he sees Aristotle and Kant as two important forerunners of such a metaphysics. Those whom Kant called speculative metaphysicians are said to have practised revisionary metaphysics.

As expressed in these terms each arm of the distinction is misleading. Strawson suggests that the aim of descriptive metaphysics is simply to describe our conceptual scheme – an account of the matter which has given rise to some speculation about who the 'we' in question are. It is in any case clear that Kant, considered as a precedent for this type of metaphysics, was concerned to do more than merely *describe* reality as it manifests itself to the human understanding. His 'critical philosophy', as he saw it, involved synthetic *a priori* judgments, and Kant thought that such judgments must, because *a priori*, have the character of necessary truths. Hence he was not concerned to maintain that such and such is how reality appears to the understanding; he wished to claim that it *must* be like that. I think that the same sort of thing is true, although in a less obvious way, of Aristotle, and, when the implications of what he has to say are worked out, of Strawson himself. It is the claims to necessity that are involved which make it implausible to say that the aim of such philosophers is simply to describe 'our conceptual scheme', whether or not we can make sense of that notion.

The term 'revisionary metaphysics' is equally misleading, although in a different way. When Leibniz, for example, said that the true substances which lie at the basis of reality, the ultimate constituents of reality (to use Russell's phrase), were monads – absolutely simple things which, he said, correspond to the ego, 'le moi', in each of us and are therefore not material in any obvious sense – he was not trying to revise our ordinary ways of thinking about the world. He was led to his conclusion by way of an argument one of the premises of which is that what basically exists must be simple, because anything complex presupposes the constituents which go to make it complex and cannot in consequence be basic. Leibniz's conclusion that the only true substances are monads may well be thought strange, if only because nothing in experience directly suggests such a thing. But one who argues along such lines is philosophizing, and it seems clear that the philosophical view that Leibniz puts forward can properly be opposed only to a rival philosophical view. Hence if he is proposing a revision of anything it is a revision merely of other philosophical views on the same matter; and he does that because he thinks, rightly or wrongly, that he has sound reasons for doing so. There is in this no revision of what we ordinarily think, no revision of our conceptual scheme. Indeed it is questionable whether it makes sense to speak of how we ordinarily think on such matters, independent of argued philosophical theories. Furthermore, while there are no doubt many concepts which many of us use, it is not clear which of them we *all* use; so that it is very unclear what place there is for speaking of 'our conceptual scheme' or of revision of that.

Despite these criticisms, there is something in what Strawson has to say that reflects a real distinction. What is common to Strawson, Kant and the Aristotle that Strawson has in mind is that they all start from some very general feature of the relationship that we human beings may be taken to have with the world. Strawson starts from the fact that we as speakers may identify things for hearers and *vice versa*; Kant starts from the fact that we make judgments about things in virtue of a common sensibility and understanding; and Aristotle starts from the fact that the language in which we express our judgments about the world involves certain word–world relations. They then ask what must be the case with regard to the world, or with regard to what there is, if this is to be possible.

I spoke just now of the Aristotle whom Strawson has in mind; for what I have said applies to Aristotle's *Categories* and other early works. It is arguable that in the later written central books of his *Metaphysics* a different strand of thought begins to emerge, although it is not yet sufficiently different in a relevant respect for it to be classified as falling into the second kind of metaphysics that I shall distinguish. One of the main conclusions of the earlier strand of thought is that the world must contain substances and that it is only because of that fact that there can be other kinds of thing – qualities, quantities and the other so-called categories. One thing that Aristotle seems to be doing in the central books of the *Metaphysics* is to ask what sorts of thing deserve primarily to be called 'substance'. The result of this is that some things which are called 'substance' are seen as substances only in a secondary way. Even so Aristotle does *not* say that such things are not really substances at all. In the case of eighteenth-century rationalism the situation is different. Leibniz, for example, asks what real substances must be like, and answers that if, as he thinks, true substances must be absolutely simple, no ordinary thing can be a substance properly speaking – only monads. He thus takes the essential step into the second kind of metaphysics.

This second line of thought, in its full-blown form, presupposes in effect a distinction between appearance and reality, but one drawn for philosophical reasons in an other than common-sense way. Hence one might say that the distinction with which we have been concerned is a distinction between a type of metaphysics which sets out what must in a very general way be the case about the world and about ourselves if some known relationship between the two is to hold good, and a type of metaphysics which holds that only things answering to certain criteria are real, with the result that there are distinct realms to be called 'appearance' and 'reality' respectively. The first kind of metaphysics involves an account of certain necessary features of the world and of ourselves considered both as part of the world and as related to it in certain evident ways. That is in effect what Aristotle's science of being-*qua*-being comes to, and even when he argues that only certain things, e.g. God, can be substances in the primary way, he shows no inclination to draw a line between appearance and reality in any other than a common-sense way. For the distinction between what is primarily and what is secondarily X is not the same as the distinction between reality and appearance. With a philosopher like Leibniz the situation is quite different. Leibniz does suppose that ordinary things are merely appearance, merely phenomena, even if they constitute well-founded appearances (*phenomena bene fundata*). Hence the second kind of metaphysics, of which Leibniz is a representative, presupposes that distinction between appearance and reality. The thought that there may be reasons for distinguishing between what is primarily and what is secondarily X leads towards the second kind of metaphysics, but the final step is taken only when a distinction between two realms of appearance and reality is made also.

Philosophers from Aristotle to, say, Husserl have produced ontological classifications of entities on one basis or another. Such classifications are as interesting as the basis on which they are constructed. But when a philosopher says that such and such are the things that basically or ultimately exist, as opposed to other things which are to that extent secondary or derivative in their existence, something more is at stake. I have already noted Aristotle's claim for the primacy of the category of substance over other categories. Other philosophers have made bids for the primacy of different categories, not always the Aristotelian ones. Whitehead, for example, has emphasized the importance of *events*, on a certain construal of them. Moreover, there are dimensions of a different kind with respect to which primacy may be claimed. The claim for the primacy of particulars over universals has, for example, been very common in the history of philosophy, as has been the even more radical claim instanced in Locke's remark that everything that exists is particular. I shall discuss that in Chapter 5, indicating that various considerations are relevant to that view, including ones concerned with the economy of ideas and Ockham's razor (i.e. the thesis derived from William of Ockham that entities should not be multiplied beyond necessity). In general it is as if by establishing the ontological primacy of this or that one acquires a better key to the intelligibility of reality.

That is not to say that there is nothing to such claims. Nevertheless each claim of this kind requires examination, and we shall be concerned with examination of such claims at many places in what follows. It must be noted, however, that even if it can be established that such and such a kind of thing is primary within a given domain, perhaps because the concept of a thing of that kind has primacy for understanding things within that domain, it does not follow that the kind of thing shown to be primary is real while other kinds of thing are not. That is to say that this approach does not bring with it a distinction between appearance and reality. Aristotle, who says that substances have priority over things in other categories, that particular substances have priority over general substances if any, and perhaps that substances the nature of which is completely determined by their form have priority over substances of other kinds, does not thereby suggest that the things that are secondary are not real.

However, once given a distinction between appearance and reality this is a fairly easy step to take. As I indicated earlier, Leibniz, who argues that ontological priority must be given to simple substances or monads, does want to say that only these are real or *entia realia* and that complex entities constitute appearances or *phenomena*, even if *phenomena bene fundata*. Furthermore, if the primary thing or things are meant to provide a rationale for what is secondary then, once again, it may seem appropriate to give it or them the honorific title of the divine and that may encourage the feeling that they have a greater claim to reality. Yet, strictly speaking, nothing implying degrees of reality follows from the use of the honorific title, and certainly not the suggestion that only what has that title is real. (It is also worth noting again how little the use of such an honorific title has to do with straightforwardly theological issues.)

What I have said, however, may give the impression that the only aim of a metaphysics concerned with ontology in this way is to establish what basically exists and what is secondary. But a metaphysics of this kind would not be worth the name if it did not try to spell out the relations between different kinds of entity and put them in a framework which does justice to how things are in the world. Thus it is natural to expect a metaphysician to say something about space and time, the two all-pervasive frameworks within which the world in which we exist fits. I shall have something to say about them in Chapter 7. It is also natural to ask whether there are any other radical distinctions to be made between those things that have been shown to be basic, and in particular to ask what place *we* have in it all. I shall discuss issues of that kind in Chapters 8 and 9

My own approach to the subject might be put as follows: one way of construing metaphysics is to say that it is concerned to set out in the most general and abstract terms what must hold good of conscious beings and the world in which they live if that world is to constitute reality for them. For this purpose the metaphysician has to set out in the most intelligible form what that reality consists of, given an adequate framework of representation of what it is for something to constitute reality for someone. That will certainly entail saying something about things, their spatio-temporal framework and the persons, or at any rate selves, for whom they are things. I shall try to work out in subsequent chapters what that means.

Chapter 2 will discuss in greater detail the metaphysics of appearance and reality, and Chapter 3 the general nature of a philosophical ontology. Chapter 4 investigates the notion of substance – the kind of thing that has often been claimed as basic for ontology. I shall be concerned with the necessary features of substances and how they affect other matters such as their individuation. One commonly recognized characteristic of substances is particularity, and that will lead me in Chapter 5 to discuss the distinction between the particular and the general and also the general problem of universals. A characteristic that is sometimes thought, although mistakenly, to belong necessarily to sub-stance is simplicity of an absolute kind, and on that idea whole systems have been erected, particularly those of monism and pluralism (when the latter constitutes a reaction to the former). I shall illustrate that fact in Chapter 6 by reference to the monism of absolute idealism as found in Bradley and the pluralism of the logical atomism of Russell and the early Wittgenstein. I shall do that because apart from the relative unfamiliarity of these systems to some readers they afford a com-paratively recent example of the opposition between monism and pluralism. They also illustrate one particular working-out of metaphysics in the style of Hegel together with a reaction to it.

I shall then proceed in Chapter 7 to an examination of the frameworks in which substances are generally taken to exist; the frameworks provided by space and time. I shall not there consider all questions that might be asked about space and time, since some such questions belong more appropriately to philosophy of science. The questions raised will be those that fit in with the conceptions of metaphysics expounded in the chapters leading up to Chapter 7. In Chapters 8 and 9 I turn to ourselves, discussing first the notion of mind and the place that the mind has in the scheme presented, and second the conception of selves or persons for whom the reality outlined is what it is. A final epilogue will put the issues in perspective and explain why certain questions sometimes discussed under the heading of metaphysics are not discussed here (which is not to say that they should not be discussed).

Appendix – the possibility of metaphysics

If I had been writing this book a few decades ago it would certainly have been necessary for me to start with a justification of the whole enter-prise, to meet the accusation that metaphysics has no sense. From time to time in the history of philosophical thought philosophers of a positivist tendency have produced criteria of meaningfulness by which metaphysics could be shown to be nonsense at one fell swoop. Hume, for example, wished to consign to the flames anything that contained, in effect, pure *a priori* reasoning, except for 'abstract reasoning concerning quantity and number'. Later philosophers, such as Ayer, have claimed that because metaphysical theses are not verifiable by reference to experience and are not merely logical or mathematical in content they are nonsense. In neither of the cases which I have mentioned is there much of an attempt to examine metaphysical arguments closely, and some of Ayer's characterizations of metaphysical positions verge on the caricature.

Verificationism is no longer the force that it was and it is probably no longer necessary to justify the pursuit of metaphysics on grounds of meaning. The proof of the pudding seems to me to lie in the eating. There are no doubt some pieces of metaphysics that are rubbish, but not because, or not simply because, they contain unverifiable statements; it is rather because they do not contain any good arguments. I do not know of any *a priori* considerations which will show that metaphysics is possible or that it is impossible. One can only examine any putative candidate and see; and that is a matter of examining the argument. If there are no good metaphysical arguments there is no good metaphysics. That may be good reason for consigning a book on metaphysics to the flames, if one wishes. But in advance of an examination of the argument it would be foolish to suppose that any adequate judgment on a piece of metaphysics can be made. Hence a judgment about the possibility of metaphysics ought to be made at the end of this book, not at the beginning, and then it would be best made by others.

2. Appearance and reality

Appearance, reality and idealism

In our everyday lives most of us work with a rough and ready distinction between what is real and what is appearance. Austin[1] said that in the case of the real/unreal distinction it is 'unreal' that 'wears the trousers'; that, in other words, we understand by 'real' what is not unreal, and we understand 'unreal' by reference to a number of prototype situations and cases. A real duck is one that is not unreal and that is likely to mean one that is not fabricated, 'mock' or 'pretend'. A toy duck used as a decoy is not a real duck, for two such reasons. Nevertheless, it would be odd to use the words 'apparent' and 'appearance' in connexion with it, even if the aim of using it as a decoy is to present an appearance of a duck to whatever it is that is being decoyed. A toy duck is not an apparent duck, nor is it in itself the appearance of a duck; all the same it is not a real duck. Such considerations might suggest that appearance does not constitute a straightforward contrast with reality.

When I say that in our everyday lives most of us work with a rough and ready distinction between reality and appearance, I do not mean merely that we have a rough and ready understanding of how to use 'real', 'unreal', 'apparent' and 'appearance', let alone 'is' and 'appears'. Most of us do recognize that some parts of our experience do not go with the rest and are not 'of' the real world as the rest is; they take the form of dreams, hallucinations, illusions and the like. When we wake up we realize that what we dreamt was not real; and similar considerations apply to hallucinations and, up to a point, illusions.

This is not to say that we could thereby give an adequate account of what the distinction comes to; it *is* to say that we have the intuition that there is a distinction. A philosopher who is concerned to develop a metaphysics based on the concepts of appearance and reality relies on that intuition, but he extends what seems to be implied in it so as to set against each other two whole realms of experience, the one to be called 'appearance', the other 'reality'. It is an extension because it is not clear

---

[1] J. L. Austin, *Sense and Sensibilia* (Oxford: Clarendon Press, 1962), pp. 70–1.

that anything like that or as much as that is implied in the original intuitive distinction. As far as that is concerned, it is simply, as I have said, that some parts of our experience do not fit in with the rest and are seen not to do so. It is not that 'appearance' denotes a whole area or realm of experience which is quite different from the area called 'reality' in the way that one geographical tract may be different from another enabling us to ask of any given thing to which area or tract it belongs. To say that the metaphysical distinction between appearance and reality is an extension of the original intuitive distinction in this way is not to say in itself that it is illegitimate. Whether it is so can be seen only by considering how it is used and to what conclusions it then leads. It must nevertheless be recognized that it *is* an extension of ordinary ways of thinking.

Once given an extended distinction of this kind, it is possible to ask whether things other than those which we might initially think of as unreal and therefore appearance do in fact belong there. To allocate an item to appearance must inevitably involve something of a relegation. It may suggest, for example, that we need not consider that item seriously any longer. There is a clear sense in which, although we may have to take the *fact* of having hallucinations seriously, we do not need to take *them*, their content, seriously. They are not, we might say, part of reality. The question is whether there are items which we might not at first sight want to put with these 'appearances' but which may be sufficiently like them to put them there all the same. It is characteristic of a metaphysics based on the distinction between appearance and reality that one finds arguments directed specifically to that end, in ways that we shall examine later.

In the case of some philosophers, however, while *we* might describe them as trying to relegate a whole area of experience to appearance, that is not how they put the matter themselves. Parmenides, for example, *may* say at the end of the prologue to his poem (it depends to some extent on what one takes the text to be) that ordinary men think that 'the things that seem' are all that there is. If he does say that, what he means is that ordinary men simply take what appears to exist as all that does exist. (There is a dispute among scholars as to whether 'exist' is the right interpretation of the verb 'to be' but that does not matter for present purposes.) In the subsequent part of his poem, known as 'The way of truth', he argues that one can speak and think only of 'what is' and that this means that very little, if anything, can be said of 'what is' other than that it is. In the final part of the poem, known as 'The way of opinion', he offers an account of what ordinary men believe and what is implied by that, but he adds that there is no truth in it. It would be tempting to say that what he is arguing for is the thesis that what the senses tell us of is mere appearance and that reason tells us that reality is quite otherwise. At no point, however, does he actually say that. If we think that such a gloss is reasonable all the same it is because we see Parmenides in the context of later ways of thinking which are nevertheless not strictly speaking his.

In Plato's *Republic* we are taken part of the way towards the later mode of thinking, but not the whole way. In Book 5 of that dialogue, Plato distinguishes between philosophers and 'lovers of sights and sounds'. Exactly what the distinction amounts to is controversial. Plato associates the distinction with that between knowledge on the one hand and belief or opinion on the other, knowledge being concerned with 'what is', belief with that which is between 'what is' and 'what is not'. (The Parmenidean echoes are perhaps obvious.) In the subsequent similes of the Sun, Line and Cave which are set out towards the end of Book 6 and into Book 7, it is made clear that 'belief' is equivalent to sense-perception. The similes of the Sun and Line provide both parallels between the sun and the intellect and a contrast between the intellect and the senses; at the same time they offer analogies between what the intellect is said to make clear to us and what the senses tell us, combined with a doctrine of degrees of reality, with images of one kind or another at the bottom of the scale provided by the line and Forms at the top. (Forms are, roughly speaking, ideal entities which act as standards against which sensible things are to be seen but which are also general in their nature and so constitute universals.)

By a doctrine of degrees of reality I mean a doctrine to the effect that some things are, for certain reasons, less perfect or less independent in their status than others and are thought for that reason to be less real than those others. This doctrine is in effect illustrated in the final simile – that of the Cave. In it Plato sets out in the form of an analogy or parable an account of an ascent from mere images to the Forms as a process of education. We are told at the beginning of the exposition that 'our state' as regards education is that of prisoners in a cave bound so that they can see only shadows on the end-wall of the cave; these shadows are cast by things being carried along a wall behind them by the light of a fire behind and above that. It is easy to construe the simile as saying that our state is that of people whose experience is confined to images or mere appearances and who therefore think that that is all there is.

Nevertheless, Plato does not quite say that the so-called sensible world is mere appearance. He does imply that the sensible world is in some sense less real than the Forms and in the simile of the Cave he does say that our state is *like* that of people for whom shadows, images or appearances are all there is. (And to judge by the later dialogue, the *Theaetetus*, Protagoras may have said that in fact things actually were that way.) Plato does not say, however, that the sensible world and what the senses tell us *is* mere appearance. Moreover, nothing in what I have reported him as saying gives sufficient reason for believing that he does. The similes provide analogies with forms of sense-perception; they do not build upon any theory of sense-perception which itself has as a constituent part the thesis that sense-experience is confined to mere appearances.

Even the theory of Protagoras, referred to above, which, as Plato reports it, is to the effect that everything is as it seems or appears to a man, does not amount to that. Plato associates Protagoras' theory with a certain account of perception in order to give weight to the theory. Although that account (which brings in a certain conception of the causal processes involved) has as a consequence the thesis that we do not perceive things as they are in themselves but rather as they appear as the result of their interaction with the sense-organs, it does not, strictly speaking, imply that we are restricted in sense-perception to a realm of *appearances*. To say that in perception we become aware only of how things seem or appear to us is not in itself to say that the only objects of perception are appearances.[2] (It is perhaps worth noting indeed that the Greek phrase which might be thought to be appropriately translated as 'appearances' – *ta phainomena* – literally means 'the things appearing' or 'the things that seem'; although there is no word for things in that Greek phrase, merely the neuter form of the definite article, the implication nevertheless is that it is *things* which appear or seem.)

It is at least arguable that the thesis that sense-perception is confined to appearances and the thesis that there is a distinct realm of appearances which is all that experience gives direct access to could not emerge until something which makes idealism a possible thesis also emerged. This something is what underlies Descartes' dualism – the thesis that we have a more direct access to, and a clearer and more distinct idea of, our own minds than we do in relation to the body and the bodily.[3] On this view, what we have direct access to in sense-perception is at best the mental

---

[2]   That, however, is a move that has often been made by sense-datum philosophers. See, e.g., A. J. Ayer, *The Problem of Knowledge* (Harmondsworth: Penguin, 1956), p. 96. Cf. my *Theory of Knowledge* (London and Basingstoke: Macmillan, 1971), pp. 164ff., and my *Sensation and Perception* (London: Routledge and Kegan Paul, 1961), pp. 174ff.

[3]   See M. F. Burnyeat, 'Idealism and Greek philosophy: what Descartes saw and Berkeley missed' in G. N. A. Vesey (ed.), *Idealism Past and Present*, Royal Institute of Philosophy Lecture Series 13 (Cambridge: C.U.P., 1982), pp. 19–50.

representatives or representations of things. Idealism is so called because it involves the thesis that all that we can be aware of (and therefore all that what we are aware of can consist in) is such representations or ideas.[4] At all events a full-blooded distinction between appearance and reality which presupposes a distinct realm of appearances depends on the presupposition that the notion of such a distinct realm of appearances makes sense. The thinking that eventually leads to idealism seems to provide that sense because it suggests that what we have direct access to is not real things but merely the representations of them in our minds, and hence, by comparison with those real things, appearances of them only. Idealism as such simply adds to the thesis that what we have direct access to in this way is all that there is.

In sum, therefore, Descartes' distinction between the mental and the physical, made perhaps for the first time in terms of the differences between the kinds of access that we have to them, provides the basis for the identification of a realm of appearances as distinct from reality. In that context at least, the notion of a distinct realm of appearances makes sense, because the mental, which includes ideas or representations which have the epistemological status of appearances, itself constitutes a distinct realm.

If that is right, dualism and the thought that we have direct access only to the mind constitute essential elements in a metaphysics based on a distinction between appearance and reality as distinct realms; and if we speak in these terms of theories, such as those of Plato and Parmenides, where those notions do not apply, it can only be by an extension, not altogether legitimate, from theories where they do apply. Strictly speaking, therefore, an assessment of such metaphysical theories should presuppose an examination of both dualism and the whole idea that we have direct access only to mental representations. I shall discuss dualism later, in Chapter 8, in a more general context. What requires emphasis here is that in Cartesian dualism the distinction between two kinds of thing with distinct natures is inseparable from the epistemological claim that each of us has direct access to our own states of mind in a way that we do not to the physical. The mental thus involves so-called privileged access. That is a thought which in this century has met with wholesale criticism

---

[4] In seventeenth- and eighteenth-century usage the term 'idea' does not mean merely 'concept' but any mental item which is, so to speak, *of* something. It is worth noting also that Plato's so-called Idealism is a quite different thing from the idealism which we are now considering; it is a theory to the effect that sensible things, the objects of perception, are to be explained by reference to Ideas or Forms, the ideal entities postulated by Plato and already referred to. The Greek word '*idea*' has no necessary connexion with ideas in the mind.

from many directions but which is still persistent in its influence. Why it had to wait until Descartes for its expression and why Descartes came to express it is an interesting historical question that has not, perhaps, received a convincing answer, but that is a matter which need not concern us now.

Once given the thought that we have direct access only to the mental, it is an easy step to the thesis that the mental constitutes in some form the only reality. For, although I have spoken of *direct* access in this connexion, it is difficult to see how on the view in question there could be access of any kind to anything else but the contents of our minds. For what principle of inference is there that could take us from the so-called mental representations to anything else, despite the seductive suggestions in the notion of *representation* which may make us think that there must be something for these mental entities to represent? It is natural, therefore, particularly for one of an empiricist turn of mind, such as Berkeley was, to deny any reality beyond ideas.

Nevertheless, anything that undermines the central thoughts of Cartesian dualism must *ipso facto* undermine idealism also, since the latter depends on the former. If there is validity in the Wittgensteinian claim that a concept of sensation, and thereby a concept of the mental generally, is possible only given a public understanding and a share in public forms of life, this will undermine idealism, just because it indicates that the existence of a public frame of reference is presupposed in the very attempt to employ the terms on which idealism depends. Idealism presupposes, therefore, the very thing – the public frame of reference –that it seeks to deny (as a consistent idealism must do if it is to assert, as Schopenhauer puts it, that the world is *my* representation). Indeed, many of the philosophers who follow Descartes in accepting the same terms of reference as idealism may similarly be accused of begging the question about publicity. For, despite the essential egocentricity (and in effect solipsism too) that Descartes' point of view involves, he and those like him simply *assume* that what holds good for me holds good for others too. When Schopenhauer, for example, says that the world is my representation, he still assumes, despite what that way of putting it seems to imply, that what is representation for me can be so for others too. The same might be said of Kant despite his avowed programme of showing that what is true for me is true for all men.

If modern critics, such as Wittgenstein, are right therefore (and I think that they are), idealism involves a certain incoherence and is for that reason a non-starter. But – to sum up what I have been saying –what is fundamentally wrong is the thinking that lies behind it, i.e. the thought introduced by Descartes that we have direct access only to ideas or mental representations. Since these do not constitute a reality of public and physical objects they can be thought of as a realm of appearances only. Idealism stems from this with the additional thought that, since we do not have access to anything beyond ideas, the only reality which we have any justification in assuming is those ideas, the appearances themselves. I have not said in this that idealism itself is a necessary condition of the possibility of a metaphysics of appearance and reality, but the framework of thought that leads in this way to idealism *is* a necessary condition of that kind of metaphysics. It might indeed be said that idealism, however incoherent in itself, is the only rational position for one who embraces the distinction between appearance and reality on the Cartesian basis.

It is desirable, however, to examine the kinds of positive consideration that have been adduced in favour of idealism, and to try to see what is involved in its counterpart, realism. That is what I shall do in the remainder of this chapter.

Arguments for idealism

The basic underpinning of classical idealism lies, as I have suggested, in the thought that, once given the Cartesian frame of reference, no other view is really possible. I am confined to my own ideas or representations. Common-sense thinking about the notion of representations may suggest otherwise. For is it not natural to think of representations being brought about, in many cases at least, by what they are representations of? From that point of view the reality that idealism speaks of is just appearance; reality proper lies beyond. That line of thought is to be found not only in Descartes and Locke, who are not, properly speaking, idealists, but in some post-Kantian idealists too (and I shall come to considerations about *them* in the next section). It involves a certain concession, however partial, to common-sense, and it might be said with some justice that throughout the metaphysics of appearance and reality can be found these twin pulls, towards on the one hand full-blooded idealism and towards on the other hand common-sense. Nevertheless, as I have suggested, idealism may be said to be the only rational position for one who accepts the line of thinking that presupposes direct access only to the mind.

What independent reasons are there, however, for accepting the story about ideas and representations in the first place? One gets the clearest view of that from Locke and Berkeley. Locke's arguments for the subjectivity and therefore ideal status or at any rate idea-dependence of so-called secondary qualities like colour, taste and warmth turn on the circumstance-dependence of our perception of these qualities of objects. The colour that objects are seen to have varies with the illumination, their taste may depend on what is done to them, as almonds change in taste when pounded in a pestle, while the warmth that objects are perceived to have varies with our distance from them. Locke thought that such considerations show that colour, taste and temperature cannot be real properties of things, and Berkeley generalized the matter by pointing out that the same or similar considerations apply to the perception of other supposed properties of things, including Locke's primary qualities, such as size and shape.

Schopenhauer appeals to similar considerations in the course of a general argument for idealism, claiming that the perception of all properties is dependent on the brain, and must therefore be products of the brain. It does not in fact follow from the undoubted fact that perception of various things is dependent on the satisfaction of certain conditions, including conditions about the brain of the perceiver, that we do not perceive objective properties of things but only the products of those conditions. All perception is subject to conditions. We need further arguments if there is to be any plausibility in the suggestion that the conditions noted are so special as to undermine the claim to the objectivity of the perception.

Both Locke and Berkeley attempt to provide this additional argument by assimilating such forms of perception to experiences which there is independent and better reason to characterize as subjective – experiences such as pain, which are not generally taken to provide objective knowledge of the world, or at least not by themselves and not without reference to other information, such as what characteristically produces experiences of that kind. Locke, for example, asks why anyone should suppose that warmth, the feeling of which is produced by a fire, is in the fire, while at the same time supposing that pain, which may equally be produced by the fire, is not in it. Berkeley too points out that a feeling of intense heat is indistinguishable from that of pain [5] (an argument that goes back to Anaxagoras, who held that pain is just the product of any intense form of stimulation).

On these grounds it is inferred that just as pains are mere sensations so are perceptions of different qualities of objects, so called. Hence there is nothing objective in any form of perception; all that we are aware of is sensations. If they *seem* to be of 'things without the mind', as Berkeley

---

[5] J. Locke, *Essay Concerning Human Understanding*, II.8.16; G. Berkeley, *Three Dialogues between Hylas and Philonous*, I (Everyman edition, pp. 203ff.).

put it, that is appearance only. What we are really aware of is representations (to use terminology which is perhaps more characteristic of Kant and other German philosophers – *Vorstellungen*); but on the strict idealist view that Berkeley embraces there is nothing to represent. In effect perceptions are assimilated to images, which are like sensations in their subjective status, but supposedly representational in that it at least makes sense to speak of them as being *of* something. It is concluded by idealists that because we are aware of nothing but such representations they are all the reality that there is.

None of these arguments is valid. Their form is that of progressive assimilation. Something, e.g. pain, is taken as the prototype of a subjective experience, and because it takes place only when certain conditions are satisfied other forms of experience are assimilated to it when conditions which are to some extent similar are requisite for their occurrence. That, however, makes the argument one from analogy, and in all such arguments the argument is as good as the analogy. These particular arguments stress similarities; they pay no attention to differences. It is true for example that brain processes and other physiological processes have to take place for there to be sensations of pain and genuine perceptions alike. There is also external stimulation in both cases, or may be. Those facts, however, take no account of possible differences both in the nature of the physiological processes and in the character of the stimulation. In other words, there are differences as well as similarities between the two cases of sensation and perception, and when one considers these it will become apparent that the analogy is not sufficiently great to support the conclusion that is drawn.

Schopenhauer, in the same connexion, adduces another, negative, argument which is of some interest. This is to meet what may seem an obvious counter-argument that an objective world with objective properties would surely exist whether or not there existed perceivers or conscious beings to perceive them, and this would imply a reality independent of minds. Schopenhauer (*The World as Will and Representation* II.1) tries to argue that the supposition that an objective world would exist whether or not there were any knowing beings involves at its heart a contradiction; because if we try to give a real sense to that supposition we must realize that we are presupposing the very opposite of what we tend to suppose. For the objective world in question must, if the idea is to be given any real content, involve at least one knowing being – the one who is trying to suppose it. As it stands the argument is a bad one. It does not follow from the fact that it is impossible to conceive of a world without a conceiver existing that the conceiver in question has to be part of the world conceived; the existence of the knowing being is not part of the content of what is thought. There is nevertheless a more fundamental point at issue. That is the question of what sense can be given to the notion of a reality independent of the conditions under which the conception of that reality is to be given application. That is in effect the issue involved in the current dispute between realism and anti-realism deriving from Michael Dummett's advocacy of the latter. I shall return to that issue in the last section of this chapter.

What emerges from a consideration of the arguments that I have surveyed is that there seem to be two general types of argument directed towards idealism, or at least towards a rejection of its opposite, realism. The first dwells on the characteristics of sense-perception, when that is construed in such a way as to assimilate it to sensation or at all events to the occurrence of private mental entities after the pattern of Cartesian dualism. That alone, however, is not enough to sustain idealism. We need also the premiss that only what we are aware of in sense-perception constitutes reality. Then, if what we are aware of in sense-perception can only be the experiences themselves, as must be the case if sense-perception is akin to sensation, it follows that there can be no reality except that which is, so to speak, internal to some mind. Since from a more common-sense point of view the last may be characterized as appearances or representations, it may be said from that point of view that reality reduces itself to appearances or representations alone; and that is one way of stating idealism.

It must be evident that there is much at fault at every step of the argument. In any case, for one who thinks that there must be a distinction between representations and what they represent, a distinction between reality and appearance re-emerges, and to meet that point idealists must have recourse to the second type of argument. This says in effect that it is all very well saying there must be a distinction between representations and what they represent, but, since all that we have direct access to is what we have called representations, no sense can be attached to what they represent except what can be spelled out in terms of the representations themselves. Hence, if a distinction between appearance and reality is wanted all the same, the only place for it is within appearances or representations themselves.

This last type of argument is in effect verificationist, in that it presupposes that the sense which is to be attached to claims about the world must be specifiable in terms of what can be verified by reference to experience alone. Whatever one may think of that consideration, it must be emphasized that if an argument expressed in these terms is to

result in idealism it must also involve, explicitly or implicitly, the premiss that the only things to which we have direct access are experiences
themselves, these being construed as intrinsically mental on the Cartesian pattern. Modern forms of opposition to realism are more sophisticated, especially in what they take to be the conditions of sense or
meaningfulness. Since, however, it is the additional premiss which I
have noted that is important for idealism and this is requisite in both
types of argument if idealism is to be inferred from them, it seems evident that a general opposition to realism on verificationist grounds need
not lead directly to idealism (which requires that additional premiss).
Idealism thus depends on the kind of thinking presupposed in Cartesian
dualism in a way in which other forms of opposition to realism need not
– realism itself being defined for the sake of argument simply as the
view that there is a reality independent of the mind and independent of
conscious beings. The impetus towards realism comes in turn from the
common-sense reaction that there is surely more to what exists than
what is simply within our own minds (and also perhaps, as I indicated
earlier, from the more sophisticated thought that the kind of thinking
which idealism derives from could not even be expressed unless something like realism held good).

Transcendental idealism

The thought that there is more to what exists than what is simply within
our own minds is implicit in Kantian reactions to the more subjective
forms of idealism such as that of Berkeley. As a matter of historical fact
even Berkeley was a qualified idealist. For he thought that there must be
something which was not itself an idea or composed of ideas to sustain
such ideas as do occur – our minds or that of God, what Berkeley called
'spirits'. Hence for him there *is* something apart from ideas or representations; but he did not accept that there was substance in the physical
sense, since he did not think that anything within experience gave content to that thought, while we have 'notions' of ourselves and of God.
Hume was much more radical in that respect. For him there is nothing
but impressions and ideas. Hume tries to distinguish between impressions and mere ideas, not in terms of what they are of (since they are not
of anything, strictly speaking), but in terms of the clarity and vivacity of
the former compared with the latter. Berkeley had in fact tried to do
something similar by appealing to the passivity of ideas of perception, as
well as their strength and liveliness. In fact, however, no such property
as the relative clarity or vivacity of one set of experiences as compared
with another seems adequate to provide a clear and definite distinction

between what is real and what is appearance. For one thing, that latter distinction is an absolute one, while the former is relative only.

As compared with these philosophers Kant goes along with the impetus towards realism to the extent of positing a reality distinct from and beyond experience – what he calls 'things-in-themselves'. If it is asked *why* Kant does that, one can point only to the feeling that experiences must be grounded in something, that there must be some reason, not why experiences take the form that they do, but why there are experiences at all. Because such a ground necessarily lies outside experience Kant thinks that we have no basis for saying anything further about it. Hence the nature of things-in-themselves is something that we can have no inkling of. The notion of a thing-in-itself is therefore the notion of a limiting case – to which at best only a set of negative characterizations is applicable.

Kant nevertheless thinks that a distinction of some kind between appearance and reality can be drawn within experience, within appearances or representations. This is made possible by the fact that an appreciation of the content of experience involves judgment, and this in turn involves bringing what Kant calls intuitions (in this case sensible intuitions or experiences of sense) under concepts. Moreover, Kant thinks – and this is one of his chief glories – that within judgments it is possible to distinguish those which are objective from those which are merely subjective, by reference to certain principles of the understanding which govern the former. More than this, Kant also thinks that it can be shown that the very possibility of setting down certain judgments as subjective presupposes that it is possible to accept others as objective. The argument for this is not the one that I mentioned earlier as put forward by Wittgenstein, since Kant, in his construal of experience, still operates to some extent within Cartesian terms of reference, to the extent of accepting that kind of epistemological apparatus. There may in any case be genuine dispute concerning the validity of the Kantian argument to be found in the 'Transcendental deduction of the categories' and the 'Refutation of idealism'.

If Kant's argument were valid (and given what I have said about his operating within the Cartesian terms of reference, this must be at least very doubtful, despite his rejection of much of Descartes' actual philosophy), it would be something of very great philosophical importance. The position reached is what Kant called 'transcendental idealism'. From the point of view of experience, idealism holds good; we are confined to representations even if there is in fact a reality of things-in-themselves beyond them to which experience can have no access. Nevertheless, there is room within experience for a further distinction between what is objective and what is subjective, as expressed in the two forms of judgments; hence there is another kind of distinction within experience between reality and appearance. The objective world as we ordinarily take it to be is, Kant thinks, empirically real but transcendentally ideal. From the point of view of experience it is real by comparison with merely subjective experiences such as those which are the product of the imagination, but since it is still a matter of representations, however organized in judgment, it is ideal by comparison with things-in-themselves.

How can a work on transcendental idealism contain, as Kant's does, a refutation of idealism? It is Berkeleyan idealism which Kant seeks to refute, and his own idealism is different from that of Berkeley in two ways in particular. In the first place, according to Kant there are not just ideas or representations; there are things-in-themselves too. Hence a distinction between appearance and reality is maintained without having recourse merely to relative differences between the characters of the experiences themselves. (It might be objected that for Berkeley too there are more than just ideas; there are spirits too. But according to Kant, selves which is what Berkeleyan spirits are, are, if treated in the Berkeleyan way, things-in-themselves, though not the only ones.) Secondly, the Kantian theory of judgment, and of the principles that judgment involves, makes possible, putatively, a distinction between the objective and the subjective within experience which is not merely a matter of the relative character of the representations themselves. Hence, whatever one may think of transcendental idealism as a theory, it amounts to a thesis quite different from the idealism which Berkeley professes.

It might be suggested that Kant wants to have the best of both worlds. He can certainly be criticized for starting from the Cartesian terms of reference which he inherited from his predecessors (even if it was natural for him to do so). That perhaps is the most obvious criticism for contemporary philosophers to make. To Kant's immediate successors, who were still inheritors of the same Cartesian legacy, it was the notion of things-in-themselves which was the really problematic thing. Schopenhauer thought that he had good reason for identifying them with the will (arguing too that there could only be one thing-in-itself). The general tendency, however, was to see whether one could retain a transcendental idealism without things-in-themselves, by providing a sound basis for a distinction between the objective and the subjective within experience. That in effect was the course taken by Fichte. It is difficult to see how such an attempt with those terms of reference *could* be successful. A sceptic can always respond by saying that even if conformity with such and such principles is a necessary condition of the possibility of objective judgment it is not sufficient. Even in the case of Kant himself, it might be argued that the 'Refutation of idealism', construed as an attempt to refute a merely subjective idealism in favour of one that leaves room for the objective, achieves only the demonstration that calling something subjective presupposes our having the *concept* of the objective. It does not show that there actually is something that falls under that concept, nor how the distinction between the objective and the subjective is actually to be applied. The same would be true of any analogous argument.[6]

Absolute idealism

The 'absolute idealism' espoused by Hegel and other philosophers inspired by him introduces another dimension. Hegel's philosophical system is immensely complex and there are some who wish to play down the idealism in it. Whatever I say about it will inevitably be over-simplified and perhaps not readily intelligible; it may, however, be worth noting certain lines of thought that it entails. The opening sections of Hegel's *Phenomenology of Spirit* (and the same is evident in Bradley's *Appearance and Reality*) make it clear that experience, or the fact that there is experience, is in a certain sense taken as a 'given'; and in that way the Cartesian legacy lingers. Hegel, however, learnt a lesson from Kant that Kant himself was not entirely willing to learn. In Kant's view experience has a sense only to the extent that it is expressible in judgment. That in turn involves bringing representations given to us in experience, or, as Kant calls them, intuitions, under concepts. But, Kant says, intuitions without concepts are blind, and that is right since having an intuition need not involve thought with content; for that, what Kant calls a concept is required as well. The whole story about representations, however, suggests otherwise, because a representation can have a separate identity only if it has a content to give it that identity.

Hegel takes that point seriously. He takes it as a datum that we have experience, but there can be no immediate sense-knowledge by that means; for knowledge we need to bring in concepts. That, however, raises the question what principles there are which can determine what can be brought under what. What determines whether experience can suitably be brought under any putative concept? No such principles are

---

6   It may be claimed that the form of the argument is that of one from 'polar opposites', for which see my *Theory of Knowledge*, pp. 16ff.

provided by experience itself. We might perhaps think that we could look for such principles in other concepts, but that simply raises other problems. Suppose, to use the example employed by Bradley in *Appearance and Reality*, Chapter 2, we attempt to provide the rationale for thinking 'White', 'Sweet', 'Hard' by saying that we are concerned with a lump of sugar. What then makes the thoughts 'White', 'Sweet', 'Hard' etc. into the thought of a lump of sugar? What unites the first set of thoughts to make them amount to the second thought? That, Hegel says, raises the ancient problem of the one and the many – the problem of how a single thing which is one can also manifest plurality, and *vice versa*.

Hegel seeks to solve that problem by invoking the notion of force – roughly, the idea of lawlikeness. The connexion between the properties of a thing so as to make up the whole is in some sense lawlike, so that the whole is a function of the parts in accordance with a law of nature. That, however, raises problems about the basis and rationale of the law; and the attempt to deal with that raises other problems – and so on. What this amounts to is that the process of trying to explain how the understanding organizes experience in a rational and coherent way involves a progressive recession; and the same applies when reason is brought in as well. Hegel seeks to show that the regress must go on until some overriding and all-comprehensive principle is reached – the so-called Absolute Idea or Concept. There is no possibility of stopping short of that – short of something that guarantees the unity of the system of ideas that has been invoked. It remains true that nothing in experience itself justifies the application of that system of ideas, even if we can know *a priori* that the reality that the system reveals to understanding and reason is experience.

It is implied by this line of thought that what are seen to be unsatisfactory ways of organizing experience under concepts may nevertheless receive something of a rationale (or at all events the fact that we so organize experience may receive a rationale) in some higher principle of organization. If reality is ultimately determined by the highest principle of organization, that does not mean that less coherent principles of organization have nothing at all to do with reality. That implies a doctrine of degrees of reality (commensurate with a doctrine of degrees of truth) which is central to the kind of thought that Hegelianism involves. What then is appearance? For on this view no appearance can be absolutely false, and therefore in absolute contrast with reality, despite the natural opposition between the concepts of appearance and reality. From the Hegelian point of view appearance can be only a less coherently organized form of reality; the supposed contrast that the terms 'appearance' and 'reality' suggest is thus, officially, a matter of degree, not strict opposition. For Hegelians, therefore, reality is in a sense both other than and inclusive of appearance. Reality both transcends and also includes its appearances.

That is a very difficult notion. In Kant's philosophical system sensibility and understanding in some sense constitute 'givens'. That is to say that sensibility and understanding provide the framework relative to which all knowledge is to be seen as such, and they cannot therefore themselves be subject to a demand for a further rationale. They provide the *a priori* forms that all experience must take. Something similar is true of Hegel, although with considerable qualifications. In the first place, although the fact of sensibility constitutes a 'given' for Hegel, as we have seen, it has no *a priori* form as a 'given'. For all considerations of form and structure involve subsumption under concepts, and thus go beyond sensibility alone. Secondly, Hegel does not think that what Kant takes as a 'given' at the other extreme from sensibility – the *a priori* principles of the understanding – do provide the kind of limit to the possibility of knowledge that Kant supposes. Reason, he thinks, can provide rationalia and principles of explanation beyond the limits that Kant thought were presupposed.

Nevertheless, it is a 'given' for Hegel that there is a final rationale for things. That is what makes Hegel's philosophy so supremely rationalistic, and is one thing that the Existentialists reacted against. Hence, despite the qualifications that I have referred to, there are in Hegel's system limits at both ends – limits imposed by sensibility and reason themselves. Sensibility, however, has no *a priori* form; nor indeed, by contrast with Kant, has the understanding, since the understanding does not by itself constitute a limit, being transcended by reason. Hence the necessities that reason is supposed to discover as the result of the Hegelian method of argument – the so-called dialectic – are not, as with Kant, necessities that govern possible experience, but necessities within the rational structure which a philosopher reflecting upon experience may supposedly discover as belonging to reality.

In our ordinary life what reality is for each of us is determined by what experience reveals to us, and our ordinary distinctions between what is real and what is not apply. To say that the things which we take as real in this way have in fact only a low degree of reality is to speak as a philosopher interested in what place such things have in the most rational construction of reality (or, better perhaps, *re*construction of reality, since it is not clear that reality is a matter for construction). That is a point worth emphasizing. In the first chapter of *Appearance and Reality* Bradley appeals to considerations concerning primary and secondary qualities (the distinction between which I shall discuss further in Chapter 4), following in this respect Locke and Berkeley. That is to say that he appeals to the fact that perception of so-called secondary qualities, such as colour and taste, are circumstance-dependent, and then follows Berkeley in generalizing that consideration so as to make it applicable to primary qualities, such as shape and size, as well. For Berkeley the conclusion to be drawn is that reality consists solely of ideas (apart from God and spirits generally), so that from another point of view it might be said that reality and appearance are conflated. According to Bradley, the conclusion to be drawn is that 'experience is not true', for the arguments seem to him to show that experience constitutes appearance only, and that reality is something else; at the same time, since the *fact* of experience is a 'given', while experience is not true it is not completely false either. The two positions sum up subjective idealism and absolute idealism respectively. Alongside them must be put the Kantian transcendental idealism, according to which experience can be true but such that there is nevertheless a reality beyond it in things-in-themselves.

Although there are these differences between subjective idealism, transcendental idealism and the absolute idealism of the Hegelians, they have in common the thought that there is no access to reality other than what the mind reveals to us, and the conclusion is drawn that reality is, except in the case of the Kantian things-in-themselves, mind-dependent in one way or another. Two observations on that are in order. The first is the one that I have made repeatedly – that a premiss requisite for drawing the conclusion is the Cartesian one that we have direct access only to the mental. It may seem something of a truism that there is no access to reality other than what the mind reveals to us (although it is important in that respect to note what only the body makes possible).[7] It is not a truism, however, that we have direct access only to the mental; it is indeed false. But the conclusion cannot be drawn without supposing the truth of that Cartesian premiss.

The second observation is in a way connected with the first. It is to the effect that even if the truth of the Cartesian premiss were granted it would not follow directly that reality is mind-dependent. That could be taken to follow only if it were allowed that from the supposed fact that we have direct access only to the mental it could be inferred that we do

---

[7] As has been argued by philosophers as different as Wittgenstein and Merleau-Ponty. See L. Wittgenstein, *Philosophical Investigations* (Oxford: Blackwell, 1953) and M. Merleau-Ponty, *The Phenomenology of Perception*, trans. C. Smith (London: Routledge and Kegan Paul, 1962).

not have access *of any kind* to anything else. That could not validly be inferred, however, unless it could be shown that there is no form of indirect access to a non-mental reality, and that needs argument. It must be admitted that it is not easy to see what principles of inference there might be which would justify any inferential move from the mental to the non-mental unless there was some independent form of access to the latter. There have, however, been philosophers who have maintained that as a matter of fact we make the move any way without there being valid principles of inference to justify it, and that there is a good reason why we should do so. Schopenhauer is a case in point, since he maintains that the understanding makes the move from sensations given in experience to their cause in the world, according to the principle of sufficient reason, but in a non-inferential way. It cannot be said that the idea is a happy one but it is worth noting its existence.[8] It is impossible to go further into these complications here. It is enough to note that there are disputable premises in any argument for idealism and that there are disputable steps that have to be taken if one is to reach it as a conclusion.

Realism

It might be thought that if idealism is unsatisfactory the only possible course of action is to accept *realism*, as the only viable alternative. Such a conclusion might, however, be premature, as is indicated by the contemporary prevalence of views which are called, after Michael Dummett,[9] anti-realist, but which are such that their authors might not accept the title of idealist. It is important, therefore, to be clear about what is involved in realism and objections to it.

Realism involves at least the claim that there is a reality independent of us and our minds, and that what we think, understand and recognize does not necessarily exhaust what that reality involves. The facts may go beyond anything that we are capable of ascertaining, but the truth is so by virtue of those facts and that reality. In recent times, however, philosophical concern with realism has had to do with its connexion with theories of meaning, because it is taken to be the case by many philosophers that the meaning of propositions is a function of what makes them true or false. The question at issue, therefore, is whether what is to be understood in any proposition lies simply in what sort of fact makes it true – in other words in its truth-conditions. Anti-realism holds that what has to be understood is more than that. To understand a

[8] See my *Schopenhauer* (London: Routledge and Kegan Paul, 1980), pp. 18–21.
[9] M. Dummett, *Truth and Other Enigmas* (London: Duckworth, 1978).

proposition we need also to know its verification-conditions; we need, that is, a recognition of when the truth-conditions apply, and when we are justified in holding that they do. It follows, given this view of what is to be understood in a proposition, that there is no sense to be attached to the idea of facts going beyond what we are capable of ascertaining. This involves a kind of generalization of the issues concerning realism and idealism that I discussed earlier. I do not intend to make any claims to a thorough assessment of anti-realism, since that would involve technical considerations about, for example, the status of intuitionist logic and the principle of excluded middle, and such considerations are peripheral to the main metaphysical issues. Some appreciation of the issues can, however, be gained without that.

One way to get a purchase upon the issues is to consider something that was one of Dummett's earliest concerns – the reality of the past.[10] Many philosophers have suggested that the past (and even more, perhaps, the future) does not have quite the same status as the present. (I shall return to some of those suggestions in Chapter 7.) 'What is past is past' is a truism; it is rather less of a truism that what has happened in the past has gone for ever and cannot be retrieved. It depends entirely on what that is taken to say. If it means that what has happened has happened and that the very same event cannot happen again even if an event just like it may do so, well and good; but the proposition in question is susceptible of other interpretations. Similar things apply to the claim that the past, *qua* past, is inaccessible to us in the present. We cannot, of course, gain consciousness of, as present, what is past. Nevertheless, we do have knowledge of the past; we have memories, and there are even ways of reconstructing the past on the basis of evidence available to us now. It might be objected that memory and these ways of getting to the past are all fallible. That is true, but all ways of getting to know things are fallible (which is *not*, incidentally, to say that we cannot be certain of anything). If I labour these points it is because it is sometimes said that statements about the past are verification-transcendent, i.e. that what they claim goes beyond the evidence that counts as their verification. It is doubts about the intelligibility of statements that have verification-transcendent truth-conditions that lie at the heart of anti-realism, for it is thought that the meaning of a statement ought to be capable of being spelled out in terms of what would verify it, and not simply in terms of the conditions of its *truth*.

If it were claimed that statements about the past *are* verification-

---

[10] See his 'The reality of the past' in *Truth and Other Enigmas*.

transcendent this could only be because a very specific conception of verification was presupposed, i.e. the conception which implies that the verification must be construed in terms of what is available to consciousness *now*. (It is worth noting the similarity of that preconception to the one that I said lay behind idealism proper; one might even call the view that I am now concerned with 'temporal idealism'.) It is clear enough that we generally accept the intelligibility of whole hosts of statements that are not verifiable in *that* way. Are there not, however, many statements about the past that are not verifiable at all? In that case have we not a class of statements the truth-conditions of which are such that we have no idea how to determine whether they obtain or not? Yes, but they form merely a sub-class of a wider class of statements of which we have, at any rate in principle, some idea of how they might be verified. If there is a difficulty about the sub-class it is a practical difficulty of some kind; it is not a difficulty of principle.

It would seem from all this that the real problem arises, if anywhere, where there are putative statements the truth-conditions of which are such that there is no way, even in principle, of determining for statements of that general class which truth-value applies. That hardly holds good of statements about the past as a class, since it is clear that we *can* determine, in the case of some statements of that kind, what their precise truth-value is. If it were suggested otherwise, that would entail a false epistemology with regard to possible knowledge of the past. The same applies to many other cases which have exercised the minds of verificationist philosophers of an earlier generation, e.g. statements about other minds. There are well-charted ways of approaching these problems.[11]

It is, however, possible to approach the issue in a much more general way and ask, without reference to specific cases, what we should say about putative statements the truth-conditions of which (considered as a class) are indeed verification-transcendent. Dummett claims that one of the most fundamental underpinnings of his thesis is the Wittgensteinian thesis that meaning is use. There is perhaps much to argue about in that thesis,[12] but even if one were to accept that knowing the meaning of an expression is knowing its use in the sense of knowing the circumstances in which a statement involving it would be true, it does not follow immediately from that that one has to be able to recognize those circumstances when in them, as would have to be the case if knowing the use entailed being able to recognize verifying circumstances.

[11] See, e.g., my *Theory of Knowledge*, pp. 60ff., 188ff., 215ff.
[12] See again my *Theory of Knowledge*, pp. 64–8.

Let me raise some related issues the presentation of which owes more to Putnam than to Dummett.[13] Suppose that we had the best possible theory about something (not merely the best available theory but the best *possible* one, if such a notion may be accepted for the sake of argument). Would it make sense to raise the question of whether the facts may not be different from what the theory suggests? It might be thought that there is no reason why they should not be. The thought that lies behind the suggestion that the facts could not be different is, in effect, not only that before we can decide what is so and what is not so we must conceptualize the issue, but, as it is sometimes put, that any conception of reality presupposes an already existing scheme of concepts,[14] so that in a way the very conception of reality and of the facts presupposes a theory. It may be possible to get outside the scheme of concepts with which we operate at any one time (and scientific progress often occurs by that very means), but it is not possible to get outside concepts altogether. Whether or not it is happy to put the issue in terms of the notion of a *theory*, it remains true that one cannot get at reality except from within some system of concepts. The question then arises as to whether there is anything to the notion of reality itself which is not specifiable in terms of those concepts.[15]

That last question is not quite the same as the questions whether reality could in fact be different from anything specifiable in terms of our concepts, or in terms of the best set of concepts (according to some criterion for the 'best'), or in terms of some conceivable set of concepts, but there is a connexion between at least some of these questions. For if there is nothing to the *notion* of reality which is independent of the concepts in terms of which reality is construed, it cannot be the case that reality might be different from anything specifiable in terms of some conceivable set of concepts. The converse relation, however, does not hold. It seems evident that reality could certainly be different from anything specifiable in terms of *our* concepts – or at least such a thing is logically possible, however unlikely it may seem in fact over a great range of our experience. As for the question about the 'best' set of concepts, there is inevitably a problem about what is to count as 'best' and why.

There is a similarity between the questions raised and that asked by some idealists as to whether conceptual thought must necessarily falsify

---

[13] See H. Putnam, *Reason, Truth and History* (Cambridge: C.U.P., 1981), chs. 3 and 6.

[14] See my *Theory of Knowledge*, p. 72 and pp. 136ff.

[15] Consider the way in which a Kantian thing-in-itself is not specifiable in terms of any concepts that we have, except of course the concept of a thing-in-itself, if there *is* such a concept.

what is brought under it in the process of conceptualization. (There is this suggestion in the Hegelian line of thought that I surveyed earlier.) Could our best ways of thinking still be false? Must they be? There is certainly no 'must' about it, despite what idealists have said (and I shall return to that and similar issues in Chapter 6). To suppose otherwise is to think of concepts as, so to speak, distorting lenses. But why should they be thought of in that way? They may, as some philosophers have suggested, be compared with sieves or nets, but there is nothing intrinsically distorting about sieves or nets. Is it possible, however (to continue with this analogy), for the best possible net to fail to catch the fish? A net's ability to carry out its function may of course be limited by what is possible in a given material, e.g. by whether the holes are small enough or the material strong enough. But even if that aspect of the comparison is taken seriously, all that follows is that even our best thought may not be sufficiently refined or subtle to catch all aspects of reality. Nevertheless, it would be only in that sense, i.e. as being beyond the scope of our minds to comprehend, that reality might be other than that which is specifiable even in the best set of concepts. That is a different matter from the suggestion that those concepts might be distorting. Hence, given these terms of reference there seems nothing wrong with the suggestion that there may be more to reality than we can conceive of. It is another matter with the suggestion that it might be *different*, since there is no possibility of our having any idea of how it might be different from *any* way in which we might conceive it. That suggestion is thus empty.

Realism nevertheless involves the suggestion of something's being set over against our ways of thinking. It provides at least the idea of a limit on those ways of thinking, and to the extent that that idea is plausible so is realism. It might be thought that all this by-passes the considerations raised by Dummett, since its concern is with the sense that is to be attached to 'realism' and to a reality distinct from our ways of construing it. But in a way it simply provides the most general and fundamental case that an anti-realist would have to deal with. For realism so construed implies the possible existence of something that may lie beyond any means of conceptualization by us, and therefore beyond any possibility of the verification or otherwise by us of statements which have to do with it. Dummett's concern with the realism/anti-realism issue, as is the case with some other modern philosophers, including ones on the other side of the fence, is with whether a theory of meaning involves reference to more than truth-conditions, in the form of verification-conditions. Behind that concern, however, is a metaphysical concern with the question of the extent to which reality is confined to what we understand. If there is a similarity between anti-realism and idealism, it is transcendental idealism that is the relevant form of idealism, as that way of putting the issues indicates.

The truth in all this lies in the truisms that we cannot think that which we cannot think, and we cannot understand what lies outside the concepts that we have, let alone those which we, as human beings, might have. If anti-realism is any different from straightforward verificationism (and it is often claimed that there is a distinction), then it relies on those truisms and infers from them that there is no reality outside our concepts. But there is a difference between saying that we can have no conception of a reality that is not mediated by our concepts (even if we have a conception of reality as set against our concepts) and saying that there is no reality outside our concepts. To maintain the latter is in effect to maintain a form of Hegelianism, but a Hegelianism which does not even recognize the contrast between concepts and the fact of experience. If that is not how it is, it is hard to see a difference from classical verificationism.

3. Ontology

What there is

If someone raises the question 'What exists?' or 'What is there?', it may be supposed that the most direct way of answering the question is to give a list of things – people, trees, animals, houses, etc. Any such answer, however, presupposes some system of classification into kinds of things. If it is thought that that conclusion can be avoided by simply listing particular things, perhaps by name, the questions still remain of what counts as a particular thing and how we are to identify particular things. The answers to those questions bring in issues about the criteria of identity for the kind of thing in question. Hence the reference to kinds of thing seems unavoidable. It follows in turn that the question 'What exists?' must, either directly or indirectly, involve also questions about the *kinds* of thing that exist.

It is clear that some questions about the kinds of thing that exist are questions which should properly be addressed to particular kinds of specialist, e.g. questions about the existence of quasars, quarks, chalones, abominable snowmen, conditioned responses or democratic governments. It is not clear that such questions are appropriately addressed to philosophers, although philosophers *have* had things to say about some of these, if only in a negative way to the effect that there cannot be things of such and such a kind because there is an incoherence in the concept involved. On the other hand, if one turns to one modern philosopher who has had much to say about ontology – Quine – one finds a preoccupation with questions about whether there are abstract entities, as opposed to concrete ones; whether, for example, there are classes, numbers and propositions, as opposed to particular things, numerals and sentences. In that sort of context a tough-minded philosopher will eschew anything that smacks of the abstract in favour of the hard world of concrete, particular, physical objects, and will depart from that only where problems cannot be solved otherwise.

In Quine's case one controlling thought in relation to these issues is provided by the belief that the questions involved are on the same continuum as those of natural science. That belief presupposes the further belief that there is no such thing as the analytic/synthetic distinction, so that any philosophical thesis to the effect that philosophy has as its domain a realm of necessary, or at any rate analytic, truths is untenable.[1] Quine also seems to think that physics is the dominant natural science and that the physical world must be accepted as a starting point for any inquiries into ontological issues. Finally, in Quine's view, knowledge and its acquisition must be construed in terms of a psychology which is fundamentally behaviourist, or at least whatever the latest way of thinking takes to be 'scientific psychology', and thus based on what are ultimately physical concepts. To accept this is to construe questions about knowledge in terms of what Quine calls 'naturalized epistemology'. That is to say that the proper questions to ask about knowledge are not ones about the *justification* of claims to knowledge, but about how the acquisition of knowledge, either by the individual or in general, are to be *explained*. The slogan which sums up the position from which Quine's approach to ontology is derived is 'To be is to be the value of a variable.'[2] What exists is what can be quantified over, i.e. what can be substituted for the variable of an acceptable quantified formula which could form part of a scientifically acceptable theory about the world. What exists is thus what is presupposed in the apparatus of the best theory about the world.

Anyone with a keen sense of philosophical history will see that there is a difference between these concerns (and the ways of resolving them) and those which have figured under the heading of 'ontology' in much of the history of philosophy. If that is the case, Quine might be accused of simply changing the subject; and the same might be said of naturalized epistemology in relation to traditional epistemology. I mean by this that the questions that Quine seeks to answer are not the same questions as those which have preoccupied more traditional metaphysicians and epistemologists; and this does not mean that the more traditional questions do not have to be answered. That there are differences between Quine's approach and that of more traditional metaphysicians can be seen from two considerations about the main traditional strand of metaphysical thinking about ontology, when that is *not* based on a distinction between appearance and reality. In saying that I wish to indicate that our concern from now onwards will be with the first of the two

---

[1] W. V. Quine, 'Two dogmas of empiricism' in *From a Logical Point of View* (Cambridge, Mass.: Harvard U.P., 1953).

[2] For 'naturalized epistemology' see the paper with that title in *Ontological Relativity* (New York: Columbia U.P., 1962). For the slogan 'To be is to be the value of a variable' see the paper 'On what there is' in *From a Logical Point of View*.

kinds of metaphysics that I distinguished in Chapter 1, i.e. that which is not concerned with appearance and reality.

In the case of the first consideration that I shall mention it may seem at first sight that I am wrong to say that a distinction between appearance and reality is not presupposed. It is that metaphysicians have generally been concerned not simply with the question 'What exists?' but with the question 'What basically exists?'. It is true that those questions have sometimes been conflated. Wittgenstein, for example, begins his *Tractatus Logico-Philosophicus* by saying 'The world is all that is the case. The world is the totality of facts and not of things.' That sounds as if he is saying that there exist facts but not things. Further consideration of the *Tractatus*, however, reveals that he would better be interpreted as saying that things have a merely secondary existence in dependence on facts. Other philosophers have given other accounts of the primacy and posteriority of different categories of things. Nevertheless, to say that certain things or certain kinds of thing are those which primarily or basically exist is not to say that the things which are secondary constitute mere appearance. Hence, there is in fact no distinction between reality and appearance presupposed here. As we saw in the last chapter, even to say that X is more real than Y is not to say that Y constitutes appearance.

On the other hand, the question of what basically exists or even the question which we noted in Chapter 1 as put by Russell about what constitutes the ultimate furniture of the universe[3] may suggest something that goes part of the way towards Quine's position – namely that there is at least a continuity between these questions and those asked by physicists concerned to identify ultimate particles. Russell attempts to disarm such a comment by saying that his atomism is a *logical*, not a physical, atomism. Without further explanation, however, such a characterization of his project is not very enlightening. Nevertheless, it seems clear that Russell and a whole host of earlier philosophers have not thought of their inquiries as being, in any real sense, continuous with those of natural scientists. I shall return directly to what Aristotle in particular has to say on these matters.

The second consideration that I have in mind in distinguishing traditional philosophical concerns over ontology from those of Quine is that philosophers practising traditional ontology have generally thought that their claims had the status of necessary truths. Quine would reject that on doctrinal grounds, particularly the one previously mentioned –

[3]   B. Russell, 'The philosophy of logical atomism' in R. C. Marsh (ed.), *Logic and Knowledge* (London: Allen and Unwin, 1956).

that the analytic/synthetic distinction is untenable. Yet when Wittgenstein, to revert to the example mentioned earlier, said that the world consisted of facts and not of things, he did not mean to suggest that it was a merely contingent fact that that was so – something which could have been otherwise. The same applies to other claims about what basically exists and to other claims concerning the structure of what exists. An assessment of such claims ought not to depend solely on doctrinal issues of a quite general kind, such as those which underlie Quine's views, but on the validity or otherwise of the arguments for them. To get a clear view of that will involve setting out, at least in schematic form, some specimen ontologies. It should be evident, however, that the traditional ontologist is concerned neither with something akin to natural history nor with something akin to basic physics.

One further point needs to be made by way of prolegomenon. Even a casual survey of ontological theories will indicate that the principle of economy and 'Ockham's razor' play a large part in the exercise. Ockham's razor, as it is called, involves in itself an ontological claim, if taken in the original version of 'entities are not to be multiplied beyond necessity'. There is obviously something unsatisfactory about the proliferation of supposed entities if such a proliferation does not do a useful job, does not solve any problems, or is without any valid ground. Economy is a useful principle within science or within any discipline that seeks for explanations of things. Its utility is, however, relative to such an end, and economy has no particular virtue for its own sake. The cardinal rule must be not to postulate additional entities if those already postulated will perform whatever explanatory function is pertinent. As we shall see in Chapter 5 there arises in the context of theories of universals the question of whether one needs to postulate real, abstract, general entities called 'universals'. Those who are termed 'nominalists' have opposed the postulation of such things, claiming, for example, that the only general things are words, and they have often appealed to considerations of economy in favour of their view. The real issue, however, is whether it is possible to explain the possibility of our thinking and speaking about the world in general ways without supposing that entities of a general kind exist. If it is not possible, considerations of economy have no force.

Being-*qua*-being

As I noted in Chapter 1, Aristotle raises in his works the question of whether it is possible for there to be a science of being in general, or a science of 'what is' for its own sake, as distinct from sciences concerned with particular forms of being, such as physics, biology or psychology. Put in that way the question perhaps suggests an affinity with Quinean questions about the continuity of philosophy with natural science. The Aristotelian conception of a science, however, is not quite 'our' conception of a natural science. For him the aim of a science, as a branch of knowledge, was simply to arrive at the principles underlying a certain subject-matter and to show how explanation of that subject-matter is to be produced by their means. There is no conception of a natural science pursued by means of an experimental methodology. It has been suggested by scholars, particularly G. E. L. Owen,[4] that Aristotle's answer to his question was initially 'No', but that as a result of certain refinements in his presuppositions he came to see that a certain kind of 'Yes' was possible after all.

The refinements were in his theory of meaning; they involved the idea that where many things are called 'X' it may be that one of them is called 'X' primarily and the others are called 'X' in some way derivatively from it. This led him to say that while many things are said to be (and I stress the words 'said to' in this in order to bring out the point about meaning) it is substances which are said to be primarily. (The reasons for this conclusion will emerge as I discuss the issues further.) In addition, though this is more controversial, he seems to say that while many things are said to be substances, one kind of substance – that which is exemplified in God and perhaps only in God, since it provides in some sense its own rationale – is said to be substance primarily. If this is his view, it follows that there is a sense in which by studying God one studies the primary kind of substance, and by studying substance one studies the primary kind of entity – so that in God one finds the best view of what it is to be an entity. Aristotle could thus say (*Metaphysics E* (6).1) that theology and the science of being-*qua*-being can be identified with each other.

Much of this account of Aristotle is perhaps arguable or disputable. What is not subject to argument is that Aristotle was very much concerned with ontology before he came to any such conclusion. Thus in the *Categories* (which is generally recognized as an early work) he produces a classification of 'things that are', although the context reveals that while he opposes 'things that are' to words he has in mind by the term things insofar as they are picked out by words. Hence a certain conception of the relation between words and the world is presupposed,

---

[4]   G. E. L. Owen, 'Logic and metaphysics in some earlier works of Aristotle' in J. Barnes, M. Schofield and R. Sorabji (eds.), *Articles on Aristotle* (London: Duckworth, 1979), Vol. 3; also his 'The Platonism of Aristotle' in *Articles on Aristotle* (London: Duckworth, 1975), Vol. 1.

and the basis for the resultant ontology is the relation that we have to the world as exemplified in our ways of talking about it. I shall return to that point later. Aristotle takes it for granted that we pick out things in the world by our words and we say things about those things that are picked out as the subjects of our discourse. He thus presupposes that our linguistically expressed thought has a certain structure – that of subject and predicate. In a similar way Frege and his descendents, such as, in this respect, Quine, presuppose that the basic structure of our language (the deep structure, one might say, in Chomsky's terms) conforms to the apparatus of variables and quantification. That is to say that all forms of proposition are derivable from certain basic ones which can for that reason be thought of as representing the basic or deep structure of language: on the Fregean conception that basic logical form is provided by the apparatus of predicates and variables governed by quantifiers.

Given these kinds of assumptions, Aristotle distinguishes two relations that the things picked out by the predicate expression may have or fail to have with whatever is picked out as the subject. These relations are those of being said of a subject (where being said of is something that can hold good of a *thing*) and being inherent in a subject. Given that those relations can either obtain or fail to obtain, Aristotle is enabled by these means to distinguish between substances and non-substances and between particular things and general things. If something can be said of a subject it is general; if not it is particular. If it can inhere in a subject it is not a substance; if it cannot it *is* a substance. Since something may be both substance and particular, or just one of these, or finally neither, we have as a result a distinction between four kinds of entity – particular and general substances and particular and general non-substances.[5]

Particular substances are those things which are neither said of nor inherent in a subject; hence, within these terms of reference, they may be seen to have the highest claim to the title of 'subject' itself. They are basically what is there to be talked about; for these purposes they are what basically exists. Later in his works Aristotle adduces other considerations which reinforce that claim and which are therefore taken to lead firmly to the conclusion that particular substances, e.g., as he puts it, this man or this horse, are what primarily exist. In the *Categories* Aristotle next distinguishes between the various kinds of thing which can be said of or be inherent in such a subject, so producing a list of what he calls 'categories'. He does this apparently on the basis of a survey of the various questions that can be asked about a particular substance as

[5]   See, e.g., the notes by J. Ackrill in his translation and notes on Aristotle's *Categories and De Interpretatione* (Oxford: Clarendon Press, 1963).

subject – questions such as 'What is it?', 'Of what sort is it?', 'Where is it?' and so on. The categories, which are said to be ten in number, are thought of as ultimate kinds of being (ultimate genera of being, Aristotle sometimes says, being itself not comprising a genus since the categories are not related to it as species to genus and are, *a fortiori*, not distinguishable from each other in terms of differentiae). Aristotle nevertheless argues for the differences between the categories and he does this in effect by attempting to show that there are things that can be said of one or other of them that cannot be said of the others. The treatment of these matters which is actually provided in the *Categories* is however neither thorough-going nor comprehensive; the text is in any case incomplete. Nevertheless, the differences that he detects between the categories cannot amount to differentiae in the formal sense, for the reason that I have mentioned above.

What emerges from all this is that in Aristotle's view there are ten ultimate kinds of way in which a thing may be said to be – as substance, as quantity, as quality, as relative, and so on. Apart from substances all things so characterized depend for their existence on their inherence in particular substances, which are themselves instances of species and genera of substances. Hence it is particular substances which primarily exist. Things such as qualities and places exist but only in a secondary way, in the sense that if there were not particular substances there would not be things of those kinds. It is possible that part of the motivation for the theory is Aristotle's wish to counter Platonism, which, in Aristotelian terms, might be characterized as asserting that the primarily existing things are not particular substances such as a particular man or horse, but general, although ideal, entities, i.e. Forms. Aristotle is in effect saying that if one considers what is involved in the expression of our thought about the world it must become evident that such things as goodness and beauty could not constitute the self-subsistent Forms that Plato supposes them to be; they can have only a secondary existence, in dependence on particular substances which are their instances. They cannot therefore have the status that Plato claimed for them.

The Greek word '*ousia*', which is conventionally translated as 'substance', means more literally 'being', or, if construed as an abstract noun, 'being-ness'. That fact, which does not emerge from the conventional translation 'substance', reveals Aristotle's concern in all this with 'what is'. Why then should not the whole thing be considered as part of a science of being-*qua*-being, since it is manifestly concerned with being and 'what is' and it is equally manifestly *not* concerned with any specific kind of being? Aristotle does not raise that question in the work called

Categories itself. If, however, he had some reluctance (as perhaps remarks elsewhere suggest) to call what he had been doing an exercise in the science of being-*qua*-being, it might be because neither the arrangement of the subject-matter nor the method pursued in its investigation conformed to what he thought requisite for a science. The subject-matter was not arrangeable in terms of species and genus, strictly conceived, and the method used was not that of demonstration (i.e. the strictly deductive derivation of necessary truths from necessary principles according to the rules of a first figure syllogism in Barbara). However that may be, Aristotle did come to think that a science of being-*qua*-being was possible, largely perhaps because, as suggested earlier, it could be identified with the science of theology, if God is the primary instance of substance and substance the primary kind of being.

It might be objected, however, that in coming to that conclusion Aristotle had changed his views very considerably. While the argument of the *Categories* can be regarded as directed to the conclusion that it is particular substances that primarily exist and that other kinds of thing exist in a secondary and dependent way, can it plausibly be suggested that the later line of thought is directed to the conclusion that it is God who primarily exists and that other particular substances, let alone other kinds of thing, have a secondary and dependent existence? For does that not suggest that particular and ordinary things are less than real? The answer to these questions is that there is no objection in principle to such an interpretation of Aristotle as long as he is *not* taken to say that the other things are not, properly speaking, real. This kind of metaphysics does not involve a distinction between appearance and reality, and speaking of what primarily exists and of what exists only in a secondary way need have no suggestion even of differences in degrees of reality, let alone of a relegation of the secondary to a realm of appearances. Certainly there is no implication in what Aristotle has to say that substances are more real than things in other categories. Similarly the superiority to other things that Aristotle attributes to God is not a superiority on the scale of reality, and not one that implies a contrast with a realm of appearances, even if it is the case, in his view, that in God we see what it is to be in a primary way.

The influence of Aristotle and the metaphysics of substance, involving as it does the attempt to identify the primary kind of substance, is persistent in Western philosophical thought, even when, through Descartes' influence, the metaphysics of appearance and reality has been introduced as well. There is a considerable similarity between the status of God in rationalist thought, e.g. in Spinoza, and the status of God in Aristotle. In the case of the seventeenth- and eighteenth-century rationalists, however, the distinction between appearance and reality plays its part as well, and that is not the case with Aristotle. By no means all philosophers have been satisfied with the Aristotelian doctrine of the categories, and I shall return to certain criticisms of it later in this chapter. It is possible, however, to argue for kinds of word–world relation other than that which gives rise to the category of substance and the other Aristotelian categories, and thus to argue for other categories. What, for example, of the category of events, which lies at the heart, even if in a technical sense, of Whitehead's metaphysics, and which has recently been re-invoked, in a more ordinary sense and for different reasons, by Donald Davidson.[6] Davidson's motivation is not really metaphysical, but for Whitehead events are certainly the fundamental category and things are, as he puts it, 'ingredient into' them. That is a very difficult notion, which it would not be profitable to explain here, but it is clear enough that for Whitehead things in the ordinary sense have a secondary status, not the primary one that they have for Aristotle. Whitehead thinks in effect that this view is implied by the language of science.

By contrast, Russell and Wittgenstein in their Logical Atomist period suggested, as I have already noted, that it is the category of facts that is the fundamental category. Things in the ordinary sense are constituents of facts. The reason for lighting upon the notion of facts as the fundamental category lies in the thought that it is the proposition that is the basic unit of discourse and of meaning, not the individual word as Aristotle seems to suppose. That is a thought common to a number of late nineteenth-century philosophers, particularly perhaps Frege, although he himself had no truck with facts. It is summed up in Frege's dictum that it is only in the context of a proposition that a word has a meaning[7] – a dictum taken over by the Wittgenstein of the *Tractatus* with the modification that 'meaning' (*Bedeutung*) is taken in the sense of 'reference' in accordance with a later Fregean doctrine. The concept of a fact reflects a certain kind of words–world relation in that a fact is what is statable by means of true propositions or statements. Hence, when Wittgenstein says that the world is the totality of facts and not of things he is in effect

[6] See A. N. Whitehead, *Process and Reality*, Corrected edition, edited by D. R. Griffin and D. W. Sherburne (New York: Free Press, 1978), and *Science and the Modern World* (New York: Macmillan Co., 1926). For Davidson see his *Essays on Actions and Events* (Oxford: Clarendon Press, 1980), pp. 103ff.

[7] G. Frege, *Foundations of Arithmetic*, trans. J. L. Austin (Oxford: Blackwell, 1950), p. x.

spelling out the implications of that words–world relation and of the thought that it is basic. Facts must be the basic category of existents, it is suggested, if that view of what is basic to language and meaning is true.

Putting matters in that way suggests that the necessity of an ontological claim of this kind is relative to a certain conception of what makes meaningful discourse possible. That is what is implied in the words 'if that view of what is basic to language and meaning is true'. A possible objection to any such claim is therefore that alternative conceptions of what makes meaningful discourse possible can surely be produced. I shall be considering in the next section but one possible objections of that kind and their implications. Before I do so, however, it will be as well to distinguish what is at stake in this respect from the Quinean thesis of ontological relativity, which seems superficially similar. Given what I have already said about Quine I can be brief.

Ontological relativity

Quine's thesis of ontological relativity is associated with his doctrine of the indeterminacy of translation and with what is for him the connected doctrine of the underdetermination of theory by data (although Quine has not always had the same view of the exact relation between these doctrines). One way of stating the relation between the two latter doctrines is the following. Quine holds that whether one is concerned with translation from another language or the interpretation of what is said in one's own language (what he calls the heterophonic and homophonic cases respectively), such translation or interpretation is a matter of putting a theoretical interpretation on the noises made or marks inscribed. The interpretation is thus made on the basis of data available to sense-perception. At this point Quine brings to bear a thesis derived from Duhem[8], that alternative and even conflicting theories are always possible with respect to a given set of data, and there is no fact of the matter which is right. Theories are thus underdetermined by data.

The way in which this applies to the interpretation and translation of language is this. When, to use Quine's own example, someone using an alien language says 'Gavagai' in the presence of a rabbit, he may be referring to a persisting rabbit or only to what Quine calls a 'rabbit-stage', and the data do not determine which. The same applies to the use of 'rabbit' itself. Some may and do think (as I do) that this way of construing what it is to understand another person involves an almost absurdly

[8]   P. Duhem, *The Aim and Structure of Physical Theory*, trans. P. P. Wiener (Princeton: Princeton U.P., 1954).

artificial way of presenting the facts. Must the interpretation of
another's words be a matter simply of constructing a theory to explain
the noises made? Could we not ask the person concerned what he was
referring to? If that rather simple-minded (though nevertheless pertinent) objection is ruled out (as it must be in any case in the heterophonic
case where a linguist or anthropologist is trying to interpret an unknown
language), could we not gather from the circumstances what is at stake?
Can we not assume that we are concerned with human beings with
human needs and interests with human ways of satisfying them, so that
human and personal relations with others are possible?

If the situation is construed in Quine's excessively abstract terms, it
may indeed seem to follow that as far as we are concerned there is no
fact of the matter about what is being referred to; for the data do not
determine which theory is correct. Quine therefore concludes that
reference is, as he puts it, 'inscrutable'. But questions about reference
and questions about ontology go hand in hand; hence if reference is
inscrutable this must have a consequence for ontology. That thought
leads directly to the Quinean thesis of the relativity of ontology. First,
the question of what exists is now seen as a matter of what our theory
commits us to. Second, as Quine says,[9] 'Specifying the universe of a
theory makes sense only relative to some background theory, and only
relative to some choice of a manual of translation of the one theory into
the other.' Thus, in the case of the man saying 'rabbit', the question of
what he is committed to is a matter of decision about what he is referring
to, and that decision is relative to the theory with which we approach the
case and relative too to the manual of translation which we use in interpreting what he says in terms of our own language (which may or may
not, of course, be the same as his). In Quine's view, the same applies to
ourselves also since, as he says,[10] 'Commonly of course the background
theory will simply be a containing theory, and in this case no question of
a manual of translation arises. But this is after all just a degenerate case of
translation still – the case where the rule of translation is the
homophonic one.'

This means, then, that (to put the issue clumsily) what we can take
both ourselves and others to take to exist is relative to the theory and
language that we bring to the situation. That presupposes but goes
beyond the thesis that to be is to be the value of a variable. The latter
implies that what we can take to exist is simply what we can quantify
over. The thesis of ontological relativity is concerned with what we

[9] W. V. Quine, *Ontological Relativity*, pp. 54–5.
[10] Ibid., p. 55.

understand when we or others speak of what exists. To determine what we should commit ourselves to ontologically is a matter of determining the best theory of these things. Thus Davidson's claim that in order to understand the logic of action sentences we need to invoke the notion of an event[11] is part and parcel of the thesis that the best theory of what we say in speaking of actions is one that involves quantification over events. To this Quine's thesis of ontological relativity adds that because of the Duhem thesis there is no finally true theory, so that there is no saying what we say exists in an absolute way.

Whether or not the Quinean thesis of ontological relativity is correct (and it is worth observing that its truth or falsity could be independent of the considerations that he adduces in its favour), it presupposes considerations about what for certain purposes we should take ourselves as committed to – whether, for example, in order to understand the facts of mathematics we need to take ourselves as committed to the existence of numbers, whether in order to understand the facts of these we need to take ourselves as committed to the existence of classes, and so on. This may suggest a certain relativity in ontological commitment; but in fact it is still a matter of what is the best theory. The thesis of ontological relativity goes beyond this, holding that it is indeterminate in fact what people, including ourselves, say exists. Any thesis about that is relative to the language and theory that is brought to it. The relativity that I hope to show as attaching to traditional theses in ontology is not of that kind.

The relativity of philosophical ontologies

When Aristotle says that the things that basically exist are substances he clearly thinks that some necessity attaches to that assertion. It is not a merely contingent matter, not even a bare matter of fact. Yet when one examines what is at stake, as I tried to do earlier, it becomes apparent that a certain point of departure is assumed in the exercise, a certain point of view about language and its relation to the world. If, then, the conclusions have the character of necessity it can be so only relative to that point of departure. I think that that thesis is generalizable so as to apply to ontologies in general. One might indeed say that the argument that is presupposed in setting out such an ontology has a character similar to that which Kant called a 'transcendental argument'.

There is much argument in the literature about exactly what a

---

[11] D. Davidson, *Essays on Actions and Events*, pp. 105ff.

transcendental argument is and how much it can achieve.[12] The waters are muddied because Kant's own arguments and his use of the term 'transcendental' had to do with the possibility of objective experience, and Kant would not have contemplated a transcendental argument having to do with other matters; it would have gone against what he took to be the meaning of 'transcendental' as having to do with the conditions of possible experience. One can nevertheless identify a common form which transcendental arguments as Kant conceived them have, apart from their having to do with possible experience. In respect of this common form they have to do with showing that something must be so because it constitutes a condition of the possibility of something else. If it is put like that it is hard to see that such an argument *could* show that something must be so in an absolute sense. If X constitutes a necessary condition for the possibility of Y, then if Y is to be possible X must exist. But an argument along these lines cannot show that X must exist, except on that condition. On the other hand, if one has good reason for thinking that Y *must* exist, so much the better for the existence of X.

When I set out in an earlier section the sort of thing that Aristotle was trying to do in the *Categories*, I indicated that in inquiring about what there is he starts from a certain word–world relation which is implied when language is construed in a particular way. That is to say that he assumes that words get their meaning by picking out things, so that things can to that extent be seen in the mirror of language. Indeed one might say that what he is concerned with as far as ontology is concerned is simply things in so far as they are picked out by words. To put the matter in that way, however, might make the limitations of the exercise too explicit. In any case, since words do not normally occur by themselves but in certain grammatical structures, an account of the semantics of language must make reference to those structures as well as to the meaning of individual words. In conformity with this Aristotle takes it that when we speak we say things *about* things as subjects. One might say that this presupposes that propositions are of subject–predicate form, but the point that he is making is not one simply of grammar; the thesis is about what we are doing when we speak. Moreover, behind the language that we use are our thoughts; hence the thesis is not simply concerned with how we speak about the world, but how we think about it too.

[12] For recent discussions of transcendental arguments see, e.g., B. A. O. Williams, 'Knowledge and meaning in the philosophy of mind', *Philosophical Review*, Vol. LXXVII, 1968, pp. 216–28 and R. Harrison, 'Transcendental arguments and idealism' in G. N. A. Vesey (ed.), *Idealism Past and Present*, Royal Institute of Philosophy Lecture Series 13 (Cambridge: C.U.P., 1982), pp. 211–24.

Nevertheless, the way in which Aristotle puts the issue invites a criticism that has sometimes been made by grammarians – that Aristotle's thesis about subject and predicate is the product of a limited acquaintance with languages; it is simply a generalization from Greek. How do we know that there are not languages which do not have a subject–predicate structure? That criticism may be disarmed to some extent if it is true that Aristotle's thesis is in fact about how we think, not merely about how we speak. Noam Chomsky has indeed claimed that the notions of subject and predicate correspond to features of the deep structure of language and therefore reflect linguistic universals which are and must be common to all languages.[13] That claim is too complex to assess here, but it amounts to the claim that picking out something and then characterizing it in some way is an activity which is fundamental to human thought and thus to human language. That thesis, however, invites the question why it must be so. Why should such a form of thought and form of language to be taken to be fundamental? Might there not be other forms of thought which have an equal or better claim to be basic?

Similar considerations apply to the views of Frege, who is often represented as presenting a very different point of view from that of Aristotle, and one that constitutes a considerable advance.[14] As I have previously indicated, Frege is one of a group of philosophers who, towards the end of the nineteenth century, suggested that the proposition (or in some cases the judgment) was the basic unit of meaning and thus the fundamental unit of thought. In many ways this was a reaction against the view dominant in earlier empiricism that thought comprises ideas and that the basic unit of meaning is the word. (In this respect Aristotle's position represents a compromise, since, although he puts a great deal of weight on the notion of predication, it is arguable that at bottom he still thought of a proposition as a complex of names, inheriting Plato's problem of how, as it was put, one thing could have many names.) Frege's theory of meaning was more sophisticated than the theory of those against whom he was reacting, in that he saw that different components of a proposition contribute to the meaning of the whole in different ways.

His model for his conception of the proposition was the mathematical function; he construed propositions as analysable into function and argument, and the whole might have one of the alternative values – the

[13] N. Chomsky, *Aspects of the Theory of Syntax* (Cambridge, Mass.: MIT Press, 1965) and *Language and Mind* (New York: Harcourt Brace and World, 1968).
[14] See M. Dummett, *Frege* (London: Duckworth, 1973), pp. 257ff.

true and the false. This led to a fundamental distinction between concept and object, the notion of a concept corresponding to the functional aspect of a proposition (in Aristotelian terms to the predicate), and that of an object corresponding to the argument of the function (in Aristotelian terms to the subject). Frege said that functions are, by contrast with their arguments, 'unsaturated'. They contain an empty place to be filled by the argument and are therefore incomplete. The same feature carries over to concepts by contrast with objects. From the functional expression 'is red' one can of course derive the expression 'redness', and that expression names an abstract object, although not a concrete object such as whatever it is that is red. All this is possible, however, only because there is the concept *red* which goes with the expression 'is red' and under which fall various concrete objects such as pillar-boxes.

It is often suggested that it was a discovery of fundamental importance that the predicate parts of propositions correspond to concepts, not objects, and that abstract objects are in general parasitical on concrete objects, in the sense that there would not be redness if it did not at least make sense to speak of things as red. And so in many ways it was. We are given thereby a pair of fundamental categories which are presented as basic to thought – those of concept and object. Aristotle, it is said, failed to see that predicate expressions do not correspond to objects, but to concepts. (And it might be added, although I am not sure that it ever has been, that the Aristotelian categories, considered as ultimate genera and so as ultimate forms of predication, ought to be regarded as kinds of concepts under which concrete objects fall.) It might nevertheless be asked, by way of criticism, why, first, it should be accepted that thought must necessarily conform to this function/argument structure, and why, second, it should be accepted even so that the basic kind of object must be concrete. Why cannot thought have some other structure which is not parasitical on the function/argument structure, and what is the rationale, whether it can or not, for the belief that it is concrete objects that are fundamental among objects? (Whether or not Frege himself held the latter view, others have done so.) Is it enough to say that that is what thought and language are like?[15] Do they *have* to be?

There are, after all, philosophers who have been willing to contemplate the possibility that our ordinary ways of speaking may be founded on and reducible to what is called a 'property-location language', in which the basic form of discourse will involve the identification of a property and the assertion of its incidence at a certain place at a certain

---

[15] Cf. J. Searle, *Speech Acts* (Cambridge: C.U.P., 1970), p. 120.

time.[16] Such views at least demand consideration. Moreover, Bradley's theory of judgment in his *Principles of Logic* involves the conception that judgment always entails bringing reality under ideas. Although the distinction between reality and idea might be assimilated to Frege's distinction between object and concept, Bradley is led in the end to the suggestion that what might be supposed to be ordinary concrete objects are really what he calls 'concrete universals' – collections of ideas characterizing reality in a particular way when taken together. Hence, in Bradley's view, there is a sense in which concrete objects are analysable in terms of abstract objects, i.e. universals. I shall return to these specific issues later, e.g. in Chapters 5 and 6. For the moment it is enough to indicate that the points of departure presupposed by Aristotle and Frege for their ontology need further justification.

Something like that further justification is provided by Strawson's discussion in the opening chapters of his *Individuals*. Behind Strawson's discussion lie further sophistications over meaning and reference (although these have in turn come in for further criticisms by more recent logicians, such as Kripke and Putnam).[17] Basically Strawson views meaning as arising from what we *do* with language; behind that perhaps lies the Wittgensteinian slogan that meaning is use. Reference arises from the fact that we identify things in discourse in order to communicate things about them. Hence Strawson takes as his point of departure the idea of speaker–hearer identification. In discourse the basic activity involved is that of one person identifying things for others. Strawson then asks what is necessary for the possibility of that activity, what has to exist basically for that activity to be possible. His answer to that question is (without reference to the arguments used to support it) that what basically exist are ordinary material objects in space and time (so-called basic particulars) and persons (although persons themselves have to be thought of as 'owning' bodies, which are a kind of material object). There are also various kinds of secondary particulars and general things or universals. The exercise that Strawson carries out might therefore be characterized as an attempt to provide a rationale for Fregean and Aristotelian claims about the primacy for ontology of particular concrete things; and that rationale is sought in what is necessarily presupposed in human communication considered in terms of speaker–hearer identification.

[16] Cf. A. J. Ayer, *Foundations of Empirical Knowledge* (London: Macmillan, 1947), ch. 5, and the discussion provided by P. F. Strawson in his *Individuals* (London: Methuen, 1959), chs. 6 and 7.
[17] See S. Kripke, *Naming and Necessity* (Oxford: Blackwell, 1980) and H. Putnam, 'The meaning of "meaning" ' in his *Mind, Language and Reality: Philosophical Papers, Vol. 2* (Cambridge: C.U.P., 1975).

It might be said that if Strawson's conclusions are presented thus, they are not very surprising. For are not the parties to speaker–hearer identification persons and are they not, at least in part, material objects related to each other in spatio-temporal ways? Is it not also the case that from the point of view of identification it is objects that have pride of place? Nevertheless, Strawson goes further than Frege and Aristotle in seeking a rationale for their attempts to base ontological conclusions on considerations concerning language and meaning by further reference to a characteristic human activity, a form of communication, from which language and meaning get their life. In other words, the answer to be given to the sceptic in this context is to appeal to what is necessarily involved in the relation between ourselves and the world if there is to be thought and language about the world. In that sense the Strawsonian investigation digs more deeply than that of the others whom I have mentioned.

There is room, however, for further scepticism. It might be said, as I have in effect already suggested, that one gets out of this kind of exercise only what one puts into it in the first place. I said earlier that the kind of argument that is involved in these attempts to set out the necessary conditions for the possibility of whatever is at stake is one that can be termed 'transcendental' in something like the Kantian sense, with the qualification that it is not restricted to the conditions of possible *experience*. For Kant the converse of a transcendental argument is what he calls the 'exposition' of a concept – the unfolding of what is necessarily involved in it. A transcendental argument seeks to show as necessary to the possibility of X what is in effect necessarily involved in the concept of X, even if it is not analytically involved. What is necessarily involved in the concept of speaker-hearer identification is that it is carried out by persons who, because they are bodily, inhabit a spatio-temporal world which is public and common to them, and who conform to common and public standards of what successful communication amounts to. It is natural for such beings that the primary objects of identification should be public, common, spatio-temporal objects.

Why, however, should such a premium be put on identification? Ought one not at least to consider seriously the possibility that what is central to human communication is that one person makes clear to another which universals are instantiated where and when? It is not entirely obvious that, for that to be possible, there must be identification of concrete objects of the kind that Strawson calls 'basic particulars'. Further argument would be required to show that it *is* necessary, and it has to be admitted that Strawson does attempt to provide it via consideration of the limitations of a language in which there is no reference to particulars. One thing that seems to me crucial here, as I shall elaborate in Chapter 9, is the apparent impossibility of our thinking of ourselves simply as bundles of universals instantiated at a given place and time. Nevertheless, it does not seem that in concerning ourselves merely with the conditions of speaker–hearer identification we have reached the ultimate basis for conclusions about ontology.

It is perhaps possible to attain further insight into what is at stake by comparing what Strawson has to say with Kant, who is the second of the two philosophers whom Strawson acknowledges as predecessors (the first being Aristotle), and whom Strawson has approached directly and critically on these issues in his *The Bounds of Sense*. Kant sees the notion of *judgment* as of central importance in considering thought about the world, and judgment, we might say, involves, as it does for Aristotle and others, reference and predication. In Kantian terms it involves bringing intuitions under concepts. Although Kant sometimes speaks as if there could be intuitions and perhaps concepts without there being judgment, it is possible to interpret what he says as in line with Frege and others in maintaining that it is judgment that is the basic unit of thought. Kant comes to that idea, however, with a scheme of faculties already presupposed – particularly the·faculties of sensibility and understanding; and his prime aim is to show how the understanding is limited to the conditions of possible experience provided by sensibility. Kant inherited the epistemological framework involved in that scheme of faculties from his philosophical predecessors, particularly the British Empiricists.

Kant is perhaps not primarily concerned with ontology in the sense which is our main interest here. Given, however, the distinction between appearance and reality which we saw as applicable to his thought in the last chapter, it is reasonably clear that if he had been asked what basically exists he would have had to say 'Things-in-themselves'. Nevertheless, within the realm of the transcendentally ideal the answer to the question of what basically exists must be to the effect that there are sensations or appearances organized by the understanding such that they are my sensations and of objects having a certain persistence through time, an extension in space, and subject to causal laws.

The argument to that effect is Kant's so-called 'transcendental deduction'. Part of Kant's motivation in that argument is to show that experiences are not such that their conjunction and sequence is a function of the imagination, as Hume in effect suggested. That is to say that the course of experience is not a subjective matter, but is in some sense objective. That is sometimes construed as saying that what holds good in this way of experiences is true for all men and not merely true for me. It is impossible, however, to see how objectivity in that sense can emerge from the terms of reference without begging the question. For the point of departure is provided by *my* sensibility and *my* understanding only. (Kant in effect brings that out when he speaks of the 'I think' accompanying all my representations. It is important that it is the '*I* think'.) It is no doubt the case that, like many other philosophers who have relied upon this apparatus, Kant simply assumed that what one discovers in oneself in this respect applies equally to others; he had no sense of an 'other minds' problem. But it is that very assumption that I had in mind when speaking just now of begging the question. Kant's starting-point is in an important sense irremediably subjective, so that from the standpoints of sensibility and understanding so construed there is no possibility of deriving a world of public objects as we ordinarily understand that. Hence, despite the implications of the account of judgment, which might put Kant with Frege, the ontology that is to be abstracted from what Kant has to say has, as a result of the idealism, only a dubious connexion with a world of public objects. That any argument can take one from Kant's starting-point to such a world is, to say the least, problematic.

For an Aristotle and a Frege a world of public objects is something to be taken for granted; they are to that extent realists. In Strawson's case the idea of a world of public objects is written into the account of the framework relative to which the ontological claims are made. The contrast with Kant in this respect is illuminating. There is, however, another point to be derived from a consideration of Kant: if, behaving as a sceptic, one were to say to Kant 'That is all very well, but all that you have claimed is that these things must exist for creatures with my sensibility and understanding, and that is a very relative matter since there could surely exist in principle creatures of other kinds', Kant would reply that that supposition is not one that can be given any substance and is to that extent empty. Human understanding and sensibility constitute the limits within which alone there can intelligibly be judgment about what is so and what is not so. Hence one can give no genuine sense, no substantial content (as opposed to purely formal content) to suppositions about alternative forms of sensibility and understanding and about what may possibly exist for them.

Strawson's point of departure is superior to that of Aristotle (and indeed that of Frege also) in going behind the forms of language to the human activities that are presupposed by them, and it is superior to Kant's in having a public frame of reference built into it. But can it be supposed that, in a way analogous to what Kant claims of sensibility and understanding, it constitutes a limit such that there is no possibility of contemplating in any useful way alternative frames of reference and thereby alternative ontologies? The answer to that question must surely be 'No', for reasons already given – that in concentrating on speaker–hearer identification it emphasizes too specific a form of commerce with the world. Speaker–hearer identification is just one of the activities that we engage in with each other through the medium of language in relation to the world. Fact-stating, which was so much emphasized by Russell and the early Wittgenstein, is another example of such activity. One might indeed describe Strawson's theory as a metaphysics of things as opposed to the logical atomist metaphysics of facts. The rival ontologies are each relative to the point of departure that they presuppose, and neither can justifiably ascribe absolute necessity to what they assert as existent or primarily existent.

We are in fact confronted here with the phenomenon that the later Wittgenstein described in terms of the notion of a 'form of life'. Whether or not it is right to think of the later Wittgenstein as in any way Kantian in philosophical tendency, the notion of forms of life plays in his thought the role of something that provides a limit on what can intelligibly be said, just as sensibility and understanding do for Kant. It is a further matter whether he thought those limits to be absolute, as Kant seems to, or in some sense relative – just aspects of the 'natural history of man', as he sometimes puts it. Nevertheless, forms of life do provide a framework, exemplified in various aspects of our commerce with the world, relative to which it makes sense to say that there is this, that, or the other thing, when such remarks are meant to have some claim to necessity. That is certainly one of the implications of Wittgenstein's *On Certainty*, where it is suggested that the existence of certain things must be accepted in the sense that their denial would entail the unintelligibility of a whole host of things that we say and hold to be the case.

Whatever is to be said about particular examples of such claims, the limits imposed by forms of a life are not such that it is possible to describe them from outside; we cannot get outside the limits. All that can be said is that when we say that such and such things must exist, basically we presuppose some form of life, some form of commerce with each other and with the world in general. Moreover, the intelligibility of such claims presupposes that there is agreement in forms of life, since it is that which provides publicity, a common acceptability of such claims as making sense. Once we try to spell out what that involves in particular cases the relativity of the ontological claims becomes evident; it is only by leaving it all implicit that an ontological claim gets the appearance of more than relativity. It is an appearance all the same. While one point of departure for an ontology may be better than another for the sorts of reasons that I have indicated in comparing Aristotle, Frege, Kant and Strawson, there is no ground for thinking that it is possible to produce an ontology which is absolutely necessary.

To say that the world is the totality of facts, of things, or of events is to lay claim to one basic concept in terms of which the world is to be seen. The working out of such a claim may provide an interesting slant on the world; it may invite us to see it in this way rather than that other, and so free us from the shackles imposed by one particular preoccupation with how things are. But it cannot be said that the world *must* be construed in that way rather than this other, unless what is meant is merely that relative to a particular way of representing our commerce with the world it must be so construed. That, however, as I have been insisting, provides a relative necessity only. While that may be illuminating in spelling out what is implied in one particular form of commerce with the world, it may also rob bold ontological claims (such as the early Wittgenstein's claim that the world is the totality of facts and not of things) of the attractiveness that they have through their very boldness.

An ontology of this kind remains an attempt to set out what is implied, as regards the existence of things, in our commerce with the world. That implies also some conception of ourselves. I say 'conception of *ourselves*' advisedly, since I do not mean simply a conception of persons. Persons are as much part of the world as are other objects. It is the implication of a whole line of metaphysical thinking, which perhaps has its origin in Kant, although there are echoes of it in the thought of other philosophers, that the 'I' is not part of the world in the sense that I have been concerned with. If that is true it must affect the 'we' too. These are perhaps cryptic remarks, but I shall return to the theme later in Chapter 9.

Formal concepts

I have made considerable use in the foregoing of concepts like those of *thing*, *fact* and *event*. These concepts, along with others such as the Fregean *concept* and *object*, are what Wittgenstein in the *Tractatus*[18] called

18 L. Wittgenstein, *Tractatus Logico-Philosophicus* (London: Routledge and Kegan Paul, 1922, 1961), 4.126ff.

formal concepts, meaning to distinguish them from ordinary concepts which serve as principles of classification of things. Formal concepts are in effect concepts of ways in which language or thought meet the world, given how we speak and think. In a sense this is evident from the way in which Frege comes to his notions of concept and object, since these notions reflect the roles performed in language by predicate and subject, or function and argument, respectively. Indeed, in his paper on 'Concept and object' Frege found himself the proponent of a paradox when he said that the concept *horse* was not a concept but an object.[19] It is an object because the expression 'the concept *horse*', as a definite description, can be construed as name-like, rather than, as one might put it, predicate-like. It is thus an argument expression not a function expression, and according to Frege's criteria it picks out an object. Yet, given the meaning that it would normally be taken to have, the expression seems to refer to a concept. Wittgenstein's suggestion in the *Tractatus* 4.126ff. that concepts like those of *concept* and *object* are not proper concepts but what he calls formal concepts in effect warns us against a failure to bear in mind what the origins of such concepts are; that is to say they reflect, not things independent of language, but certain ways in which words meet the world.

The kind of ontology that I have been considering in this chapter is in effect one that is concerned with the question of what ultimate categories of things must be supposed to exist. It is difficult to spell out exactly what a category is. Aristotle sometimes spoke as if categories were simply the widest genera under which things fall. The situation has not been improved by the fact that subsequent philosophers, such as Kant and Hegel, have used the term 'category' in different ways which have only a remote connexion with Aristotle's use of the term. It is clear, however, that if one is concerned with classification in terms of species and genera the final moves to be made in the chain of wider and wider classifications – man, vertebrate, animal, living thing . . . substance, thing – are not the same as those which precede them. I shall have more to say about the notion of substance in the next chapter, but it should be clear already that the notion of a thing, to the extent that it is the equivalent of the Fregean notion of an object, does not simply constitute the limit of a series of concepts reflecting wider and wider classes or increasing generality in classification. With the notion of a thing one has moved out of a straightforward system of classification to a notion which is in a sense a reflection of our very modes of thought and speech.

[19]   G. Frege, 'Concept and object', in P. Geach and M. Black (trans.) *Translations* (Oxford: Blackwell, 1952), p. 46.

In this sense of the word a thing is simply an object of identification, a nameable (or, in Strawson's perhaps confusing terminology, an individual); it is whatever is picked out in thought and speech. By contrast a property is simply an aspect of a thing as described or characterized – a predicable. (If we say that it is what is picked out by a predicate, or is capable of being so picked out, it must be recognized that this involves a different sense of 'pick out' than the one used for reference to objects.) An event is an item corresponding in an analogous way to a non-continuous-tensed verb, as opposed to a process or state where there is the reflection of a continuous-tensed verb of one kind or another. A fact is what is statable by means of a true proposition or statement. An attempt to produce an exhaustive, comprehensive and systematic list of such concepts would not be profitable, although philosophers have sometimes tried to produce such lists. The possible success of the project depends on whether thought and language are themselves clear-cut and systematic in their nature.

A recognition of the nature of these concepts will, however, help not only with Frege's paradox,[20] but with other putative problems. I shall mention two. The first is the question, often discussed,[21] of whether a thing is more than the sum of its properties. It seems clear that when one has given all the properties of a thing there is nothing else of that kind to mention. On the other hand, when one has done that, one has, technically speaking, merely described that thing; one has not *eo ipso* identified it, however much one may have enabled others to identify it on that basis. Hence there may exist the feeling that one has not, so to speak, grasped the thing merely by listing its properties. On the other hand, philosophers such as Russell and Ayer have insisted that there cannot be more to a thing than the instantiation of a great number of properties and that it is the non-empiricist supposition to the contrary that leads to the Lockean idea of a substance underlying the properties, such that that substance must *ex hypothesi* be unknowable and undescribable. Whether that is a correct historical judgment as far as Locke is concerned need not be discussed here; in any case it is worth noting that the point at issue is not limited to substances but applies to anything that can have properties.

Underlying the thought that a thing cannot be more than the sum of its properties is the truism already mentioned – that when one has given all the properties of a thing there is nothing more of that kind to mention. If it is felt that in that case one has still not said all there is to be said,

[20] But see contra M. Dummett, *Frege*, pp. 257ff.
[21] By, e.g., B. Russell, *Human Knowledge* (London: Allen and Unwin, 1948), pp. 310ff., and A. J. Ayer, *Philosophical Essays* (London: Macmillan, 1954), ch. 1.

it is because when one has said that a set of properties is instantiated at a given time and place one has not yet said anything about there being a *thing*. It is sometimes suggested that one needs to add to the list of properties some principle or principles of organization of those properties – involving perhaps relational properties. Such a thought also encourages the idea that things are more than the sum of their parts. Yet whether it be properties or parts that one has in mind, when one has listed them all there is nothing more of that kind to mention, and principles of organization are either additional properties or something analogous to that.

If one still feels that there is something more to a thing – the something that is more than the sum of the parts – it is not because something of that kind is missing. It is true that the properties or parts have to be brought together, but coinstantiation, however secured, is enough for that. For a thing to exist it is quite sufficient that its properties be coinstantiated, and in that sense a thing just is the sum of its properties, granted that they are coinstantiated. That, however, does not make the concept of a thing identical with or analysable into the concept of a set of properties so coinstantiated. To think otherwise is to mistake what kinds of concept those of thing and property are, it is to fail to see that these concepts are reflections of different aspects of thought – identification and description. The concept of a thing is the concept of an identifiable. The fact that identifiables are also capable of description does not make the concepts the same. Things are no more than the sum of their properties, but the concept of a thing is not the concept of a set of properties however brought together. To say that is to give due acknowledgment to the fact that the concepts of thing and property are formal concepts not ordinary concepts.

The second question which I shall consider briefly is the status of the slogan 'No entity without identity'. As Strawson says in an admirable paper 'Entity and identity',[22] it is a slogan that has 'achieved great popularity in recent philosophy'. It is indeed often suggested that there is some connexion between the concepts of existence and identity. Quine, for example, says 'We cannot know what something is without knowing how it is marked off from other things. Identity is thus of a piece with ontology.'[23] The point that Quine makes has been put elsewhere by saying that if something is to count as an entity there must be criteria of identity for things of that sort – we must know how they are marked off from other things. That thesis has indeed been used as a kind of test of

[22] P. F. Strawson, 'Entity and identity' in H. D. Lewis (ed.), *Contemporary British Philosophy*, 4th Series (London: Allen and Unwin, 1976).
[23] W. V. Quine, *Ontological Relativity*, p. 55.

ontological claims – things which do not satisfy it have as a consequence a lesser claim to be admitted into our ontology. Strawson indicates in his paper the sorts of things to which this test has been applied, e.g. properties, as opposed to classes. He also indicates certain kinds of thing to which the notion of a criterion of identity does not seem to apply, e.g. colours, where no general account is available of what marks them off from each other.

This point about colours is connected with the fact that the relation between individual hues and colour in general is not that between species and the genus of which they are species (for, as Aristotle insisted, species are distinguished from each other under a genus by differentiae, and there are no differentiae which distinguish red, for example, from other hues). The relation in question is in fact that which W. E. Johnson in his *Logic* called that of determinates to determinable. To say that, however, is merely to make the point that not all relationships between the general and the more general are species–genus relationships. That point could be generalized so as to take account of the sort of thing that Wittgenstein had to say about family resemblances.[24] Indeed Wittgenstein's anti-essentialism, which the point about family resemblances introduces, could be interpreted as an insistence that conceptual relationships take many forms. More recently, essentialism has achieved, once again, something of a vogue, in the form of the thesis that things, or some of them, e.g. natural kinds, have distinct essences; they have necessarily a certain nature, a certain set of essential properties, which they could not do without. I shall return to that issue in the next chapter, and indicate that the thesis is at best a thesis about substances and not about things in general. Analogously, 'No substance without identity' is a more promising slogan than 'No entity without identity', even if it sounds less good.

There are at least two different things which may be at stake when we are concerned with identity. First, there may be the question, as I have in effect been suggesting, of what identifies things of a certain kind so that they can be distinguished from other things. To be concerned with this question is to be concerned with the identification of a kind of things, something that goes *pari passu* with their distinguishability from things of other kinds. In this sense the thesis of no entity without identity is the thesis that there is no entity which does not belong to a kind the distinguishability of which from other kinds depends on determinate criteria. Second, there may be the question of what makes two putatively different individuals numerically the same or identical. In the

[24] L. Wittgenstein, *Philosophical Investigations* (Oxford: Blackwell, 1953), §§67ff.

terms that Strawson uses in *Individuals* this involves a concern, not just with the identity or identification of things, but with their re-identifiability – the possibility of this being recognized as the same as that.

These two issues that I have distinguished are connected but they are not the same. As we shall see in Chapter 9, when philosophers are concerned with, for example, persons as a kind, they are concerned at least with the question of what marks off persons from other kinds of thing. The answer could not be 'spatio-temporal continuity', although that answer has been given to the question about the criteria of personal identity. In this latter case the question seems to be what determines whether two putatively different persons are really the same. Of course, in order to answer that question satisfactorily one has to know what sort of thing a person is, something that might be put in terms of the question 'What are the criteria of identity for persons?'. While that is necessary, however, it is not sufficient for dealing with the question of what determines whether two putatively different persons are the same, even if it may enable us to rule out certain answers as inadequate. This second concern with identity affords a second sense to be given to the slogan 'No entity without identity', although it may not be the sense that is generally given to it, i.e. no entity without the possibility of its re-identification.

Unfortunately, it is not *clear* that an entity need admit of re-identification. There seems nothing incoherent in the idea of an entity which exists only for an instant. Sense-data have sometimes been thought to be entities of that kind, although in his lectures on 'The philosophy of logical atomism' Russell, while distinguishing them from the 'old notion of substance', denied that they had the kind of instantaneous existence that I have mentioned, saying that they exist merely 'for a very short time indeed'.[25] It is clear, however, that if the notion of an entity, like that of a thing, is a formal concept, there is no necessity that entities should have any form of persistence through time. For the notion of an entity is simply that of the correlate of identification, and unless further considerations are brought to bear there is no reason to believe that what can be identified must also be capable of being re-identified.

On all scores, therefore, there seems little to be said for the slogan 'No entity without identity'. It may, as I have already said, be a different matter with 'No substance without identity', and to these considerations I shall turn in the next chapter.

[25] In R. C. Marsh (ed.), *Logic and Knowledge*.

4. Substance

The traditional conception of substance

The term 'substance' is one of the most confusing terms in philosophy. For Aristotle, at least some of the time, the paradigm cases of substances were, as he put it, 'this man, this horse', i.e. particular things of that kind. For complicated historical reasons, however, substance has sometimes come to be equated with what Aristotle called 'matter'; thus iron and sulphur, and other stuffs, have come to be called 'substances'. For further complicated historical reasons substance came to be regarded by e.g. Locke as the underlying something or other which is supposed to give support to the properties that inhere in it. Indeed the Latin etymology of the term 'substance' will suggest to anyone having a sensitivity to it that notion of something standing beneath the properties. Locke thus called it a 'something I know not what' – a suggestion that is not conveyed by either of the other two usages. The situation is complicated still further by the fact that the Latin etymology is relevant only to those modern discussions which rely on the term 'substance'. The Greek word which Aristotle used – 'ousia' – and which is traditionally translated 'substance' has none of the suggestions that the Latin etymology of 'substance' provides, but has additional suggestions of its own, particularly a connexion with *being*. (The feminine present participle of the verb 'to be' in Greek is *ousa*; *ousia* has the form of an abstract noun and is for that reason naturally to be translated 'being' or 'beingness', but Aristotle often uses the word with an article to indicate a particular kind of being, a particular kind of thing.)

For present purposes one needs to note these points only to put them on one side. As I shall indicate later, what Aristotle means by *a* substance is roughly what Strawson calls a 'basic particular', and for similar reasons. Considered as a kind, substance is, according to Aristotle, one of the categories, one of the ultimate kinds of being. If one takes, for example, a particular man (the 'this man' referred to above) and asks what it is essentially, the answer will ultimately be 'substance'. If one were to ask other questions such as 'What is it like?' or 'How big is it?', one would expect immediately other answers, such as 'White' or 'Six feet tall'; and if one asks what the things so specified are essentially, one will ultimately get the answers 'Quality' and 'Quantity'. In this way one gets a list of categories or ultimate genera of beings. Whatever is thought of the method used to achieve this result and whatever is thought of the comprehensiveness and refinement of the list that Aristotle himself produces (an issue on which there have been many criticisms), it becomes evident that substance as a category has a status and importance over and above that of the other categories. Indeed Aristotle claims, and provides some argument to support the claim, that substances are the primary kind of beings; they are what primarily exist. Moreover, while Aristotle distinguishes in the *Categories* between primary and secondary substances, the latter being species or genera of primary substances (and it is a matter for argument whether he holds to that view in later works), he argues that it is particular substances (this man, this horse) that are primary.

In this we are given two of the essential characteristics of the traditional notion of substance – the primacy of substances among exist-ents, and their particularity. The question still remains: what sort of primacy? Aristotle says that entities in other categories apart from sub-stance are dependent on substances for their existence. He says indeed that they are inherent in substances, although there is argument among scholars about the formal criteria of inherence that Aristotle offers. Secondly, Aristotle says that general things, like species and genera, depend on particular substances as their instances, although he does not, in the *Categories*, say that they are inherent in them, and elsewhere he says little if anything about inherence at all. However this may be, Aristotle's belief in the ontological primacy of substances is obvious. It is meant to be evident in the way that subject–predicate language relates to the world, so that Aristotle can come to assert what is sometimes called the traditional doctrine that particular substances are never predi-cated of anything else but everything else is predicated of them. They thus constitute, as Strawson puts it with respect to what he calls basic particulars, 'basic logical subjects'.

Strawson's *Individuals* provides a parallel account of the matter, start-ing from the notion of a particular as an object of speaker–hearer identi-fication (as we saw in Chapter 3). The first part of the book argues that material objects are the basic form of particular from the point of view of speaker–hearer identification, and that other particulars are from that same point of view dependent on basic particulars in a variety of ways. Later, in chapter 3 of *Individuals*, persons are introduced as another kind of particular but one with a special status, even if, because persons have bodies, they are dependent on material objects.[1] The second part of the book argues for the primacy of particulars in general over other kinds of individual (where by 'individual' is meant any object of possible identification, so that non-particulars, such as justice, count for that reason as individuals). It might be said that the order of the argument in the book is an odd one. It might have been expected that, given speaker–hearer identification, there would be an argument, first for the primacy of particulars over other individuals, and second for the primacy of material objects as basic particulars over other particulars. It can nevertheless be seen that the outcome of the argument is very much the same as that of Aristotle, despite the difference in the starting-point. The basic things, whatever in the argument they are basic to, are particular material things.

If that is so there must be more to being a substance than being basic and particular; for material things have other characteristics. For one thing, to put the matter in Strawson's words, basic particulars are not only identifiable; they are also re-identifiable. That is to say, in effect, that they not only occupy space but also have a certain persistence through time, so that they can be re-identified as 'the same thing as the one which was . . .'. Aristotle puts the matter by saying that it is perhaps the characteristic most peculiar to substance that substances are the only things that can remain the same while receiving contrary qualifications, i.e. they retain their identity through change. Substances therefore have a relative permanence; they do not have a merely instantaneous form of life. For Aristotle at least there are the additional points that substances are necessarily subsumable under kinds (they are members of species which have an essence), and they are normally constituted out of some kind of stuff or matter. (That is to say in effect that they have a form and a matter.) These notions also have gone into the traditional conception of substance, so that substances come to be regarded as the building-blocks of material reality (and in the view of some philosophers, and with modifications, immaterial reality also).

There is one characteristic that has sometimes been ascribed to substances that does not appear in the Aristotelian and Strawsonian accounts. It is that of simplicity. The thesis that substances must be simple is integral to atomist theories as long as they hold that the atomicity or indivisibility of the atoms is one of principle and not merely something that holds good in fact. It might be objected, however, that such a simplicity is a relative one only, since it is a matter only of spatial nature or

---

[1]   It is well to note that fact, but the special status of persons in Strawson's account of things creates a certain awkwardness in his ontology.

size. Material atoms are simple only because indivisible. Any form of logical atomism or thesis to the effect that our thought or language depends for its intelligibility on there being objects which constitute units of meaning (something that is explicitly involved in the logical atomism of Russell and the early Wittgenstein) must invoke a more comprehensive form of simplicity.

Perhaps the clearest historical example of a theory which invokes a radical and comprehensive form of simplicity in relation to substances is Leibniz's 'monadology'. Leibniz asserted that the basic entities that exist as substances must be absolutely simple: hence the term 'monads'. They are simple, he said, in the way that the 'ego' is; they are absolutely one yet capable of representing a plurality, as the ego does in its perception of the world. This is a feature which is not exemplifiable in any material thing, so that the ultimate substances must, for that reason, be immaterial. Whatever one may think of the outcome of Leibniz's argument, there can be no doubt that one of the steps in that argument is based on the thought that substances must be absolutely simple because no complex thing of any kind could be basic; it must be secondary to whatever it is a complex of. In other words, it is supposed that the basicness of substance must itself entail its absolute simplicity. I shall indicate in Chapter 6 that something like the same idea is to be found in monist theories also – theories to the effect that in the end there can be only one substance.

If not all those concerned with the metaphysics of substance have thought that substances must be absolutely simple, this may be because they recognized that the basicness of substance is not itself an absolute matter. That is to say that in claiming that substances are ontologically primary they were, to some extent at least, explicit about what the primacy is relative to. For example, the claim that something like substance is essential to the possibility of speaker–hearer identification does not bring with it any suggestion to the effect that the examples of substance that are in question must be simple. Leibniz came to the contrary conclusion because he thought of substances as the primary existents without qualification, i.e. in an absolute sense so that they could not be thought of as dependent on anything else. It is this absoluteness of the conception of primacy that is espoused that leads to the idea that substance must be simple in an absolute sense also. It is arguable, however, that simplicity is always a relative matter (as Plato in effect saw when he said in *Republic* 7 that 'one' is a relative term, so that something can be called 'one' only if there is already available an answer to the question 'One what?'). If it is, the argument that substance must be simple lacks cogency if simplicity is construed in any other than a relative sense.

Must there be substances?

The notion of substance is sometimes represented as a hang-over from ancient and mediaeval times, and it is sometimes added that, as philosophers, we ought to have learned to live without it. To assess such a claim it is necessary to consider what alternatives there are. Such alternatives must be things in some sense – not events, facts and so on – but they must be drawn from a category other than substance. It is not obvious that a decision between alternatives can be made simply by reference to the point of departure for an ontological inquiry, as was the case with 'things' in Chapter 3. The issues that we are now dealing with are not the same as those which we considered in Chapter 3 under the heading of the 'relativity of philosophical ontologies'. There we were concerned with things versus events, facts, etc.; we are now concerned with substances versus other candidates to the title of 'thing'. The question now is whether there could be an intelligible account of the world in which we find ourselves which made no reference to substances.

In the case of speaker–hearer identification, for example, it may seem obvious that if both speakers and hearers are bodily, and thus have a spatial character and persistence through time, something of that same kind must be supposed to exist as a possible object of identification, and indeed as having primacy among possible objects of identification. How much of that, however, is a necessary feature of speaker–hearer identification? Could we deal with the facts that are implicit in that notion without invoking anything like the idea of substance? To do that, it should be noted, we should have to deal in the same way with the reference to ourselves and others that speaker–hearer identification presupposes, and that is a point that I shall emphasize later. One way of putting the question that I have raised is to ask whether we are committed to the notion of substance even if we start from the standpoint of speaker–hearer identification and what that implies about the notion of 'things'. The same applies to other possible starting-points for ontology. If we are committed to things are we also committed to substances?

Certainly some philosophers, mostly those of an empiricist turn of mind, such as Ayer and Russell, have been willing to suggest that all that is required for a coherent conception of the world in which we find ourselves is the idea of properties having a location at places at times. I referred to that idea in Chapter 3. Ayer indeed expresses his distrust of the old notion of substance, acknowledging a prejudice in favour of the idea that all there is to the existence of a material thing is the incidence of a number of properties at a place at a given time or times.[2]

---

[2]   E.g. in A. J. Ayer, 'Individuals' and 'The identity of indiscernibles' in his *Philosophical Essays* (London: Macmillan, 1954).

Part of the suspicion that philosophers such as Ayer have of the notion of substance is no doubt due to the belief that this notion includes the Lockean idea of the 'something, I know not what' which is supposed to underlie properties and support them. That, as something in principle and necessarily unobservable, is naturally an object of suspicion for an empiricist. But, as Leibniz pointed out to Locke in his *Nouveaux Essais* 23.2, acceptance of the notion of substance does not commit one to any such belief in the existence of a 'something, I know not what'. Indeed there cannot be anything that underlies *all* properties. That is true even if one believes, as do some modern essentialists (whom I shall consider in a later section of this chapter), that substances have, as Locke also suggested, a real essence distinct from their nominal essence – an essential nature which is knowable through science and which explains why substances are assigned the nominal essences they have, i.e. their classification as things of a certain observable sort or kind. Such a view does not entail that the real essence is something unknowable, as Locke also seemed to suggest; only that, if it is known, it is not known in the way that it is possible to know a thing simply as a member of an empirically determinable kind, but in the way that it is possible to know, through scientific theory, what is responsible for its being a thing of that kind. So construed, an underlying real essence, if there is such a thing, is not the same as a 'something, I know not what' underlying the properties that inhere in it.

Can it be the case, then, that all that there is to the existence of a material thing (a material substance or a Strawsonian basic particular) is the incidence of a set of properties (however organized in terms of what is essential and what is merely contingent) at places and times. The issues here are very similar to those discussed in Chapter 3 with reference to the question of whether a thing is merely the sum of its properties. It could well be said that when one has listed all the properties that have incidence at various places at various times, one has said all that there is to be said *of that kind* about a substance: there is nothing else *of that kind* to be said. On the other hand, there is certainly one thing that will not have been said: nothing will have been said about anything having *changed* over time. The notion of substance, as Aristotle observed, is correlative with that of change, in that it is substances which change and are subject to change, and it is in substances that changes take place.

It might be replied that, even if nothing has been said about substances changing or indeed about change at all when one speaks of properties having incidence at various places and times, it remains true that when substances change all that takes place is the variation of properties incident at places at successive times. The response to that objection must be to admit that nothing else *of that kind* takes place but to insist that that gives no particular credence to the suggestion that what basically exists is properties having incidence at places and times. On the other hand, the suggestion cannot be dismissed simply by saying that in any case the notion of a property is parasitical on that of a substance in that properties need substances to be properties *of*. The notion of a property is correlative with that of a predicate (whether or not all predicates entail the existence of properties – an issue to which I shall return in Chapter 5); predicates are predicated of a subject and properties belong to whatever is a subject in that way. It does not follow that all properties are properties of a *substance*. If, then, properties do not logically presuppose substances, what is wrong with the suggestion that all that is material to the notion of substances is the idea of properties having incidence at places and times?

What is missing from talk of properties having incidence at places at successive times is any reference to the notion of identity (except perhaps in the presupposition that places themselves have a certain identity over time, and that brings problems of its own, as perhaps may the idea of times being successive). The sense-data which Russell, in his logical atomist period, posited as particulars were said by him to be substitutes for the old notion of substance but lasted only for 'a very short time indeed'. To the extent that they were thought to persist at all they presumably had some identity over time. There are not available in this conception, however, any principles of connexion between particulars which are sufficient for speaking of anything having any longer-term identity. Only the notion of substance itself could supply that. It is the identity over time that substances possess which makes possible the ascription of change to them, in a way that is not possible for other kinds of thing. If one confines oneself to the idea of properties having incidence at places and times this reference to identity is inevitably missing.[3]

Must there, then, be substances? The answer to that question is: 'Yes, if one wishes to sustain our ordinary talk of and belief in change and the identity over time which is the correlate of change.' That answer, of course, provides no form of absolute necessity. There have been philosophers who have thought that the growth of science and of scientific views of the world give plausibility to the belief that the best terms

---

[3]   Chapter 7 of Strawson's *Individuals* (London: Methuen, 1959) contains a very involved, indeed involuted, discussion of this sort of issue and indicates the extent to which any attempt to provide, within a framework involving features or properties having incidence at places and times, conditions sufficient for speaking of identity must be something of a fraud.

in which to speak and think of the world are not those of substance, identity and change, but, for example, events or processes. As suggested in Chapter 3, Whitehead is a case in point. In his view science does not sustain the conception of a world of persistent substances subject to change. What earlier thought regarded as substances are best conceived as aspects of processes. Whitehead put the point by saying that objects are 'ingredient' into events; they are, one might say, logical constructions out of events and processes.

That was not an entirely new thought. One can find something like it in Heraclitus, at least on one interpretation of that early thinker. If it is true that he likened the world to a river, he may be taken as saying that material things, as we ordinarily take them to be, owe their identity to regular changes of the stuffs of which they are composed. Material things thus have no real identity, only something like the 'fictitious identity' which Hume too thought was the only form of identity to be ascribed to the bundles of impressions and ideas that physical things amounted to in his system. Such a view may present a certain vision of the world which is an alternative to the one that posits persistent substances. As Hume indicated in the Appendix to the *Treatise*, however, it is a view which it is very difficult, if not impossible, to apply to ourselves, and that is one reason why we may think that speaker–hearer identification at least must presuppose a belief in real identity.

Hume's view, like that of Russell and unlike, perhaps, that of Whitehead, does presuppose the existence of things which have a self-subsistent status, even if they are not substances. Indeed, in the chapter of the *Treatise* on the immateriality of the soul (I.iv.5) Hume says that if anything deserves the title of substance in his system it is impressions or perceptions; for they are the only self-subsistent things. Strictly speaking, however, they are not substances, since they provide no real principles of identity. In the case of bundles or collections of impressions Hume tries to substitute for identity relations such as constancy, coherence and causality in order to give those bundles something that approximates to identity – the fictitious identity that I referred to above. There are things with respect to which such an attitude towards identity has a certain plausibility, to the extent that their identity does not presuppose that their parts or constituents remain absolutely unchanging. Hume's example of a church, all the stones of which may be replaced over time, and Hobbes' 'ship of Athens', all the timbers of which are similarly replaced,[4] are cases in point, since their identity depends upon the spatio-temporal

---

[4] D. Hume, *Treatise of Human Nature*, I.iv.6, and T. Hobbes, *De Corpore*, II.8.1.

continuity of the whole rather than the strict identity of their parts.

It might indeed be argued that science has shown that this point is generalizable to all physical things, and that those things which we generally count as physical substances do not depend on strict identity, despite what I said earlier. These cases do not, however, show that it is wrong to speak of strict identity over time under some description. It *is* the same church, the same ship, the same whatever it is, and the description of the examples depends on those facts. The sameness or identity of a substance does not presuppose the literal identity of everything that has to do with that identity; it need not presuppose that the substance has the same constituents throughout its existence. Nevertheless the changes that take place must, if there is to be substantial identity, be construable as changes in one thing. It is that which Hume's framework of ideas makes it impossible for him to achieve, and in the case of the self the issue became crucial for him. The problem is worse with Whitehead's more radical scepticism over substance, since on his view there are no self-subsistent things, while on Hume's view at least impressions are self-subsistent.

Some of my preceding remarks may have provoked the thought that a substance must consist of a certain stuff and that there must be some kind of identity of stuff. It is not clear, however, that a physical substance must be composed of the same stuff throughout its history; biological substances are certainly not composed of the same matter throughout their life. Moreover, it is at least logically possible that a substance might undergo more radical, Protean, changes in the kind of stuff that it is made of. The suggestion that there must be constancy of stuff because of the principle of conservation of matter is at best a suggestion about a principle of physics and not one that a philosophical argument could sustain. (It may be of some interest in this respect that Kant's argument in the 'First Analogy' of the *Critique of Pure Reason*, which seems at first sight to be an argument for the necessity, relative to possible experience, of persistent substances, turns out to be an argument for the principle of the conservation of matter; whether or not that principle is valid, it is difficult to see that it can be defended as a condition of possible experience.)

It might nevertheless be thought that it is at least true that if something is to be a substance at all it must be constituted of some matter. That seems evident enough in the case of material substances; it is what makes them material. Is the principle generalizable, however? Does it even need to be? I am not sure of the answer to these questions. *Prima facie*, if a thing has the kind of persistence and identity over time that substances have there must be an answer to the question of what it is composed of at any stage of its history, and if there are non-material substances they must for that reason be composed of non-material stuff. That has not seemed to all philosophers evidently necessary. The Aristotelian God, who certainly falls under the category of substance, has no matter. On the other hand, the thought that substances must have a matter may be in part what leads Kant to the idea that the 'I' is not a substance. The issue does not seem to me clearly determinable.

The answer to the question set by the title of this section is, therefore, that there must be substances in any world with reference to which it is possible to speak of change and of identity through change. Such a necessity is a conceptual and relative one. I have not claimed that one can make no sense of the idea of a possible world without substances, but there are limits to what can be intelligibly said about such a world, and there are certainly difficulties about the idea that *we* could have a place in such a world, given what we are.

The individuation of substances

Given that there are substances, the question that next arises is what marks off any one substance from any other. The mediaeval philosophers called this the problem of the principle of individuation, and concern with the problem is also sometimes ascribed to Aristotle (although I have some doubts as to whether he ever raised the question). Questions about identity go hand in hand with questions about the nature of the thing or things to which identity is to be ascribed.[5] Given that, it should be evident that some substances might be individuated, i.e. given a unique identification in distinction from other things, by reference to the kind of thing that they are. Two substances of the same kind cannot be so distinguished and their individuation must therefore depend on other factors. The question underlying the problem of the principle of individuation puts the issue in its most general form – how ultimately can any two substances of whatever kind be distinguished?

One perennial answer to that question makes reference to spatio-temporal position, it being presumed that no two substances of the same kind can occupy the same space at the same time, and that it is not a necessary truth that two different things must be different in respect of some property. These presumptions cannot, however, be allowed to go unquestioned, and they have indeed been questioned at various times. The latter presumption conflicts with what Leibniz called the principle

[5] It is to be noted that that is *not* to subscribe to the thesis that identity is itself a relative matter and that what are putatively two things can be identical in one respect and not in another.

of the identity of indiscernibles – the principle that if what are putatively two different things have all their properties in common they must be identical and not different. What I mentioned as presumed not to be a necessary truth is in fact the contrapositive of this – that if two things are different they cannot have all their properties in common, they must differ in respect of some property. Leibniz seems to have thought of his principle as a necessary truth (although that did not stop him seeking empirical confirmation of it). Thus the second presumption that I mentioned involves a denial of that, or rather of its contrapositive. Since the status of one principle must equally apply to its contrapositive, it does not matter which we choose to consider. From the point of view of the principle of individuation it is perhaps best to consider the issue in the form in which I introduced it – whether it is a necessary truth that any two things that are different must differ in respect of some property.

A further complication is that it is necessary to distinguish between non-relational properties, relational properties where the relation is specified in general terms, and relational properties such that the specification involves an embedded proper-name or otherwise directly individuating expression. Examples of these properties are those of being a philosopher or being philosophical, being the pupil of another philosopher, and being the pupil of Socrates – all of which are properties of Plato. (One might also perhaps mention the property of being identical with Plato, if that is a property, although it introduces what some might think unnecessary complications.) It is clear that the last two kinds of property (those involving reference to an individual and those involving also the notion of identity) already presuppose for their understanding an understanding of the notion of identity in some form. Hence they are useless as an elucidation of the identity of an individual. It might be objected, however, that that is not to the point. The real question is whether the principle of the identity of indiscernibles or its contrapositive is necessarily true in such a way as to provide a principle of individuation. Once the issue is put in that way it becomes clear that even if it is true, and indeed necessarily true, that there is only one thing which possesses the property of being identical with Plato, and even if it is true, whether or not necessarily true, that there is only one thing that possesses such and such properties and is also a pupil of Socrates, such truths do not provide a *clear* principle of individuation since they *presuppose* the individuation of something. Hence to invoke them is merely to shift the problem one stage back.[6]

[6]   Cf. D. Wiggins, *Sameness and Substance* (Oxford: Blackwell, 1980), pp. 55–7.

Such an objection does not apply to the principles stated in such a way that the properties in question are confined to the first two kinds men-tioned above. Although Leibniz seems to have thought that the principles so stated are necessarily true, it has not always been apparent to others that that is so.[7] In recent times there have been attempts to describe what are called radially symmetrical universes to which the principles do not apply. One of the earliest of such attempts is that by Max Black.[8] He offers the description of a universe consisting solely of two spheres, which are qualitatively indistinguishable but also such that any outstand-ing feature of one is matched by an identical feature of the other, opposed to it not directly but radially. If, for example, there is a feature answering to a certain description (say 'F') on the side of one sphere facing the other together with another feature of description G related to the F feature by the relation R, the same will be true of the other sphere. The outcome will be that the features of kind F will in each case be directly opposed to features of kind G, and any description of a feature of one kind in terms of its relations to features of other kinds will be matched by a description of exactly the same kind applicable to the other sphere.

It is essential to the case that the universe should consist of these two radially symmetrical spheres and nothing else. Any introduction of a further item or an observer will introduce an asymmetry. To those who think that the assertion of the existence of two spheres of this kind requires a backing in terms of verifying circumstances it will seem essential to the specification of the universe that there is a point of view of it such as to create an asymmetry. Ayer makes such an objection with reference to his own example of a rather more restricted universe con-sisting simply of an infinite sequence of sounds ... ABCDABCD ABCDA ... in his paper on 'The identity of indiscernibles'.[9] A verificationist objection of that kind scarcely seems to gainsay the claim that the specification of a radially symmetrical universe makes sense. Strawson gives another example of a universe consisting entirely of a chess-board with nothing outside it.[10]

If examples of these kinds are intelligible (and to suppose that is to

---

[7] Cf. L. Wittgenstein, *Tractatus Logico-Philosophicus* (London: Routledge and Kegan Paul, 1922, 1961), 5.5302.

[8] M. Black, 'The identity of indiscernibles', *Mind*, Vol. LXI, 1952, pp. 153–64; also in his *Problems of Analysis* (London: Routledge and Kegan Paul, 1954).

[9] In his *Philosophical Essays*.

[10] P. F. Strawson, *Individuals*, ch. 4, esp. p. 125. Wiggins, ibid., p. 57, seems to think that it is enough to consider any object which is symmetrical about at least one plane that bisects it, but that is not evidently true.

reject the verificationist point mentioned above), then there can be two
things which have all their properties in common, where the properties
comprise all non-relational properties and all relational properties
which are specifiable in a way that does not presuppose the individuation of an individual. In that event the principles of the identity of
indiscernibles and its contrapositive are at least not necessarily true;
whether they are true depends on the facts about the universe. Hence
the only reasonable conclusion is that one does not know whether the
principles are true in fact, but that there is no question of their being
necessarily true. If that is so, the principles provide no necessary principle
of individuation for things in general; and, to the extent that what is true
of things in general must also be true of substances, the same conclusion
holds for substances.

The examples that we have noted do, however, presuppose differences
of place and time; the spheres are in different places. Hence it might be
suggested that whether or not there can be two things with all their properties in common, spatio-temporal position is sufficient to differentiate
any two material substances. We can thus revert to the first of the two
presumptions which were mentioned when we began to consider the
principle of individuation. The first point to note is the obvious one that
spatio-temporal position will not be an adequate differentiating factor
in the case of non-spatio-temporal entities, if there are any. In the case
of some putative items of this kind it may be that temporal position is
sufficient. That would be true of, for example, mental entities, if for the
sake of argument they can be allowed the status of independently existing entities (i.e. not such that they are necessarily dependent for their
existence on bodies). Whether there are entities which temporal position could not differentiate is hard to say. It is worth noting, however,
that since angels could not be differentiated by spatio-temporal considerations Aquinas had to say that each angel constitutes a distinct
species (which is to say that each angel has certain necessarily differentiating features). On the other hand, it does not seem to be a conceptually necessary truth that there is not more than one angel
corresponding to a given species, whatever may be thought about the
theological issues and the possibility of theological necessities. (It is, it
may be worth noting, a similar consideration which led to mediaeval
speculations about the possibility of an infinity of angels standing on the
point of a pin!)

Even in the case of spatio-temporal entities, however, spatio-
temporal position will individuate only if it is impossible for two or
more such entities to occupy the same place at the same time. Or rather,

that will be so only if it is impossible for them to occupy the same places throughout their history; for, even if it were possible for two entities to occupy the same place at a given time, the rest of their temporal life might be different and that would be sufficient to differentiate them. That is an important consideration because some philosophers have thought it desirable *for these reasons* to rule out the possibility of two things of the same kind ever occupying the same place at the same time. David Wiggins, for example, argues in that way in a note in the *Philosophical Review*, 1968.[11]

The two most important considerations that he adduces are as follows. First, there is the supposed fact that space is mapped only by reference to its occupants,[12] so that if it were possible for two things of the same kind to occupy the same place at the same time that would prevent proper differentiation of places and thus the mapping of space. That consideration, however, is quite invalid. It is not true that space is mapped only by reference to its occupants if that means that no place can be differentiated except by reference to something occupying that place. It may be the case that the mapping of space requires the identification of at least one thing to provide a source-point for the mapping, but that is another matter and is not enough to sustain the thesis under consideration. The occupation of a given place by two things of the same kind, if that were possible, would not prevent the mapping of space – as long as the occurrence was not too common.

The second consideration is that the impossibility of two things of the same kind occupying the same space at the same time is supposed to follow from the criterion of identity for material objects – that '*A* is identical with *B* if there is some substance concept *f* such that *A coincides* with *B* under *f* '.[13] That means roughly that *A* and *B* are the same if they share the same spatio-temporal history. There are two things to note about this consideration. The first is that it advisedly applies only to material substances; that, however, need not worry us in our present concerns. The second point is more important. It is that the criterion of identity which is offered implies only that sharing the same spatio-temporal history is a sufficient condition of identity; it does not imply that it is a necessary condition also. It is the latter, however, that would have to be the case if the criterion of identity were to rule out the possibility of two things of the same kind occupying the same place at

[11] D. Wiggins, 'On being at the same place at the same time', *Philosophical Review*, Vol. LXXVII, 1968, pp. 90–5.
[12] Cf. R. Swinburne, *Space and Time*, 1st edn (London: Macmillan, 1968), p. 25.
[13] D. Wiggins, ibid., p. 93.

the same time. The contrapositive of the criterion is that if two things are different they must not share the same spatio-temporal history throughout. That does not prevent their coinciding *sometimes*.

Attempts have been made to spell out what it would be like for two things to come to occupy the same place at the same time, in terms of the idea of two billiard-balls, for example, coming to coalesce.[14] As far as concerns things like billiard-balls, such a conception would no doubt involve changes in the laws of physics. That, however, is not a crucial objection to the conception; physicists, after all, have been willing to contemplate more radical possibilities than that with regard to elementary particles. It is not even clear that events of the kind in question should be upsetting for the physics of macro-bodies, as long as they remained unusual and abnormal events. It is a plausible view that laws of nature constitute norms, even if norms that are deviated from only because of the effect of other laws. Exceptions to a law are in that sense always possible and are not upsetting as long as the exceptions are explicable by reference to other laws.

It might be argued that when two bodies, such as billiard-balls, appear to coalesce and when that is not due to, say, the particles of one body filling the gaps between the particles of the other, we are not bound to speak of apparently solid bodies occupying the same space. We might, for example, speak of one of the bodies going out of existence in favour of the other or of both going out of existence in favour of some third (perhaps only then coming into existence). It is not a crucial objection to such suggestions that they imply a discontinuous existence on the part of some body or bodies (since *presumably* on these suggestions the original billiard-balls exist again when they cease to 'coalesce'). There *are* things, especially things composed of parts that may be reassembled temporally into other things and then taken apart again to enable the reconstitution of the original object, that thereby lead a discontinuous existence.[15] Nevertheless, it cannot be assumed that reference to discontinuous existence is always the most plausible way of explaining the phenomena in question. There might well be circumstances in which the most economical way of explaining the phenomena is to put forward the hypothesis that two things of the same kind are occupying the same place at the same time. That should not entirely upset our conception of those objects and of their identity – unless again it were to happen too often.

[14] By, e.g., D. Sanford, 'Locke, Leibniz and Wiggins on being in the same place at the same time', *Philosophical Review*, Vol. LXXIX, 1970, pp. 75–82.

[15] See, e.g., M. B. Burke, 'Cohabitation, stuff and intermittent existence', *Mind*, Vol. LXXXIX, 1980, pp. 391–405.

It has indeed been suggested by J. M. Shorter[16] that just this is the case with certain clouds – that the only way to account for the behaviour of certain masses of water-vapour when passing over areas of high ground under certain temperature conditions is to suppose that there are two clouds literally occupying the same space at the same time. If that is true, then it is not only *conceivable* that two bodies of the same kind should occupy the same space at the same time: it sometimes happens in our world. It might of course be disputed whether clouds are bodies within the meaning of the act, and there might certainly be doubt as to whether they are, properly speaking, substances. Even so, nothing in what has been said makes it inconceivable that two substances of the same kind should occupy the same place at the same time. If that is so, spatio-temporal position is not an adequate principle of individuation, although spatio-temporal history may be. If we were to allow the possibility that different things might share the same spatio-temporal history, that would indeed be upsetting for our conception of things and their identity. We should indeed have no grounds for speaking of different things in such circumstances. If anything provides the principle of individuation for substances, or at any rate material substances, spatio-temporal history does. That is to say that as far as concerns material or spatio-temporal substances difference in spatio-temporal history is a necessary condition of difference of substance. If there are any non-material substances then the differences will have to be confined in their case to temporal history, unless, as Aquinas claimed with respect to angels, it is possible to appeal to some other, non-philosophical, basis for their difference. But that, as I have said, would not be a *philosophical* matter.

Essentialism

In the last section I have really been concerned with difference rather than identity as far as concerns substances. But the implication of what I have said is that if substances X and Y share the same spatio-temporal history they are not different but the same. Questions about identity (including, as we shall see in Chapter 9, questions about personal identity) are not always raised in quite that way. They may have to do with the identity of something at one period of time with something at another period of time, or about the identity of something that exists now with something that might have existed in some way under various contrary-to-fact conditions. In these cases it is impossible to apply the consideration about identity of spatio-temporal history. That holds

16 J. M. Shorter, 'On coinciding in space and time', *Philosophy*, Vol. 52, 1977, pp. 399–408.

good, for example, for the question of the identity of Hume's church or Hobbes' 'ship of Athens' – examples which I referred to earlier; in both those cases one is asking about the identity of things over an interval of time. One is concerned in such cases with the various kinds of change that either have or might have gone on during that interval. What changes in a substance are compatible with its remaining the same substance?

It is obviously the case that there are some changes which are entirely compatible with the substance's remaining the same substance; for, as we saw earlier, one of the distinguishing features of a substance is its potentiality for remaining the same while undergoing changes. A Proteus – something that undergoes repeated and perhaps rapid changes in its character – is not a logical impossibility, and many things do undergo very extensive and frequent changes in the course of their history. All that matters is that they are of the kind of thing the criteria of identity for which allow of changes of that kind and to that degree. When I say that a Proteus is not a logical impossibility, however, the question still remains whether the changes that Proteus was supposed to undergo were compatible with Proteus being a *substance*. That should be the question that concerns us now.

If the answer to the question is 'Yes' the next question that will naturally arise is 'What substance?' These questions are in effect questions about the nature of the thing under consideration. They are not, it should be said, questions simply about the semantics of the word 'Proteus'. I make that point because in recent philosophical literature questions about what is called 'essentialism', questions about whether, as Wiggins put it, 'every natural thing *x* satisfies throughout its actual existence some sortal concept that those who single *x* out have to treat as invariant',[17] are very much mixed up with questions about the semantics of proper-names and words for natural kinds (what Saul Kripke has called 'rigid designators' – words which have the same designation in all possible worlds).[18] Indeed much recent discussion of these issues involves also discussion of issues concerning reference and modality – matters involvement in which would take us too far from our main purpose.

Are there, however, limits to the changes that a substance can undergo? Must there be something that a substance essentially is? Can, on the other hand, a substance of one kind turn into one of another kind, and what, if anything, does the answer to that question show about the

[17] D. Wiggins, *Sameness and Substance*, p. 117.
[18] S. Kripke, *Naming and Necessity* (Oxford: Blackwell, 1980).

answer to the previous question of whether there is anything that a substance essentially is? By way of answering questions of these kinds
Wiggins indicates that the question 'Could this rat turn into a toad?' is
not the same as the question 'Could this rat have been a toad?,[19] and
claims that the relation between the two questions is that 'whether a
thing can submit to a certain kind of change depends on what it essentially is'. The question of what a thing essentially is is connected with the
question of what it could have come to be from, whether it must
necessarily have a certain sort of origin; the thesis that a substance must
have a certain sort of origin has become known as the thesis of the
'necessity of origin'. That thesis has a good Aristotelian ancestry, since
according to Aristotle the species that a substance belongs to, the form
that it has, determines and delimits the lines of change that it can be subject to, and equally the fact that a substance belongs to a certain species
determines and delimits the kind of origins that it had or might have
had. These putative necessities arise from the fact that it is part of the
nature or essence of a substance that it is a member of a certain species;
hence essentialism.[20]

We see, then, that essentialism involves the view that the limits upon
the changes that a substance may be subject to are due to the essential
nature of the substance, and that essential nature explains why it is as it
is. The essential nature is not merely a matter of what Locke called the
'nominal essence' of a thing – a matter of what is conceptually involved
in classifying a thing as a member of a certain observable kind. The real
essence has in some way to explain why a thing which is taken to be a
member of a certain observable kind is as it is. Thus, to use Putnam's
example in his paper 'The meaning of "meaning" ',[21] the essential
nature of water – the water that we all recognize as such – is its being
H_2O, whether we know it or not; and if there is a stuff on a 'twin earth',
called by all concerned 'water', and looking like that, it will not be water
if it is not H_2O. Water is a natural kind which has that essence.

At the back of this conception of natural kinds with distinct essences
to which things of necessity belong is, no doubt, a view of science and
natural law (though also a semantic theory which seeks to explain
reference to natural kinds through what Putnam calls 'the division of
linguistic labour', according to which the reference of terms such as

[19] D. Wiggins, *Sameness and Substance*, pp. 215–16.
[20] But the fact that things have a matter also affects the issue, and it has been denied, in part
because of this, that Aristotle was an essentialist in practice. See D. Balme, 'Aristotle's biology
was not essentialist', *Archiv für Geschichte der Philosophie*, Vol. 62, 1980, pp. 1–12.
[21] In, as with other references to Putnam, *Mind, Language and Reality: Philosophical Papers, Vol. 2*
(Cambridge: C.U.P., 1975).

'water' may be fixed by experts with the aid of theories that the ordinary man may know nothing of). An anti-essentialist would reject that whole conception of natural kinds, at any rate as implying anything fixed. To be an anti-essentialist, however, it is not necessary to want to claim that 'anything goes' with respect to a substance. An essentialist of the kind that I have been discussing must hold that because substances have an essential, if underlying, nature there is necessarily something constant about them. The opposite extreme to this would be a theory that saw nothing constant in a substance, and to the extent that it recognized identity it might base that identity on the changes in question, perhaps in something of the way in which Heraclitus made the identity of a river depend upon the changes of its waters. Whether that sort of thesis makes sense if given a literal interpretation is open to question. It is of course true that something is not a river if it does not involve constantly changing waters, but its identity as a river does not depend solely on that fact; it has banks and a distinct course, which may change, but nevertheless remain relatively constant. This suggests the possibility of views in between the extremes of essentialism and anti-essentialism however specified.

One possibility is the following. Wittgenstein held, at any rate on one interpretation, that membership of a kind (the one that he had in mind being that of a game) might involve nothing more than a family resemblance between its members, without there being necessarily any one thing in common apart from membership of the kind. Analogously, a thing of a certain kind might presumably undergo changes such that there was nothing literally in common between the stages of its existence, but only a family resemblance. It would be a mistake, I think, to suppose, or to take Wittgenstein as supposing, that all concepts are family resemblance concepts. It might equally be a mistake to suppose that all substances are such that their membership of a kind goes along with stages of existence between which there is only a family resemblance. Moreover, if there were substances of that kind, the question would naturally arise whether there was not in fact some underlying nature which explains why the stages of the substance's existence take the form that they do. It cannot, however, be assumed that there must be such an underlying nature, and whether there is or not must surely be a scientific question. In the case of Proteus, where there is, presumably, spatio-temporal continuity, but no relationship between the phases, it would be arguable, without prior knowledge of Proteus, whether one should speak of one substance undergoing radical changes or a succession of substances coming to be and passing away. Some relationship between the changes of the kind that I have mentioned in speaking of family resemblance might be enough to clinch the matter in favour of a single substance. In that case the question whether there is an underlying nature, whatever be the norm, must be one for science to answer. Could a rat, then, turn into a toad? Not as far as I know, but only science can provide the answer.

It might be held, however, that substances with a constant nature are the norm, and it might be argued that that is in some sense a condition of the possibility of discourse about the world. That would imply a transcendental argument to the effect that a condition of the possibility of meaningful discourse about the world is that there should be reference to items of which certain necessities hold good that are *de re* (i.e. they are features of the things in question and of their nature rather than, as is the case with *de dicto* necessities, features of our way of talking about those things). Kripke's form of argument for essentialism might be construed in that way (as might some, but not all, of Putnam's methods of argument). For he argues in effect that objects of rigid designation (i.e. those objects which, as I explained earlier, are, as picked out by rigid designators, the reference of those designators in all possible worlds), are such that certain things hold good of them by what he calls metaphysical necessity and not merely epistemic necessity. (A metaphysical necessity is *de re*, as explained above. It is now suggested that *de dicto* necessities bring in issues about our knowledge of, or belief about, the things in question and are for that reason epistemic.)

The point argued for is that successful reference depends necessarily not on certain things being known or believed about the objects in question, or at all events not on that alone, but on the objects themselves being such that certain things about them are metaphysically necessary, i.e. they are necessary *de re* and hold of their very nature. It is suggested that this is the case with the 'necessity of origin' (that *this* desk could not have been made of some other stuff) and the 'necessity of constitution' (that *this* desk here and now could not be composed of ice). Whatever one thinks about such particular cases and examples, it might certainly be argued with plausibility that the world could not be totally Protean; there must be *some* constancies and necessities about things if there is to be successful reference to and discourse about them.[22] It is less clear, however, whether such arguments lead to any controversial essentialism, since the conclusion to which they are directed is merely that there must be *some* constancies and necessities; we are not committed

---

[22] Plato seems to argue in that way against Heraclitus at *Theaetetus* 183aff.

thereby to the view that every substance must have an underlying essential nature, even granted the premiss that reference is in fact successfully achieved.

In surveying possible kinds of change Aristotle was inclined to say that there was no such thing as change of substance and that what might be so termed was really the ceasing to be of one substance and the coming to be of another. (I say that he was inclined to say that because he does not appear to be altogether consistent on the issue.) That could be made into a merely verbal point – that when X changes into Y there is first X and then Y and nothing we can refer to as existing throughout the process and so speak of as changing. To put the matter in that way, however, would be to beg the question, since, as we have seen, it is not clear that every substance must persist in an identical form and that this is a condition of successful reference to it. For this purpose what must be ruled out is that what we are concerned with is merely a process with differing stages or phases. It is true, therefore, that, as Wiggins says, a substance must satisfy throughout its existence some sortal concept (and that is not necessarily true of a process). But one could not conclude that that is true of all substances from a consideration of the conditions of possible reference; one could only conclude that it is true of *some* substances. Moreover, the view that a substance must satisfy some sortal concept throughout its existence does not lead directly to any conclusion about underlying natures. All that we have is the thesis that there must be enough, in some way or other, about a substance, for us to be justified in holding it to be of a certain kind throughout its history. What else that entails about the substance depends on the nature of the kind. As it stands it is a very minimal form of essentialism.

Essentialism in what is generally taken to be the Aristotelian sense (and which I believe Wiggins takes himself to be following despite the minimal nature of the account by him that I have considered) holds that substances are always members of kinds or species which do have essential properties; these properties put limits upon the changes that substances can undergo and limits upon the kinds of things which can produce them or which they themselves can produce. Within biology the function of a living substance is to reproduce things which are like it in kind, and that certainly presupposes that biological entities fall within natural kinds which are not merely a matter of *our* systems of classification or our understanding of words. Even with respect to systems of classification it is plausible to maintain that we must eventually run up against classes or kinds which are natural,[23] and that classification depends on the

---

[23] Cf. A. Quinton, 'Properties and classes', *Proc. Arist. Soc.* Vol. 58, 1957/8, pp. 33–58, and his *The Nature of Things* (London: Routledge and Kegan Paul, 1973).

recognition of such. A minimal essentialism therefore must insist on the point that not everything can be a matter of convention in classification. Aristotelian essentialism goes far beyond that in holding that things have *de re* necessities irrespective of systems of classification.

Even a thesis of that kind must not be hardened in such a way as to preclude the possibility of there being members of a kind which are, by some standard, defective. Biological species do after all evolve; there are mutations and sports. Even Aristotle, who knew nothing of the evolution of species had to allow the existence of defective members of species (due, in his way of thinking, to the fact that things do not merely have form – one word for which is the same as that for species – but matter also). As Balme points out,[24] there is a respect in which for Aristotle a female is already thereby something that falls short of the essence of the species (since in his view it is the male that in reproduction contributes the form, the female contributing the matter). It has also been argued by John Dupré[25] that modern biological thinking does not presuppose the rigid essentialism that is sometimes attributed to it. It remains true that whether essentialism of this kind applies in biology or to the world in general must in the end be a scientific question and not one to be answered by a philosopher *a priori*.

To sum up: (1) It seems true that there must be attributed to a substance some sortal concept under which it falls throughout its history. Only if that is true can one speak, even granted spatio-temporal continuity, of the same substance which persists through various changes. Thus and in that sense the slogan 'No substance without identity' seems valid, if not the 'No entity without identity' which was discussed in Chapter 3. (2) It may be that it is a condition of possible reference and thus of thought and language engaging with the world that some substances, as objects of reference, must be such that further *de re* necessities hold good of them. It may even be the case that this is the norm. The argument for this conclusion cannot, however, sustain also the thesis that the conclusion holds good of *all* substances. It is only the point under (1) that holds good generally. So far we have a minimal essentialism at best. (3) There is a more thorough-going essentialism to the effect that substances must have an underlying nature *qua* members of a natural kind. Is it, however, clear that every substance is a member of a *natural* kind? In any case, the extent to which this more thorough-going essentialism holds good and the question whether, as with Aristotelian essentialism, it brings with it theses about the necessary limits upon the possible origins of substances and upon the possible changes that they

[24] D. Balme, 'Aristotle's biology was not essentialist', p. 2.
[25] J. Dupré, 'Natural kinds and biological taxa', *Philosophical Review*, Vol. XC, 1981, pp. 66–90.

can undergo seems not to be an *a priori* matter and must therefore in the end be something determinable only by science.

Primary and secondary qualities

Locke, who is in some ways a progenitor of modern essentialism because of his distinction between nominal and real essences, is also largely responsible for an emphasis on a distinction between primary and secondary qualities of things – between qualities such as shape, size, motion and solidity and qualities such as colour, smell and taste. A similar distinction is to be found, in one form or other, in Democritus, Plato and Aristotle. Aristotle, for example, distinguishes between those properties of things which are perceptible by one sense only and are thus special to that sense and those which are perceptible by more than one sense and are therefore common to those senses. That aspect of the distinction is retained by Locke, but he adds also the suggestion that primary qualities are those without which a material object could not exist, the same not being true of secondary qualities. Indeed, Locke is sometimes taken to hold that the latter are not really qualities of objects at all but merely ideas produced in us by such objects and the primary qualities that they really have.

In a way that thesis connects up with essentialism, since it maintains that there are certain kinds of property that are essential to material substances, even if those substances can vary in respect of the particular form that those properties take in their case. It is important to take account of the latter qualification. Descartes argues in his second *Meditation*, with respect to a lump of wax, that extension is an object of intellectual intuition, on the grounds that when the wax is melted it loses its hardness, smell and colour, whilst its extension remains. To argue in that way, however, is not to compare like with like; it is to contrast the generic property of extension with the more specific properties of hardness, smell and colour. It is not after all clear that it loses the generic properties of smell, colour and perhaps solidity, as opposed to the more specific forms of those properties that the unmelted wax may have. It may nevertheless seem obvious that properties like those of extension, solidity and motion or rest *are* properties without which a material substance cannot exist and that they are therefore essential to it.

It might be argued in return that material substances must have colour in some sense of that word (such that colour is not restricted to chromatic colour and includes transparency) and perhaps other secondary qualities as well. Hence, even if there is reason for distinguishing between the two kinds of quality in the way previously indicated (in terms of their perceptibility by means of one or more senses), that is not a reason for saying that primary qualities are essential to material substances in a way that secondary qualities are not. One possible reply to that is to point to the fact that physicists are willing to contemplate the existence of particles which have extension, or at any rate position, but which do not have colour. Indeed, one of the things that may have influenced Locke in making his distinction is the fact that primary qualities have a place in physical theory in a way that secondary qualities do not. It is not clear, however, how crucial that consideration is for the ordinary material substances which we come across in our everyday lives.

It has been argued by Jonathan Bennett that there is nothing in the case of primary qualities corresponding to defects such as colour-blindness, and that that is a further reason for making the distinction in a way that makes primary qualities essential to bodies.[26] To argue in this way is not to say that we cannot make mistakes in our perception of, for example, the sizes of things. The point is rather that a colour-blind person may lack awareness of a whole range of properties and distinctions that apply to bodies, but is not thereby prevented from finding his way round the world or from having an understanding of bodies. By contrast, if there were such a thing as size-blindness it would prevent both those things; there could not be size-blindness and yet a proper awareness of the world and the bodies in it. If that is true it may be because size is perceptible by more than one sense and a 'blindness' in respect of it would be perceptually far more disrupting than colour-blindness, with corresponding consequences for the understanding.

What such arguments certainly point to is the fact that, given that we are creatures with bodies, the interrelationship between those bodies and other bodies has a fundamental part to play in our perception of the world and explains the weight that is put on those properties of things which figure in such interrelationships.[27] It is not clear, all the same, that those considerations should lead us to put a premium on primary qualities and say that these are essential to material bodies in a way that secondary qualities are not. Many scientists have been known to follow Locke in claiming that secondary qualities are not really qualities of objects at all, but merely sensations that are produced in us by those

[26] J. Bennett, 'Substance, reality and primary qualities', *American Philosophical Quarterly*, Vol. 2, 1965; also in C. B. Martin and D. M. Armstrong (eds.), *Locke and Berkeley* (London: Macmillan, 1968), pp. 105–17. See also his *Locke, Berkeley, Hume: Central Themes* (Oxford: Clarendon Press, 1971), ch. 4.

[27] See my 'Perception and agency', *Monist*, Vol. 61, 1978, pp. 536–47; also in my *Perception, Learning and the Self* (London: Routledge and Kegan Paul, 1983).

objects. That view involves a confusion. It is just as much an objective fact about post-boxes that they are red as that they are round; and that is not gainsaid by the fact that our perception of the redness of the boxes is subject to conditions of perception which are not applicable in the same way to our perception of roundness. Berkeley argued against Locke that the context-variability of secondary qualities applies equally to our perception of primary qualities. He was right to do so, but wrong to draw the conclusion that for that reason primary qualities were as subjective as secondary qualities. He was influenced by Locke in that. He could have drawn another conclusion, and should have done so – that they are equally objective.

That is not to say that there is no distinction to be made between primary and secondary qualities. There is still Aristotle's distinction between special and common objects of the senses. That distinction has no particular relevance to essentialism, however, unless to that variety of essentialism which insists on underlying natures which, if discoverable by physics, will have nothing to do with secondary qualities. Indeed on this latter view the possession of secondary qualities by substances may well have to be explained by reference to underlying mechanisms the setting out of which will involve reference to primary qualities only. Apart from such considerations, however, the validity of the distinction between primary and secondary qualities does not warrant the claim that material substances have primary qualities essentially in a way that they do not have secondary qualities. There is, finally, what may be the obvious point that the distinction has really more to do with what it is for something to be material than with what it is for it to be a substance.

5. Particular and general

The distinction

I indicated in Chapter 4 that particularity would generally be accepted as one characteristic of substances. I did not argue for that thesis, although I referred to arguments presented by Aristotle and Strawson for the conclusion that it is particular substances, or their Strawsonian equivalent, that primarily exist. Indeed Aristotle claims in the *Categories* (2b5) that unless particular substances existed it would be impossible for their corresponding species and genera and non-substance properties to exist. Strawson argues for a similar conclusion regarding material objects as basic particulars from the point of view of speaker–hearer identification.

It is arguable that later, in the *Metaphysics*, Aristotle came to a different conclusion because of further refinements in his view of what must hold good of a substance. He says that the primary cases of substance must be identical with their essences, and that amounts to their being self-explanatory, *causa sui* as Spinoza puts it. It is sometimes said of this later view that it amounts to the identification of substance with form, and because the word for form is the same as that for species it implies that Aristotle came to give greater priority to species than to particular instances of them.[1] If such a view seems esoteric from the point of view of common sense, it should be noted that, if one attaches importance to what is permanent and persistent in the world, species have by that criterion a greater importance than particulars. For it is species or forms that are constant, and it might be argued that the function of the particular is to give rise (e.g. by reproduction) to things like it in form and thus to preserve the species. It might be objected that such a view pays too much attention to what may be the case in biology and generalizes from that unduly.[2] Even so it is a view that needs to be considered seriously.

I said that from the point of view of common sense such a view might

---

[1] See, e.g., G. E. L. Owen, 'The Platonism of Aristotle' in J. Barnes, M. Schofield and R. Sorabji (eds.), *Articles on Aristotle* (London: Duckworth, 1975), Vol. 1.

[2] But remember what was said about thoroughgoing essentialism in Ch. 4.

seem esoteric, but I am not sure to what extent common sense is in this regard a product of culture; the view in question may well seem less esoteric in some parts of the world than in others. It cannot be denied that there is endemic in Western philosophical thought what might be called a prejudice in favour of the particular, with the result that Locke's claim that everything that exists is particular is likely to meet with considerable agreement. To reject the claim one would first have to maintain that besides particulars there also exist general things or entities. It would be a further claim to maintain that such general things have in some sense a primacy for existence. It is this latter thesis which is represented by the view that I said might be attributed to the later Aristotle and it is certainly part of Plato's theory of Forms or Ideas; for the latter, whatever else they are, are undoubtedly general and so constitute universals. It would be a further step again to move to the thesis that *only* what is general exists, or perhaps really exists. It is doubtful in fact whether the last thesis could be intelligibly maintained except against the background of a distinction between reality and appearance and except in the form of the thesis that particulars are mere appearance, general things constituting the true reality. I shall not consider that thesis any further, but the other views mentioned need to be taken seriously.

It would perhaps be as well, first, to be clear about the distinction between the particular and the general itself. Strawson claims to give an account of the distinction in Part 2 of *Individuals*, but that account is mixed up with other matters from which it ought to be disentangled. I said in Chapter 4 that from certain points of view the argument of *Individuals* might seem to be presented in the wrong order. Individuals are for Strawson simply objects of identification or individuation, so that anything that can be picked out and identified by some linguistic means counts as an individual. We pick out in language in this way not only particular things of varying kinds but also general things such as justice or wisdom. That is a fact about the phenomenology of our language but it is one that Strawson takes seriously. He is concerned with two questions: which individuals are basic from the point of view of speaker–hearer identification, and if particulars then which particulars? He deals with the latter issue first.

We can now confine our attention to the former issue, the order of priority to be given to particular and general things, as that provides the context for the account of the distinction between the particular and the general itself. That context Strawson expresses in terms of the ancient (in fact Aristotelian) thesis that while either particulars or general things can serve as subjects of subject–predicate discourse only general things and never particulars can serve as predicates and thus be predicated of subjects. The outcome of the discussion is the claim that particulars deserve to be counted as paradigm logical subjects. The basis of that claim is an affinity that Strawson discerns between the status of subjects and that of particulars – an affinity expressed in terms of the idea that they both have a certain completeness. Subjects, by comparison with predicates (and in conformity with the parallel Fregean claim for the 'saturatedness' of the argument of a function by comparison with the function itself),[3] constitute complete items for thought in a way that something expressible in terms of being a such and such does not. Particulars equally have a completeness because their identification presupposes knowledge of a complete fact.

Whether the senses of 'completeness' involved in this train of thought are the same, and what remains of the argument if they are not, are matters for debate. In my opinion the senses in question are not the same and that vitiates the argument, whatever is to be said independently about its conclusion. Moreover, Strawson complicates matters by distinguishing between what he calls the conditions for the introduction of particulars and general things into propositions, and the conditions for their introduction into discourse. That rather opaque distinction could be put, roughly speaking, into other words by saying that the first is concerned with the conditions for identification of particulars as opposed to universals given already a prior understanding of those notions. By contrast, the second is concerned with the conditions under which particularhood and universalhood have application at all. Strawson goes on to consider the second issue after dealing with the first because it might be objected that his way of dealing with the first issue is circular because of a failure to explain what particulars are at all. To provide that explanation Strawson seeks to show how the notion of a particular could emerge, given other conditions to do with identity, from a more basic (or at any rate more non-committal) way of thinking about the world in terms of what he calls 'features' (roughly speaking, stuffs) having incidence at places and times specified demonstratively.[4]

It would not be pertinent to enter here upon a close examination of the whole programme. It seems in any case a cumbersome and perhaps dubious way of showing that particulars have a priority for identification over general things. I shall return to what are perhaps more direct considerations in that direction later in this chapter. With this rough

[3] See p. 48.
[4] Cf. what I said in Ch. 4 concerning property-location languages.

idea of the context of the argument, however, let us return to the distinction between the particular and the general itself. (Any failure to understand the context of the argument will not matter much; I have summarized it simply to put Strawson's account of the distinction in its place.) I have already hinted at one feature of Strawson's account of the distinction when I said that in his view identification of a particular presupposes knowledge of a complete fact.

Strawson's own summary of that account (which, he stresses, is *very* summary) is as follows: 'Knowing what particular is meant entails knowing, or sometimes – in the case of the hearer – learning, from the introducing expression used, some empirical fact which suffices to identify that particular, other than the fact that it is the particular currently being introduced. But knowing what universal is meant does not in the same way entail knowing any empirical fact: it merely entails knowing the language.'[5] Thus the distinction is made by reference to the conditions for meaningful identification of items corresponding to the terms in question. On the account offered, knowing what particular is meant by the term 'Socrates' involves knowing some fact which serves to identify Socrates, such as that he was the teacher of Plato; while knowing what universal or non-particular is meant by the term 'wisdom' does not involve knowing any such fact but merely involves understanding the language.[6]

It might be argued that the attempt to make the distinction between the particular and the general in terms of what has to be known for successful identification of items under those headings involves a somewhat odd procedure, even if it fits into the context of Strawson's general argument. For does not the identification of things under those headings presuppose an understanding of the headings themselves? It has to be remembered, however, that it is not Strawson's concern at this point to distinguish particularhood from universalhood (that is the aim of the later stage of the general argument); it is to provide what are in effect criteria for the identification of things as particulars and universals, given a prior understanding of particularhood and universalhood. For that purpose it is clear that it is necessary to associate the two kinds of thing with different conditions for their identification. Does the account work, however?

The point about particular-identification is in effect an aspect of

---

[5]   P. F. Strawson, *Individuals* (London: Methuen, 1959), p. 185.
[6]   I abstain from any comment on the claim that the facts presupposed in the identification of particulars must be empirical; but see the Critical Notice of Strawson's book by B. A. O. Williams in *Philosophy*, 1961.

Strawson's theory of reference, according to which a condition of successful reference is that it is presupposed that there is some known description under which the thing actually falls. Thus successful reference to Socrates presupposes knowledge of a description such as 'teacher of Plato' which applies to Socrates. Recent theories of reference, such as that of Kripke in *Naming and Necessity*, have made the point that the use of a name to refer to something need not presuppose the applicability of any description or even a cluster of alternative descriptions. There may be intelligible names in cases where nothing is known of the thing in question other than that it is so called, although there may nevertheless be explanations available of how the use of the name has come about. Hence it is at least arguable that knowing what particular is meant by a name does not entail knowing any fact about it other than that it is so called.

It might nevertheless be held that a distinction remains between conditions of reference to particulars and conditions of reference to general things, whatever be the correct account of reference to particulars – but should the distinction be made in Strawsonian ways? Philosophers who start from the Fregean conception of the distinction between object and concept (corresponding in turn to argument and function) are likely to point to the fact that generality enters the situation via concepts. It may also be held that abstract objects such as justice or wisdom are parasitical on the corresponding concepts. Wisdom, that is to say, is parasitical upon 'being wise'.[7] Hence, it might be said that what Strawson says about identification of universals presupposing knowledge of the language, or knowledge of what the corresponding expression means, is really an account of the identification of concepts, not objects.

Dummett indeed criticizes Strawson for offering a pre-Fregean account of the matter in presuming that the aim of the exercise is to offer criteria for a distinction between two kinds of *object*.[8] He also goes on to argue that within these terms of reference (which he rejects) whether or not there is an abstract object corresponding to a concept is not something that can be ascertained simply through consideration of whether or not the concept expression is understood. In this connexion he offers as a relevant example Hume's case of the missing shade of blue. In considering the question whether every idea corresponds to an impression Hume admits that we might have the idea of a shade of blue in a series of shades without ever having experienced that shade and therefore

---

[7] Cf. J. Searle, *Speech Acts* (Cambridge: C.U.P., 1970), esp. p. 120, where there is a criticism of Strawson in those terms.

[8] M. Dummett, *Frege* (London: Duckworth, 1973), pp. 257ff.

without having had that impression. It might indeed be the case that the shade of blue is never to be found in any object. Is there in that case a universal specified by the description of that shade of blue? According to Strawson the answer must presumably be 'Yes' (although it might be said that in this case there is also a fact about the shade which has to be known for its identification, namely its position in the series of shades – but that is dubiously an *empirical* fact). In Dummett's view, according to what he takes to be the Aristotelian position, the answer ought to be 'No', because there is nothing that exemplifies the shade. His own view on the matter, however, is that the initial question asked, presupposing as it does a distinction between two kinds of object rather than one between an object and a concept, is misconceived.

Within the Strawsonian terms of reference an alternative position to the one adopted by Strawson is, therefore, that whether a universal exists is a question which depends for its answer on whether there is anything which satisfies the corresponding description. In that case what universals there are depends on the facts about objects, on what there is in reality. In this spirit David Armstrong[9] maintains an *a posteriori* theory of universals, or, to be more exact, an *a posteriori* realism over universals. Thus in Chapter 2 of his book, for example, he argues against what he calls predicate nominalism, the theory that what universals there are is simply a matter of what predicates there are – although, historically, it should be noted, nominalism has often involved the rejection of universals altogether. In those terms Strawson (strangely enough, given that he accepts the existence of general things) is a predicate nominalist, although technically he approaches the issue not from predicates but from the names of the abstract objects derived from them. On that presupposition Strawson would be right only if nominalism is a tenable theory of universals, and that is a matter to which further consideration will be given later in this chapter. Although the terms of reference are obviously confused at this point, it is evident that the acceptance of a 'nominalist' criterion for universalhood is scarcely compatible with the generally realist terms in which Strawson discusses the issues. That is to say that it is not compatible with the idea that the exercise as a whole is concerned with the conditions for the identification of two kinds of object, both thought to have a real existence.

From this point of view, therefore, Dummett is surely right in his criticism of Strawson, not because Strawson's way of discussing the matter is pre-Fregean, but because the answer that he provides is not really consistent with the presuppositions of the approach that he does adopt.

[9] D. M. Armstrong, *Universals and Scientific Realism* (Cambridge: C.U.P., 1978).

On the other hand, there is something unsatisfactory about relying on the concept/object distinction to make the distinction between the general and the particular. The claim that universals as abstract objects depend on concepts presupposes the truth of the prior claim that the structure of our thought necessarily conforms to the Fregean pattern, as we saw in Chapter 3. Even so, the suggestion that universals as abstract objects are derivative from concepts implies that the basic objects that fall under concepts are concrete objects, and what else is a concrete object but a particular? That implies in turn that particulars are the basic entities that exist and that what universals exist depends on what can be truly thought about particulars. If all that is true, the concept/object distinction implies a prior acceptance of the notion of particulars; or if that is not strictly true, in that the distinction between concept and object is simply a reflection of the two aspects of a proposition (function and argument) and nothing more, then there is being grafted on to that purely 'formal' distinction a thesis about how our thought relates to the world.

It is perhaps worth noting that when Dummett comes to consider abstract objects in their own right,[10] he too offers criteria for distinguishing abstract objects from concrete objects, in terms of the part played by ostension in the identification of the latter and in terms of the possibility of their standing in causal relations – neither of which is applicable to abstract objects. The trouble is that the latter criterion is problematic because of an uncertainty about what causality involves; once again it is likely as a criterion to turn out to be circular. The former criterion is problematic because of doubts about ostension in general unless all sorts of other things are presupposed.[11] Does ostension with regard to particulars, for example, presuppose their characterization as instances of universals? If so the criterion once again presupposes the distinction that it is meant to elucidate. It is necessary to emphasize once again, however, that these considerations have nothing specifically to do with the concept/object distinction itself; they involve additional issues. (However, it may be that not all abstract objects are derivative from concepts, e.g. numbers, and for that reason considerations about abstract objects may inevitably go beyond those appropriate to concepts. That does not affect what has been said about the relation between the particular/universal distinction and the object/concept distinction.)

It has to be admitted that no argument has been as yet put forward to show that criteria for the particular/general distinction cannot be pro-

---

[10] M. Dummett, *Frege*, pp. 488ff.
[11] See my *Theory of Knowledge* (London and Basingstoke: Macmillan, 1971), pp. 40–2.

vided. It remains unclear, however, what sort of criteria these might be if circularity is to be avoided. The notions of the particular and the general look like ultimate 'categories', and if that is so the programme of trying to provide criteria for these notions does not make sense. All the same, the distinction between the particular and the general is endemic in our thought, whether we think of it as a matter of being given objects and bringing them under concepts or whether we think of it as a matter of being given universals and applying them to reality, as some philosophers have done. That is a matter of whether particulars or universals should be taken as basic for thought; the truth is probably that they both come together. Thought certainly presupposes some distinction between the particular and the general, and to the extent that thought can be considered objective it seems that there must be something about the world which fits that distinction. Whether that is really so is an issue to which I shall return as this chapter goes on.

'Everything that exists is particular'

In the discussion above I frequently referred to the supposition that it is particulars that are basic for existence in some sense or other. This has not been a universal belief among philosophers. I mentioned, towards the end of the last section, that there have been philosophers who have regarded universals as the primary things as far as thought is concerned. That seems true of Bradley, and it is perhaps characteristic of the whole Hegelian tradition. That tradition, however, not only presupposes a distinction between appearance and reality; it also sees reality as in effect something *constructed* via processes of thought, even if with the proviso that experience is a given, although not in such a way as to provide a basis for the construction. (Indeed, if one starts from the idea that our thoughts are general in their character it is a problem how on that basis alone thought of particulars is to be conceived of as taking place.)

Strawson, as we have seen, argues for the thesis that particulars are paradigm logical subjects and therefore primary existents from the point of view of speaker–hearer identification. From that point of view it must be regarded as a cardinal fact that speakers and hearers are themselves particulars and indeed must conceive of themselves as such if they are to be a party to speaker–hearer identification. A condition of their identifying other things is that they must identify each other in a spatio-temporal framework and see themselves as part of the same framework. Ultimately, therefore, the reason why particulars are basic for speaker–hearer identification is that to see the world with those terms of reference is to see it as it is *to* certain particulars, who must regard themselves and each other as particulars.

For one who starts from the question, whether explicit or implicit, about how things are for thought, the situation will be different. For there is nothing about thought as such which puts a premium on particulars and much that puts an emphasis on what is universal or general. It might be argued that it is wrong to ask how things are for thought just like that, since there is no thought without thinkers; it is simply an unreal abstraction to speak of how things are for thought without paying attention to the forms of life of which thought is a part. That has indeed been one reaction to Hegelianism. If it is correct (and it is clear that there is a sense in which it must be), it reinforces the point that the reasons for attaching importance to particulars lie in an aspect of the form of life relative to which these matters become an issue. Once again the aspect in question must be that those who share in that form of life are themselves particulars and must inevitably see themselves as such. For even if we can by an effort of thought or imagination try, and perhaps succeed, to see the rest of the world around us as mere bundles of universals (and some philosophers have argued that that is how we ought to see it), it seems impossible for us to see ourselves in that way.

The claim that particulars are basic for a conception of the world, however that conception comes about, and the lesser claim that particulars are simply indispensable for the same purpose, are both much less than the claim that everything that exists is particular. This last claim is one that is to be met with fairly often in the history of thought, however it is expressed. There is a sense in which it is obviously false; yet it is essential to understand the impetus towards it. It is false for the reason mentioned at the end of the last section – that if there are aspects of our thought that involve generality and if thought can be objective, it is difficult to resist the conclusion that the same generality must apply to reality, or to the reality in relation to which thought is objective. To say that is not as yet to commit oneself to the idea of universal entities with a distinct and independent status (*that* I shall consider later); it *is* to suggest that there must be an aspect of reality which is general. The acceptance of that, however, is enough to rule out the bare claim that everything that exists is particular.

It might be thought, however, that its acceptance is compatible with allowing that no independently existing entity is universal or general. That would be to say that the general features of reality all take the form of attributes of particulars – a position noted in the previous section. I shall return to a consideration of that position in the final section of this chapter. At present it may be enough to suggest that there *may* be a confusion in those who claim that everything that exists is particular between that thesis literally interpreted and the thesis that everything that

has an *independent existence* is particular. That might amount to the thesis
that every substance is particular, which ought not to be controversial.
Indeed as one refines the thesis under consideration so, it seems to me, it
becomes less controversial. It is not enough to seek to support the thesis,
literally interpreted, by pointing to the fact that in the everyday commerce of our lives we put a premium on concrete particulars, even if, as
I have insisted, we cannot fail to regard ourselves as particulars. For it
does matter to us in the ordinary conduct of our lives that things have
certain general characteristics and properties, such as edibility, comfort-
ableness and rigidity. So it matters to us whether such things as these
exist. It is one thing to say that from certain, no doubt important, points
of view a premium is to be put on particulars; it is quite another to assert
that particulars are the only things that exist.

I said, however, that one must understand the impetus towards that
last point of view. It is an impetus that is coincident with nominalism, as
we shall see in the next section, and it is one that goes along with a certain putative tough-mindedness, a preference for the concrete. To the
extent that anyone has been prepared to say that everything that exists is
universal or general (and once again that is a different thesis from the
thesis that what primarily exists is universal) there appears to be a con-
centration on abstract thought and less preoccupation with the concrete
details of our lives. That certainly *seems* true of idealists such as Bradley,
who, as I have noted, approach reality from the point of view of how it is
to be brought under ideas or concepts in judgment, and for whom
ordinary particular things are to be regarded as 'concrete universals',
bundles of universals brought together and unified in some way. But the
tendency to associate thought with what is general or universal goes
back much further than that, despite occasional reactions against it (for
example in the philosophy of William of Ockham, who insists that the
mind can have dealings with particulars by way of intuition).

Nevertheless the belief that thought can be concerned only with
universals is as much a superstition in its own way as is the belief that in
our everyday physical existence we are concerned only with particulars.
It is not even true that to think of a particular one must think of it under
a description or descriptions, although it is no doubt true that to think of
a particular one must know things about it that are general.[12] Yet even if
these are superstitions they must be understood. However much they
are elaborated in theories they involve initially generalizations of what

---

[12] Even that has been denied, as my reference to William of Ockham indicates; the denial is
explicit in the Russellian notion of knowledge by acquaintance, on which see my *Theory of
Knowledge*, pp. 104–6.

are really merely emphases – the emphasis on the concrete and particular in ordinary physical life and the emphasis on the capacity for
abstraction that exists in thought.

Theories of universals

The topic of universals is, almost *par excellence*, one of those philosophical subjects which it has been customary to discuss in terms of alternative
and rival theories. Historically there have often been clashes (sometimes
violent) between proponents of those theories. In my view, however,
the reasons for those clashes have nearly always, if not universally, had
to do with things *associated* in some way with the status of universals and
not with beliefs about that status in itself. Plato's Theory of Forms, for
example, which is often presented as a theory about a world of transcendent but real universals, depends for its controversial character just as
much if not more on the fact that the Forms constitute ideal standards or
paradigms. It is indeed of some interest that in criticizing arguments for
the existence of Forms Aristotle says that the arguments are inconclusive
because they point to the existence of universals only, not Forms. Thus
in his view, and rightly, the Platonic Forms were not merely universals,
and it is because of that that he thought the Forms controversial. Similar
things are true of mediaeval arguments about universals, which had as
much, if not more, to do with theological issues such as the doctrine of
the Trinity as they had to do with the straightforward issue of the existence of universals.

A connected point is that it often seems that what the different
theories of universals *assert* is correct; it is what they *deny* that produces
controversy, and it is in that respect too that they seem to have implications for other controversial matters. That fact becomes more obvious
in the case of the extreme versions of the theories in question, whereas
more moderate versions seem less controversial because they deny less
and admit more. What then are these theories? It is usually said that
there are three of them – realism, conceptualism and nominalism –
although H. H. Price maintained[13] that one ought to add imagism to the
list, because of the place that images have in the theory of universals put
forward by some of the British Empiricists. Realists assert that there are
entities of a general kind that exist independently of us and of our ways
of thinking and speaking about the world. Conceptualists locate the
generality in us and in our minds, pointing to our ability to subsume
things under concepts, which perform a generalizing and classificatory

---

[13] H. H. Price, *Thinking and Experience* (London: Hutchinson, 1953).

role in that respect. Nominalists claim something similar for words, which are said to be, in the words of some of the British Empiricists, particular in their nature but general in their representation. Imagism is a sort of cross between conceptualism and nominalism, claiming a role for images of the same kind as is claimed for words by nominalists.

To present the theories in that way may seem, however, unduly pacificatory; for there seems nothing obviously inconsistent between the theories so presented. It is indeed obvious that if we are to think both generally and objectively about the world there must be something about all three things – the world, our minds and the mode of expression of our thoughts – which makes that possible. On the other hand, to *deny* that there is anything about the world that has to be the case if we are to think generally about it suggests an arbitrariness or conventionalism in our thought which would be incompatible with claims to objectivity. Again, to *deny* that there has to be anything about our minds that underlies the possibility of thinking generally about the world goes in the opposite direction in two respects. First, it plays down the extent to which the question of *which* general features of the world are discriminable is answerable only by reference to features possessed by human beings and their minds; second, it leaves as a general mystery how we can be aware of such general features of the world at all. To *deny* that words have any relevance in this matter is to leave as a mystery how general thoughts about the world are to be realized and above all perhaps how they are to be communicated.

This all goes to establish that it is what the rival theories deny which leads to controversy. More can be brought out about that by considering what is involved in extreme and moderate versions of the theories. For an extreme version of any such theory tends to maintain that the explanation of the possibility of our thinking generally about the world lies *solely* in the feature with which it is concerned. Thus extreme realism explains that possibility simply by positing the existence of independent universals of which we have some form of direct awareness. Such a view provokes the question of how such universals and our awareness of them are relevant to our more ordinary powers of thinking in a general way about the world. What is the connexion between such universals (sometimes called *ante rem*) and the ordinary things that are supposed to be instances of them, and what is the relation between our awareness of such universals and our seeing things as manifesting general features and properties? In so far as Plato's Theory of Forms was a theory of universals (and Forms were certainly universals whatever else they were) it raises just those questions; and the difficulties involved in Plato's answers by reference to sensible particulars participating in or imitating Forms are notorious.

Extreme nominalism is perhaps more often mentioned than actually professed. Numerous philosophers (Roscelin of Compiègne and Hobbes for example) have said such things as that the only things that are universal or general are names or words. But some of them have gone on to qualify that claim with some form of conceptualism, adding that words are signs of concepts in the mind, and some of those in turn have gone on to provide a theory about the way in which concepts themselves come into being. To do that, however, is to try to answer in this case questions which are very similar to those arising from extreme forms of realism; and in so far as answers are forthcoming the theories in question tend to be moderate rather than extreme. An extreme nominalist would have to say that generality lies solely in the relation between words and things without that owing anything either to those things or to our powers of thought of which the words might be an expression. To say that words are particular in their nature but general in their representation is all very well, but we in fact need some explanation of how that is possible. Similar things might be said about an extreme conceptualism.

In the theories of the great mediaeval exponents of rival accounts of universals (the period of mediaeval philosophy being, so to speak, the hey-day of such theories) it is often possible to detect elements of theories other than that which is officially espoused. Aquinas, the prime exponent of realism, thought of form as being a real and general feature of things in the world. On the other hand, universals do not have in his view a self-subsistent status. Rather universals are abstracted from *phantasmata* which are produced in us by things in the course of perception; the intellect forms from them concepts which are then verbalized. In this account of the matter there are clearly elements of all three aspects that the rival theories emphasize. Abelard, who may be thought of as the primary example of a conceptualist in the mediaeval world, held that universals were concepts (*sermones*). Nevertheless he combined this view with a theory of abstraction of such concepts from particular things through attention to their features. Moreover, his use of the word '*sermo*' indicates the connexion in his way of thinking between concepts and speech. William of Ockham, the great fourteenth-century nominalist, originally said that universals had only a logical existence, being the meanings of words, these in turn being conventional signs of things corresponding to concepts which are natural signs of things. The term 'universal' is what he called a term of second intention, in that it picks out the content of our apprehension (or intention) of our first-order apprehension of a class of things. That, however, presupposes that things form classes and that there is some form of apprehension of that. Indeed Ockham later came to accept something like a more straightforward conceptualism.

If it is accepted that a complete account of the possibility of general thought about the world presupposes elements of all the rival theories of universals, there will be much less temptation to ask questions such as whether, if there were no humans or other conscious beings, there would exist in the world anything else but particular things. For, similarities between such things surely exist whether or not there is anyone to recognize them. Moreover, there are no doubt far more similarities between things than are ever recognized, whether or not the recognition of such similarities is natural or not. Shoes and ships and sealing-wax, cabbages and kings do not, one might suppose, form a natural class, although the reason why they are brought together by Lewis Carroll is obvious enough from the sound of the words. The fact, however, that we have to appeal to the nature of the words makes the suggestion that we are thereby given a class a somewhat arbitrary one. If, however, we could find some similarity between the things themselves, however farfetched, that would be another matter. That similarity would exist whether or not anyone recognized it, and so would the property in virtue of which the similarity holds good. Similar considerations apply to the relation of words to the world; there are far more general features in the world than we have words to express.

It might, however, be objected that to the extent that such considerations give credence to realism (that is to say to the extent that they justify belief in the existence of real universals, even if *in rebus* – as aspects of particular things in the world) they allow of the possibility that there is an indefinite number of such universals. Such a consideration may offend against a sense of economy and invite the application of what is called, aptly in this case, Ockham's razor. The same consideration applies to the evident possibility of generating more and more classes, and thereby more and more universals, by taking into account second-order classes with first-order classes as members, then third-order classes, and so on.[14] Can one contemplate such a proliferation of universals with equanimity? What about the possibility of universals corresponding to conjunctions or disjunctions of properties,

[14] This process is sometimes likened to the argument in Plato's *Parmenides* known as the Third Man Argument. There are in fact significant differences between the two arising from the fact that Plato was not concerned simply with classes or even universals, but with Forms which were paradigms or standards as well as universals.

or to negative properties? What about relations? Some of these latter questions and others of the same kind are discussed systematically by D. M. Armstrong in the second volume of his *Universals and Scientific Realism*, entitled *A Theory of Universals*, from which it is clear that there are considerations which pull anyone attempting to answer these questions in different directions. Those interested in such matters can do no better than refer to Armstrong's discussion.

Nevertheless, such considerations may lead to the invocation of Ockham's razor and an attempt to find principles reference to which may at least bring about a reduction in the number of universals postulated. One such move is to try to find a basis for our use of general words and general concepts simply by reference to the similarity between things, without supposing the existence of universals corresponding to distinct *kinds* of similarity or to properties that things have in virtue of those kinds of similarity. Such a view is sometimes referred to as a kind of nominalism,[15] but it has been pointed out by many others that the account offered presupposes the existence of at least one, realistically grounded, universal – similarity. For it is surely presupposed by the theory in question that similarities between things are objective features of the world. It might also be said that from a truly nominalist point of view it does not matter how many realist universals one is driven to accept; one is too many, and if one is driven to accept one there is not much point in stopping there. Nevertheless, it is worth seeing whether an appeal to similarity will in fact prevent the need to accept further universals.

Realists have generally responded to similarity theorists by saying that it is not enough to appeal to similarity, since every similarity holds good in a certain respect. Resemblance is always resemblance in some respect, and the attempt to spell out the respects will entail recognition of the universals corresponding to them. It is not in fact clear that this response is correct if treated as an absolutely general claim. Some resemblances, e.g. that between red and orange, do not seem to presuppose a specifiable respect. Moreover, if there are family-resemblance concepts, there will not be a single respect in virtue of which all the things which fall under such a concept will be similar. The issue is connected with the general question of whether the principles of classification of things are always those of genus and differentia, such that species of a genus are always marked off by a differentia; or whether there is not also classification in terms of what W. E. Johnson called

---

[15] Cf. D. M. Armstrong, *Universals and Scientific Realism*, Vol. 1, ch. 5.

determinates and determinables, where the determinates of the determinable are not necessarily co-ordinate and are not marked off from each other by a differentia. Red and orange are determinates of the determinable colour. They are of course both colours, just as instances of the family-resemblance concept *game* are all games. Moreover, it can rightly be said that objects that are red and orange resemble each other in respect of colour. But red and orange, *as colours*, do not resemble each other in that respect, or indeed in any other respect. They just are similar though not *in any respect*.

However, reference to red and orange as colours, rather than to red and orange things, may be taken to imply a commitment already to the universals *red* and *orange*. Hence, if the concern is to eliminate universals or at least to reduce their number, we ought to see whether it is possible to eliminate these particular references to universals by speaking only of particular, concrete things, and if we do whether we need *in that case* any reference to the respects in which those things are similar. For if we do need to make reference to such respects, it will be clear that we cannot do without such a reference in *all* cases, and that will strengthen the realist's case. Armstrong points out that arguments put forward by Arthur Pap and Frank Jackson[16] show that the reference to a respect cannot be eliminated when trying to say in terms of particular things and their similarities what is said by 'Red resembles orange more than it resembles blue'. For if we try to analyse that proposition in terms of red objects being more like orange objects than blue objects, there may be other ways in which the objects in question stand in those relations apart from colour. Hence we cannot explain what we mean in this way without specifying the respect in which we are considering the objects, i.e. their colour. Frank Jackson has put forward a similar argument in the case of the proposition 'Red is a colour'. This cannot be equivalent to 'For all particulars x, if x is red, x is coloured', since the latter might be true for reasons other than that red is a colour; hence it does not entail 'Red is a colour'. Further details are given in Armstrong's discussion.

In sum, it does not seem possible to eliminate the reference to respects in *all* cases where it is proposed to do without reference to universals by analysing propositions which apparently make such a reference in terms of particular things and their similarity. Hence there will certainly be as many universals as are generated by such cases. If we have to have so many there seems little point in being abstemious beyond that,

---

[16] See ibid., pp. 58ff. The papers by A. Pap and F. Jackson are in *Philosophical Quarterly*, Vol. 9, 1959, pp. 334–8 and *Mind*, Vol. LXXXVI, 1977, pp. 427–9 respectively.

although the questions that I mentioned earlier as to whether there are any limits on them still remain.

One further objection to having any truck with realism over universals should perhaps be noted. In a well-known paper,[17] David Pears construes reference to universals as an answer to the question 'Why are we able to name things as we do?' and maintains that all possible answers to that question are necessarily circular and that all analogies employed to explain naming are either too like the phenomenon to be explained or too far away from it to be satisfactory. Hence, in one way or another, a reference to universals is unsatisfactory and does no real work. Putting the question to be considered in terms of naming is perhaps unfortunate, because not all names are general and thus capable of having anything to do with universals. I believe, however, that it is no coincidence that the issue is put in that way, since Pears wants to assimilate the use of general words to naming from the point of view of the kind of meaning that they have. However that may be, the second point that he makes, about the unsatisfactoriness of possible analogies, is no doubt valid; for the relation between a general word and the instance to which it applies presupposes the relation between the general and the particular, and any attempt to find an illuminating analogy to explain that relation will be fruitless if, as I believe, that relation is unique. That, however, is not an objection to the intelligibility of the relation itself.

The first point that he makes is another matter. Alan Donagan[18] has objected that the claim that it is 'too obviously circular even to look informative' to say 'We are able to call things red because they are red' is invalid. It is so because the thesis under examination should really have been put in the form 'We are able to call things "red" because they are red', and in that case there is no repetition of the same thing in the explanation and the explanandum; for the first occurrence of the word 'red' is in quotes, but not the second. Michael Loux[19] has added to that criticism the further one that Pears has in any case chosen an example which looks too favourable to his case. Loux thinks that if we said that we call people 'courageous' because they exemplify courage, there would not even be the appearance of circularity, since the words 'courageous' and 'courage' are not the same. That is no doubt true, but Pears chooses his example because he believes, as he puts it, that the only exit from the maze of words is ultimately by pointing – that is, by osten-

[17] D. Pears, 'Universals' in A. G. N. Flew (ed.), *Logic and Language*, Vol. 2 (Oxford: Blackwell, 1953), pp. 51–64.
[18] A. Donagan, 'Universals and metaphysical realism', *Monist*, Vol. 47, 1963.
[19] M. Loux, *Substance and Attribute* (Dordrecht: Reidel, 1978), p. 22.

102 Particular and general

sion and ostensive definition. We do not really explain to anyone what 'red' means if we tell them that 'red' applies to red things, we need ostension as well.

That is certainly true, and it might perhaps be said in reply to Loux that we do not say much more by way of explanation of what 'courageous' means if we tell them that 'courageous' applies to things that exemplify courage. In fact, however, the appeal to universals is not really made to answer *that* question. Even if we put the matter in Pears' terms, the question 'Why are we able to name things as we do?' ought not to be construed, if it is anything like a correct version of the question that generates reference to universals, as a question about how we are able to explain the meaning of the words that we use. The question that is at stake is in effect a 'How possible?' question. It asks how it is possible that we should think and speak generally about the world. One element in the answer to that question must be that it is possible to use general words objectively only if there is something that holds good of the world, namely that the world has general features or aspects.

The situation is in some respects like that which holds good of answering the question 'Why is a statement true?' by saying 'Because it corresponds to the facts'. There is a putative circularity in this latter case too, if the question is taken as a request for a reason for saying that any given statement is true.[20] Nevertheless, it is only because the world is such that there are facts with regard to it that statements can be true. To say that is to point to the conditions under which there can be objectivity, and that, as I have said more than once, is one of the concerns of a theory of universals. How can it be that the use of a general word reflects objectivity? Because there is a general feature of the world, a universal, which the use of that word reflects. That is not part of the explanation of the meaning of the word; it is rather a statement of the general conditions under which it can have meaning in an objective way.

The primacy of the particular

In using the words 'general feature of the world' as an alternative to 'universal' at the end of the last section, I took the first step towards answering the question of whether there can be universals if there are no particulars to exemplify them. It is implicit in the use of the words 'of the world' that a universal functions as an attribute. It is a further question, however, whether that attribute must be instantiated in particulars. It will be remembered that Dummett said against Strawson that even on his terms of reference it was not enough, in considering what universals

[20] See my *Theory of Knowledge*, pp. 136ff.

there are, to say that the answer lies in the understanding of the language. It is not enough, that is, to say that what universals there are is a matter of what intelligible general words there are or even what intelligible predicates there are. Whether there is such a universal as Hume's missing shade of blue is in that case a matter of whether there actually *is* anything of that colour. And that is an *a posteriori* question. If that view is right then what universals there are depends quite definitely on what particulars there are, and the question is not decidable in any other way.

At the other extreme is the view, in fact rarely met with, but in effect there in Plato's philosophy, that universals have a strictly independent existence, and perhaps that what particulars there are is in some sense dependent on what universals there are. (And by that more is meant than that the identification of particulars depends on the possibility of bringing them under general descriptions. That may or may not be the case, but it does not in any way imply that universals have an independent status.) Platonism in this sense about universals is not only rarely to be met with; it tends to receive little support or understanding when it *is* met with. That is understandable, and it has to be recognized that Plato's Forms were not just universals but also absolute standards to which we have to look when making decisions about particular things and particular courses of action, and to which, according to Plato, the creator has to look in bringing about the world. Thus the motivation for positing a realm of independently existing universals lies once again in something that does not belong to the notion of a universal taken by itself.

We nevertheless have two extreme views: (1) that universals exist only as attributes of existing particular things, and (2) that universals exist as independently existing things, so that it is at any rate logically possible that they should provide a rationale for particulars. In between these extremes lies perhaps the view that while universals have no independent existence in their own right and they are dependent on particulars to the extent that they exist only as attributes, there is no need for any given attribute to be instantiated in an actually existing particular for there to be such an attribute and thereby such a universal. That view is at least implicit in Strawson's claim that in order to identify a universal we need only to understand the language. For in understanding that, we understand what attributes there are, in a way that does not wait upon the discovery of what things have such attributes. As long as we have the concept of X then the universal X exists. But, of course, the question then arises of just when we have the concept of X.

Because of this last point, and perhaps for other reasons, it cannot be denied that this intermediate theory of universals has a certain awkwardness. It ought to be an objective matter whether a putative universal exists. On the theory in question, according to which our possession of a concept determines whether a corresponding universal exists, it ought similarly to be an objective matter whether we have the concept. But how is that to be decided? Is it enough that no contradiction arises from its supposition? Is that even necessary? Is there a concept of a round square, and if there is is there a universal *round square*? Or is the answer to both these questions 'No' because there is a contradiction in the notion of a round square? To suggest that there are universals only when there are particulars with the corresponding attributes certainly provides an easy and straightforward way of dealing with these problems.

Nevertheless, the answer to the question of what universals exist ought not to turn on such issues of convenience. The argument between Platonists and their opponents is really one concerning whether universals exist merely as attributes or whether they exist as independent entities – as substances, Aristotle in effect says. A second point is whether, if they exist as attributes, it is enough for that purpose that there should be the corresponding predicate (provided that it is a genuine predicate, one that makes sense). If we reject Platonism, as we surely ought to, then the whole weight of the problem comes on the second point. On that the answer surely is that there exists an attribute as a matter of objective fact only if something exemplifies it – that is to say, only if there is something that has that attribute.

To say that is not necessarily to reject Strawson's claim that the condition that has to be satisfied if there is to be identifying reference to a universal is merely an understanding of the language. For there is the further question of what is involved in understanding a language. That opens up considerable issues which occupy contemporary philosophers of language. Nevertheless, if universals exist by way of or in dependence on attributes, and if what attributes there actually are depends on what is the case with regard to the world, then what universals exist depends on what actually holds good of actually existing particulars. In that sense the thesis that there is a primacy about particulars holds good too. That, however, is not to say that particulars can exist without attributes, and it is not to say that the only things that exist are particulars. It is at most to say that particulars have a certain primacy as regards what exists independently. If there ain't no justice it is because there is nothing that is just.

6. Simple substances: Monism and pluralism

Must substance be simple?

As we saw in Chapter 4, it is not part of the Aristotelian tradition about substance or indeed of our ordinary thinking about substances (if there is any such thing) that substances are simple. It might indeed be said that they are quite the contrary. The things that we should ordinarily think of as substances are complex both in the sense that they have a multiplicity of properties and in the sense that they are spatially divisible. Moreover, it is important to note the point which in Chapter 4 I mentioned as recognized by Plato – that the predicate 'one' is a relative term so that whether something is counted as one or many must depend on the answer to the prior question 'One what?' The thought that substances must be simple is the same as the thought that they must be one in an absolute sense.

It is Leibniz, among philosophers concerned with substance, who seems most concerned also with the simplicity of substances. It is arguable that he thought that they must be simple, and not merely in possession of the spurious unity which attaches, as he put it, to sacks of pistoles (i.e. the unity of a mere collection), because he thought that this followed from the fact that substances are primary as regards existence. In other words, he thought that substances must be absolutely simple because any complex thing, whether that complexity is actual or potential, is capable of being analysed into, and is thus dependent on, the things of which it is a complex, and so cannot be primary. The simplicity of a true substance follows, therefore, from its primacy for existence.

Leibniz is by no means the only philosopher who has thought in this way. The thought is characteristic of most forms of atomism, at any rate when that doctrine is not interpreted as a merely physical theory. It is to be found, for example, in the logical atomism of Russell and the early Wittgenstein. In the *Tractatus Logico-Philosophicus* the latter says at 2.02 'Objects are simple' and at 2.021 'Objects make up the substance of the world. That is why they cannot be composite.' The same thought, though not always expressed in the same way, is to be found also in philosophers of a quite opposite persuasion, such as Bradley. The latter's argument for monism, the thesis that there is at bottom only one thing, in his *Appearance and Reality* turns on a supposed impossibility about relations, so that, as he puts it (p. 34), 'experience, where relational, is not true'. But anything that is complex involves relations between its parts or aspects; hence reality cannot be complex and must therefore be simple.

Any thesis that puts weight on the supposed absolute simplicity of substance must involve also a distinction between appearance and reality; for it is clear that ordinary things, as we ordinarily suppose them to be, are not absolutely simple in that way. If they are held not to be substances for that reason, then the fact that they *seem* to be substances must be put down as appearance, reality being quite otherwise. It is for this reason that Leibniz held that ordinary things are merely phenomena; they are *phenomena bene fundata* because they are not mere semblance, but they do not constitute reality all the same. Given this, it was incumbent on Leibniz to identify the constituents of true reality, on the assumption that they had to be absolutely simple. Moreover, it was not enough that they should be just simple. If they were to be the constituents of reality they had to provide a rationale for the world's being as we take it to be. They could not just be simples; they had to have content. In Leibniz's way of putting it, they had to be capable of reflecting a multiplicity in their simplicity.

It might seem that such a specification must inevitably involve a contradiction. How can something be absolutely simple and yet capable of the multiplicity presupposed by the necessity to provide content such that together they make up a world? The notion of simplicity seems to rule out the possibility that substances should even be spatial, since anything spatial is capable, at least in principle, of being divided and so made plural. That is a point that was taken for granted by Zeno of Elea in his arguments against pluralism, and it is one that Leibniz too takes seriously. For a time Leibniz played with the idea that the true substances of which the world is composed were 'massy points' – unextended, pointlike objects which nevertheless had physical properties. Such a notion, however, is obviously unsatisfactory, and he eventually came to posit the existence of 'monads'. Plato had invoked that notion in his *Philebus* (15d) – the notion of a single, indivisible thing – but he did not apply it in the way that Leibniz did. Leibniz thought that the only thing that could be of this kind and yet was capable of constituting a unity in a plurality (and so reflecting the world from its point of view) was something like the 'ego' ('*le moi*'). It is of some interest that he took the self or the ego as his model for a simple substance, and he is not the only philosopher to do so.[1] He took it to be an illuminating paradox about the notion of the self that it, the ego, is both simple and yet capable, through perception, of reflecting the world from a single point of view. If that is taken seriously it provides an obvious model for things that are to constitute unities in a plurality.

At the same time, it would generally be taken as paradoxical that the substance of the world should be made up of a plurality of egos or of entities analogous to egos. Such a view has in any case the corollary that our ordinary beliefs about the world are beliefs about appearance only. To say that that appearance is 'well founded' does not help to remove the paradox unless some satisfactory account can be provided of just how, in these circumstances, it *is* well founded. By comparison, Russell's simples, as expounded in his lectures on the 'Philosophy of logical atomism', are identified with sense-data; he supposes that one can give an account of the nature of the empirical world on the basis of sense-data in ways that are familiar from discussions of phenomenalism.[2] But the very possibility, if it were one, of building a world from sense-data demands that sense-data provide not only a content but also the other features of substance, including, as I indicated in Chapter 4, identity. On that Russell is somewhat ambiguous, since, while denying to his particulars (i.e. sense-data) the quality of persistence through time that is characteristic of substance, he goes on to say that a particular 'as a rule, is apt to last for a very short time indeed, not an instant but a very short time'. It is not clear in any case how sense-data could do all that is required of them and still be absolutely simple.

There does seem to be a genuine conflict between the idea that something can be absolutely simple and the idea that it can constitute the substance of reality, be one of its constituents, so to speak. The only course is to recognize the point with which I started – that there is no such thing as something which is absolutely simple. That is not just because there does not happen to be any such thing, but because the notion of absolute simplicity is itself an incoherent one. Simplicity is always a relative matter because the notion of simplicity itself is a relative one. Hence, the proper response to the question 'Is such and such simple?' is 'A simple what?' The acceptance of this does not entail that, because of Leibniz's argument that only the simple can be primary for existence, one should give up the thesis that substance is primary for existence. For even if the notion of absolute simplicity is abandoned there is no need to think that

[1] See the references to Reid given in Ch. 9.
[2] See my *Theory of Knowledge* (London and Basingstoke: Macmillan, 1971), pp. 170ff.

primacy for existence entails simplicity in the sense that Leibniz thought. There is no need to accept the argument that anything complex must necessarily be secondary, except that a complex F is obviously secondary to a simple F. But a simple F need not, and indeed cannot, be absolutely simple.

This point covers even spatial complexity and simplicity. An object which is spatially complex in that it is spatially divisible is secondary to its parts only as long as those parts can have a genuinely independent existence. The fact that something is divisible simply in principle does not, however, mean that it has a secondary status, for in that case there is no implication that it is divisible into parts which can have independent existence. For that reason the mere fact that something is extended in space does not entail that it is complex in a sense that necessarily implies the existence of something more simple on which it is dependent. Hence the point that I mentioned earlier with respect to Leibniz – that the very notion of simplicity rules out the possibility that substances should be spatial – is not a valid one. It would be valid only if the mere *possibility* of division (which is a consequence of extension) were enough to prevent a substance's being one, let alone one of the kind to which it belongs. The fact that a substance is spatial, and therefore potentially divisible spatially, does not entail that it is spatially complex, let alone dependent for its existence on separable parts. Substances can, therefore, be both extended and simple of their kind.

It is worth noting indeed that even if a substance does have separable parts this need not prevent its being simple of its kind. When Leibniz opposed true substances to 'sacks of pistoles', he was opposing true substances to mere collections which do not make up a true unity, so as to be something that is one of a certain kind. There are, however, certainly things that have separable parts which nevertheless constitute true unities in that sense. In some such cases, though I do not know if it applies to all, the parts as separated are not all that they are when they contribute to the whole (something that has led some people to say that the whole is more than the sum of the parts). Such unities are sometimes called 'organic', since the parts of an organism are, when separated from the whole, not all that they are when part of the whole; they do not, for example, perform the functions that they perform when part of the whole, they do not in separation manifest what they contribute to the whole. While organic unities exhibit such facts in the clearest way, it would be a mistake to think that they are restricted to organisms. A carburettor is not, in separation, all that it is when part of an engine. The one clear case where this sort of thing does *not* hold good is where the whole is a mere collection as is the case with Leibniz's 'sack of pistoles'.

Issues about simplicity do not therefore restrict the range of substances to things of a certain kind, such as monads or organic entities. Indeed it might be said that the whole issue about simplicity is something of a red herring as far as the topic of substance is concerned, in that it depends upon a misconception concerning the kind of concept that that of simplicity is. If it is recognized that simplicity is a relative matter, most, perhaps all, the difficulties that seem to ensue disappear. That fact, however, has not prevented many other issues being raised that turn on that conception or do so when one digs below the surface. One such issue is the opposition between metaphysical theories that embrace monism and those that in contrast assert pluralism, by way of reaction.

Monism and pluralism

My use of the words 'by way of reaction' at the end of the last section was deliberate. Simply to say that there are many things, even many substances, would be to content oneself with a thesis that is frankly boring – boringly obvious, one might think. Historically, the pluralist theses that have seemed interesting or even challenging have always taken the form of reactions to what are perhaps even more challenging monist theses. To assert with monism that there is only one thing, or even only one kind of thing, brings with it an air of paradox, the dispelling or reduction of which requires a great deal of argument. It is not surprising, therefore, that monisms have generally been backed up by arguments of a kind that may be called 'rationalist' in the sense that they turn on *a priori* considerations. By contrast, pluralisms have seemed to involve a strong dose of common sense. On closer examination, however, it may appear that the apparent support for pluralism by common sense is deceptive. I do not mean that it is not a common-sense view that there are many things, or many substances of many kinds, in the world. It is that pluralist theories generally assert the existence of many things of a very specific kind, often things which are simple.

To attain a clear view of this it is first necessary to distinguish between *substance* monism/pluralism and *kind* monism/pluralism. The ancient Greek atomists, for example, thought that there were many things – atoms – but they were all of the same kind, and apparent differences between kinds of thing were reducible to differences between combinations of things of the same kind, i.e. atoms. Empedocles, by contrast, thought that there were four (or possibly six) kinds of thing to which other apparent kinds of thing were reducible – earth, fire, air and water, plus, in a certain sort of way, love and strife. Anaxagoras thought that it was impossible to reduce apparent differences of kind to so few underlying differences of kind; and he may have thought, although this is not so clear, that there was an infinity of kinds of thing, and certainly an infinity of things. A philosopher can, therefore, be a thing- or substance-pluralist and either a kind-monist or a kind-pluralist. It is difficult to see how a philosopher who thinks that there is only one substance could also think that there are many kinds of substance, although he may believe, as did Spinoza, that his one substance has attributes of more than one kind and that there are many kinds of thing in that sense. I shall not here consider further the question of how many kinds of thing there are, although there surely are many. I shall in Chapter 8, however, be concerned with one particular issue of that sort – whether a dualism of mental and physical things is tenable.

Let us confine our attention, therefore, to the issue between substance-monists and substance-pluralists. I said earlier that such monists have generally relied upon *a priori* considerations in arguing for their views. Such considerations have not always been of the same kind, but they tend to turn in various ways on difficulties or incoherences that the philosophers concerned see in the idea of a plurality of substances. Hence they start from a consideration of common-sense observations and argue *a priori* that they cannot be accepted. It is not surprising, therefore, that monisms generally involve a distinction between how things really are and how they seem to be, although, as I sought to show in Chapter 2, that need not amount to a distinction, even if it often does so, between two realms of appearance and reality.

Parmenides, to recapitulate the example from Chapter 2, thought that he could show that there is no truth at all in the 'beliefs of mortals'; but the fact that there is in his view a distinction between the 'Way of truth' and the 'Way of opinion', the latter being what the 'beliefs of mortals' amount to, does not entail that the 'Way of opinion' gives an account of a realm of appearance. The account of the world that Parmenides gives in the part of his poem concerned with the 'Way of opinion' may be the best account of the world as ordinary men see it; it is nevertheless, he says, all false. The truth is that 'what is' is one because there is no place in it for plurality. Plurality implies difference, disparity and distinction. They all imply for their very conception the possibility of 'what is not'; for if A and B are different, where A is, B is not. Moreover, Parmenides thinks that he has good reason for the conclusion that 'what is not' is unthinkable. I shall not go further into the details of the argument; it is sufficient to see that it is a strictly *a priori* argument, leading to the conclusion that difference and for that reason plurality are impossible. Any account of the world which suggests otherwise must be false, however good it may seem. The argument and its conclusion are bald ones; they admit of no half measures.

Spinoza argues differently, though in a no less *a priori* way. He starts from the premiss that if substance is to be primary it must be its own rationale and cannot for that reason depend on anything else; it is *causa sui*. From that starting-point Spinoza argues that substance must be unlimited by anything else; hence it is infinite and for that very reason one (finiteness would mean limitation and thus something else to limit it; infiniteness precludes that). He does not, however, say that our ordinary view of the world is totally false, however inadequate our ideas of it may be. Indeed, ordinary things are in a sense preserved by the theory, but not as substances; instead they are modes of the one infinite substance, which is God or Nature. If we wish to say that on this theory our ordinary view of the world constitutes appearance, since reality consists of the one substance with infinite attributes and what we ordinarily take to be substances are really its modes, the appearance still has its basis in reality.

Very much the same is true of Bradley who argues for monism via considerations that have at first sight some affinity with those relied upon by Parmenides, yet without the conclusion strictly speaking, that what we ordinarily think is totally false. Bradley's argument, which I shall survey in more detail later in this chapter, turns in the end on an incoherence that he sees in the notion of relations. But the possibility of a plurality of things depends on there being relations between them, if only the relation of difference. If relations are incoherent and irrational, so then must be pluralism, and our ordinary view of a world of many things must therefore constitute a view of appearance only. Bradley does not, however, think that appearance is totally false. Reality must somehow include appearance, since a complete explanation of reality must also explain why there is appearance and why it is as it is.

I have emphasized certain differences between these thinkers – differences both in the mode of argument and in the outcome, as regards the relation between their monism and common sense. They have in common, however, the use of an *a priori* argument to the effect that either the very idea of plurality, or at any rate the idea of a plurality of substances, is one that cannot rationally be sustained. There must be one thing only, one substance only, in an absolute sense which rules out any possibility of complexity or multiplicity. The one thing that comprises reality must therefore be one and simple in an absolute sense, whether or not they put the matter in those terms. Reality cannot be one in a sense that rules out all possibility of plurality and yet simple in some relative sense only.

Pluralists who have reacted against such a position have not been content merely to emphasize common sense and on that basis simply assert the existence of many things. Leibniz said at one point that if it were not for the monads Spinoza would be right. It is a curious remark in a number of ways, but it indicates the extent to which Leibniz was influenced by the same sort of considerations as Spinoza was, but without wishing to accept his conclusions. To the extent that that is typical of pluralists, a pluralist is a monist with a strong dash of common sense. That holds good of, for example, the Greek Atomists in their response to Parmenides. For they accepted some parts of his argument, or at any rate some of his sub-conclusions. In particular they accepted that nothing could come into existence or go out of existence (a position that Parmenides showed to follow from the impossibility of 'what is not'), but they wanted to preserve as much as possible of the common-sense world. For that reason there is a sense in which each atom can be regarded as a Parmenidean 'one'. Hence, the Atomists might have said 'If it were not for the atoms (and of course the void) Parmenides would be right.'

Similar things could be said of the logical atomism of Russell and the early Wittgenstein, as I shall indicate in the next section. If that is the case generally, then pluralist reactions to monism can be characterized as asserting the existence of a plurality of substances having the same or similar character to that possessed by the corresponding monist's one substance. Pluralism is by that criterion a definite metaphysical position, not the re-assertion of common-sense 'prejudices'. On the other hand, it is a metaphysics deeply tinged with common sense. For that reason also, pluralist arguments tend not to be totally *a priori*; they are thus less rationalistic than those of monists. That is not surprising, since the departure from common sense that monism entails requires a more radical kind of argument than does the position that, at least in respect of the *number* of existing things, common sense is right. It must be emphasized yet again, however, that pluralism and common sense are not the same, and that a pluralist reaction to monism cannot be content merely with the position that there are after all many things in the world. For as it stands that is not a philosophical position at all, and certainly not a piece of metaphysics.

Absolute idealism and logical atomism

It is worth while to concentrate on the opposition between F. H. Bradley, the absolute idealist, and Bertrand Russell and the early Wittgenstein, the Logical Atomists, partly because the details of the opposition may be less well worked over than other examples of conflicts between monists and pluralists and partly because it involves peculiarities of its own which are of some interest. Logical atomism by that name is a twentieth-century phenomenon, but in the light of it it is possible to recognize similar views in earlier thinkers.[3] At the same time, twentieth-century logical atomism would not have taken the form that it did if Bradley's absolute idealism had not been there to react to. It must be borne in mind that Russell began his philosophical life much under the influence of the idealists.

Bradley's argument for monism has in effect two stages. The first operates, to put it in its Hegelian context, at the level of the understanding, and is to be found in Bradley's *Principles of Logic*. The second operates at the level of reason, and is to be found in his *Appearance and Reality*. Despite his rejection of some aspects of Hegel's philosophy (particularly what he referred to as 'the bloodless ballet of the categories'), Bradley remained a Hegelian in a great many respects and there are many echoes in his argument of the opening chapters of Hegel's *Phenomenology*. In the *Principles of Logic* Bradley presents his account of the understanding in his theory of judgment, the central aspects of which are laid out in the first two chapters. In Bradley's view the basic element of thought is the judgment, not the ideas which constituted the basic apparatus of the theory presented by the British Empiricists and their nineteenth-century successors, e.g. James and J. S. Mill; and some part of Bradley's argument is directed against the latter. There are no 'floating ideas', he claims, independent of judgment. That means in effect that the logical status of ideas is that of the predicative aspects of judgments, and for that reason ideas can have, logically, no independent status. In judgment we bring whatever is the subject under ideas; we bring objects, to use the parallel Fregean terms, under concepts. Such objects, considered as subjects of judgment, comprise either reality or some selected portions of reality. Selection of portions of reality for the purposes of judgment can, however, be carried out only through sub-

---

[3]   A book on Plato by Gerold Prauss is called *Platon und der logische Eleatismus* (Berlin: Walter de Gruyter, 1966). Logical Eleaticism turns out to be very like logical atomism in that the 'ones' that it refers to are atoms of meaning. Gilbert Ryle too saw aspects of logical atomism in Plato; see his articles on 'Plato's Parmenides' in *Mind*, Vol. XLVIII, 1939, pp. 129–51 and 302–25.

sumption under ideas, and that, as we shall see, has important consequences.

The aim of judgment is, in Bradley's view, to bring reality under ideas. To capture it completely in that way would in effect involve an identification of reality with some set of ideas, an identity between the two, an identity between, as Bradley puts it, the 'that' and the 'what'. But the 'that' and the 'what' are, it might be said, categorially different, in the same way as Frege's objects and concepts are. An unsympathetic critic might therefore say that there is a built-in incoherence in Bradley's conception of judgment. He, however, takes it to show the importance of the notion of identity in difference. Without that conception, he says, we come up against the old dilemma that if we predicate what is the same we say nothing, while if we predicate what is different we say what is false. Nevertheless, the outcome of the theory of judgment is bound to be, as Bradley comes to put it, that logic is not true to reality; the understanding cannot gain an adequate grasp on reality. If that is so, what the understanding tells us about reality cannot be true, or not totally so, and since the understanding tells us of a reality with many distinct objects, that conception of reality must already be under suspicion. Or so Bradley wants us to believe. The drive towards monism becomes more evident in the details of the argument concerning judgment.

Bradley distinguishes between five kinds of judgment: (a) analytic judgments of sense, (b) synthetic judgments of sense, (c) singular non-phenomenal judgments, (d) existential judgments, and (e) abstract universal judgments. The basis of that classification of judgments is not altogether obvious, and in making it Bradley uses terms in a not altogether conventional way, particularly 'analytic' and 'synthetic', which have nothing to do with the corresponding Kantian terms. He nevertheless takes the distinctions made to be exhaustive. The question with which he is then concerned is which, if any, of these kinds of judgment can provide a sure grasp of reality, or, as he puts it, which of them, if any, furnishes unconditional truth. His ultimate answer is that none of them do. Bradley argues that all singular judgments are in effect existential, because the subjects of the judgments have existential import; for that reason we do not need a separate category of existential judgments. On the other hand, all universal judgments are in effect hypothetical rather than categorical, because to say 'All As are B' is really to say 'If something is A it is B'; in consequence they cannot provide categorical truth, even if they rest on a positive ground. Hence it is only in the singular judgments that we have any hope of finding something that is a candidate for unconditional truth.

There are three candidates of that kind – (a), (b) and (c) above. Judgments of kind (a), the analytic judgments of sense, merely analyse given experience. Bradley distinguishes between various forms of such judgments, but basically, when they are expressed in propositional form, they involve picking out some part of the experience that is given by means of an indexical such as 'this', 'here' or 'now' and bringing this under an idea so as to provide an analysis of present experience. Judgments of kind (b), the synthetic judgments of sense, connect up what is given in experience with something that lies outside it, as occurs with the use of proper names, which imply reference to something with an identity through time, or the use of tenses or analogous expressions which imply a reference to something lying outside the present time or immediate location. Judgments of kind (c), the singular non-phenomenal judgments, involve reference to some kind of particular which transcends experience altogether, such as a particular history, or, more obviously, the universe or God.

Having made these distinctions, Bradley argues that none of them provides unconditional truth, since what they say is always conditional upon something else; to use Hegelian terms from the opening chapters of the *Phenomenology*, they do not provide immediate consciousness of reality, only mediate. The problem lies in the identification of the subject that the subject-term is supposed to provide. In the case of a synthetic judgment of sense, what is picked out as a subject by means of any referential item, e.g. a proper name, definite description or tense, is connected with what is immediate, present experience only by means of further ideas. In the case of proper names, Bradley insists, against J. S. Mill, that they have meaning, and their meaning is a set of descriptions that apply to the thing in question. Proper names are in effect therefore, as Russell was to say, disguised descriptions. In that case, a synthetic judgment of sense does not provide an unconditional and unique identification of that part of reality which is brought under an idea in the judgment. Such identification is conditional upon what is given in experience being capable of being brought under other ideas, other descriptions, which together go to make up the meaning of the referring expression. For that reason such judgments cannot be said to provide by themselves unconditional truth.

What of the analytic judgments of sense? They correspond roughly to what philosophers of other persuasions have called 'sense-datum sentences', and the arguments that such philosophers have had about whether a proposition such as 'This red' is incorrigible correspond to Bradley's argument about whether a judgment expressed in those terms provides unconditional truth. Bradley follows Hegel in claiming that expressions such as 'this' are really general. Hegel argues for that conclusion on the ground that indexicals of this kind are multiply applicable (they can be applied to many things) just as are general expressions of a more obvious kind, such as common names. Bradley argues positively that 'this' signifies merely relative position in a series. In effect, 'this' means 'near' in the series 'near, further away, further away still, etc.', just as 'now' signifies a relative position in the series 'past, present, future . . .' There is a good deal to be said for this view of the role of indexicals. It does not follow from it that we do not secure reference by means of such expressions, but it does follow that, if reference is to be secured by means of them, much else has to be understood and presupposed.

It follows also in Bradley's view that even granted that we are confronted in experience with the bare fact of something being given to us, any way of thinking about it involves subsumption under universal ideas. Hence while a singular judgment of sense, whether analytic or synthetic, makes reference to what is given, it does so only in a conditional way because it presupposes other understanding; moreover it says only that *if* what is given is to be brought under those other ideas it is to be brought under the idea that is made explicit in the judgment. There is nothing categorical in that, and in consequence all judgments are to that extent hypothetical. They say that if reality is S then it is P. There is in this theory of judgment some impetus towards the thought that judgment can capture reality only to the extent that the latter conforms to a system of interconnected ideas, a system brought together by internal relations (relations having a more than contingent status, as is implicit in the thought that they are expressible in a hypothetical of the form 'If S then P'); for any attempt to identify reality in terms of some idea or set of ideas will be conditional upon the applicability of some further idea or ideas. Particular things are for Bradley concrete universals; that is to say that as far as judgment is concerned the content involved in reference to them is that of a bundle of ideas given concreteness by its connexion with present experience.

There remains only singular non-phenomenal judgments, and in answer to the question of whether categorical truth is to be found in their case Bradley says: 'Either here or nowhere'. But in a footnote (p. 113, n. 66), he goes on to say that the answer must ultimately be 'Nowhere'. That indeed must be so on the theory of judgment that is put forward, since however reference is secured the categorial gap between the 'that' and the 'what' makes it impossible for judgment ever to grasp reality through the identification of it with ideas. There is therefore no direct way to reality via the understanding. The understanding can provide at best only an increasingly coherent system of ideas attached to present experience, to the extent that judgments fit together. None of this quite suggests that reality must be one in the sense that monism proper requires , but the suggestion that the most that can be achieved on the road to unconditional truth is the bringing of reality under a maximally coherent system of ideas does imply that in so far as reality is available to judgment it is in some sense a unity. But that 'in so far as' is important. We do not capture reality completely via judgment, via the understanding. The question is whether reason can do better.

Bradley's critique of the understanding from the point of view of reason is to be found in the first part of *Appearance and Reality* – the part concerned with appearance; his positive account follows in the part concerned with reality. In that second part it transpires, among other things, that reality consists of experience (hence the idealism), but is such that it transcends, while in some way also including, appearance. More important for our purposes, it is one. That it cannot be many really emerges from the critique in the first part, particularly from the first three chapters, at the end of which Bradley says, 'The reader who has followed and has grasped the principle of this chapter, will have little need to spend his time upon those which succeed it. He will have seen that our experience, where relational, is not true; and he will have condemned, almost without a hearing, the great mass of phenomena.' That comment is in fact valid, or would be if the argument itself were valid. The critique of phenomena as they present themselves to the understanding in many ways follows quite closely Hegel's similar critique at the beginning of the *Phenomenology*, particularly that to be found in the chapter on 'Force and understanding'.

Chapter 1 of *Appearance and Reality* raises issues about primary and secondary qualities which are familiar from Berkeley's criticism of Locke. In Bradley's view, as in Berkeley's, the inability to draw a firm distinction between the two such that the one constitutes objective properties of things, the other not, points towards the subjective or ideal character of both. It is in the next two chapters that the meat is to be found. Chapter 2, on 'Substantive and adjective', raises issues about the one and the many which are similar to those raised by Hegel. For Bradley the problem is how a single thing, such as a lump of sugar, is related to its qualities, and the issues are similar to those which I raised at the end of Chapter 3 of this book. The crucial question is how the plurality of qualities make up the unity of the thing, and Bradley gradually comes to suggest that the unity of the thing is provided by the qualities *in relation*. He then raises difficulties about what that can mean, difficulties which turn on how we are to understand relations. They cannot be thought of as attributes of their terms either taken separately or taken together. On the other hand, if we think of the relation as something distinct in its own right we are confronted with what has become known as Bradley's paradox of relations. If we have A, B and the relation R, the question arises how the relation R becomes attached to the terms A and B. Will we not require further relations to relate A to R and R to B? If so the problem arises yet again, so that we are confronted with an infinite regress.

It has sometimes been suggested[4] that Bradley is here criticizing external relations in favour of internal relations; that he is criticizing merely contingent relations as opposed to the necessary ones referred to earlier. There is no evidence, however, that that is so. Bradley seems to be asking what sort of thing a relation is, and finds objections to relations being construed either as attributes or as independent terms. The reader may wish to cry out 'But they are relations.' Bradley seems to be operating with a too restricted set of categories. Moreover, there is surely no general problem of the one and the many. In the case of *some* things there may be quite genuine questions about what makes those things the unities they are. But, as I indicated in Chapter 3, if we ask in general whether or not a thing is the sum of its attributes, the answer must be that when one has mentioned all the attributes of a thing there is nothing further of that kind to mention. What makes it a unity is that all the attributes fall together in that thing. Attributes may fall together in different ways in different cases, so that, to revert to Leibniz's example, there is a distinction between a true substance and a 'sack of pistoles'. This does not imply a *general* problem of the relation of a thing to its attributes; it is a problem that arises only in certain cases.

However that may be, in chapter 3, 'Relation and quality', Bradley brings a piece of Hegelian dialectic to bear on the relation between relations and qualities, arguing that 'qualities, taken without relations, have no intelligible meaning . . . taken together with them, they are equally unintelligible' (p. 30). He argues in the same way also from the other direction, that relations are unintelligible both with and without qualities. We need consider the matter from the first direction only, since the argument is essentially symmetrical. The argument that qualities are unintelligible without relations seems valid. It is to the effect that the attribution of a quality would be impossible if there were

---

[4] By, e.g., Richard Wollheim, *Bradley* (Harmondsworth: Penguin, 1959), pp. 109ff.

no relation, not even similarity or difference, between it and other qualities or between its exemplifications. We could not, that is, have the idea of a quality if there were no relations at all. The thesis that qualities are nothing even with relations requires more argument. Bradley claims that if the first limb of the general argument is accepted 'qualities must be, and must *also* be related' (p. 31). But that means, he says, that there is a diversity that falls inside each quality. 'It has a double character, as both supporting and being made by the relation.' So far so good; that does indeed follow from the conclusion of the previous argument that something is a quality *if and only if* it stands in relations. There seems nothing wrong with it.

At this point Bradley suggests that this makes a quality something that has two attributes – the double character mentioned above. In that case the problem of the one and the many which applied to the lump of sugar applies equally to the quality. If we were to accept that no rational account can be provided of the notion of a lump of sugar we should have to accept that the same applies to the notion of a quality. That is in fact just the conclusion that Bradley draws, and he argues to the same effect from the side of relations. For an Hegelian the real is the rational; if an incoherence has genuinely been shown to exist in the notions of quality and relation, then such things are irrational and cannot be real. That is why it follows, in Bradley's view, that experience, where relational, is not true. If, on the other hand, there is no real incoherence in the relation of a thing to its attributes, there is no incoherence in the notions of quality and relation either. That is indeed the correct conclusion to be drawn. It is not, however, the conclusion drawn by Bradley himself and as far as he is concerned the argument leads directly to the further conclusion that reality must be one, because any form of plurality presupposes relations. Hence, in final terms, the monism.

Following Hegel, Bradley calls his one reality the Absolute because it is the one thing that can be an unconditional object of identification. We know that it consists of experience, because that was the starting-point for the investigations that began in the *Principles of Logic*; we are *given* experience, that is the one thing that is immediate. We now 'know' that because the notion of relations is, in Bradley's view, incoherent, the reality which is experience must be one – therefore absolutely simple. (And, even at the level of understanding, judgment can be true only to the extent that it subsumes experience under a maximally coherent system of ideas, which thereby has 'uniqueness'. For Bradley, truth is coherence; there are degrees of truth and also of reality.) It is impossible, however, simply to write off all that the argument 'shows' to be appearance. The Absolute must also provide the rational grounds for appearance being as it is. Hence in the end the one Absolute must be capable of reflecting all aspects of experience, and to that extent it is a Leibnizian monad writ large.

How that is possible is a large and obscure question, discussion of which takes up the whole of the second and larger part of *Appearance and Reality*. It is neither possible nor necessary to go into the detail here, but it is worth noting that judgment cannot attain absolute truth even here – although Bradley does allow (in chapter 27 of his book) the existence of truth which is 'not intellectually corrigible' and which is absolute to that extent, even if he expresses doubt on that too in the end. (The truth in question is truth about the internal nature of reality – the metaphysical conclusion of his argument.) Since we are 'given' experience and thereby reality, knowledge of the Absolute must take the form of acquaintance (to use Russell's word), not something expressible in judgment. It is perhaps a form of intuition – although that is not a word which, to my knowledge, Bradley uses in this context.

It is a point of some significance that when Russell comes to expound his rival theory of logical atomism in his lectures on the 'Philosophy of logical atomism', he opposes his theory at the very outset to that of 'the people who more or less follow Hegel'; and at the beginning of the third lecture he insists both on the self-subsistence of what he calls 'particulars' and on their being objects of acquaintance – such acquaintance being prior to and presupposed by both knowledge by description of things and knowledge of facts. Thus Russell's reply to Bradley's insistence on the conditional nature of all judgment would be to insist in return that what Bradley says about the Absolute as a whole really applies to his particulars. In other words, because we have acquaintance with particulars there is the possibility of unique and unconditional identification of them in such a way as to provide the foundation for judgment about the world.

In chapter 5 of *Problems of Philosophy* Russell states as a fundamental axiom that every proposition that we can understand must be composed wholly of constituents with which we are acquainted. There are perhaps obstacles in the way of a modern reader's understanding that principle, some of which arise from Russell's use of the term 'proposition' to denote in this context, not just what the lectures on logical atomism call a 'symbol', but what the symbol says or describes as a possibly objectively existing state of affairs. Nevertheless, what the principle implies is that anything that can be said must be capable of analysis into items which uniquely individuate objects of acquaintance. In *Problems of*

Philosophy objects of acquaintance included sense-data, but also, among other things, universals. According to the 'Philosophy of logical atomism', the simplest form of proposition, an atomic proposition, asserts relations of varying orders between particulars, these being confined to sense-data. Qualities are to be construed as monadic relations – a somewhat curious notion. Russell was no doubt influenced in his view of these matters by Wittgenstein, who in the *Tractatus* thought of states of affairs as consisting of objects standing in a determinate relation and of propositions as picturing such states of affairs. In their completely analysed form, therefore, states of affairs consist of nothing but objects standing in relation, and atomic propositions mirror these. How propositions asserting a quality of something are to be analysed in that way remains obscure, but there is no suggestion of monadic relations, a notion which, as Russell uses it, gives the impression of being something of a cheat.

Nevertheless, the picture of reality conveyed by both Russell and Wittgenstein is one of simple objects standing in merely external relations. It is a picture totally opposed to that presented by Bradley; yet there are many points of connexion and similarity. At the level of judgment or the understanding, the crux of the issue between them lies in what Bradley calls analytic judgments of sense. It will be remembered that such judgments involve indexicals or their equivalent, and it is Bradley's claim that such expressions do not provide unconditional identification of reality or any portion of it. For Russell it is quite the contrary. Such expressions are, in his view, the prime candidates for the status of being what he calls 'logically proper names', the criterion for which is that if they do not name particulars they are not names at all, but just a noise.[5] Their use is such that they cannot fail to pick out what they purport to refer to. They are thus infallible expressions of identification. Ordinary proper names are really disguised descriptions; there is nothing about them which ensures that they pick out an actually existing and unique object of reference.

On that point, as we saw earlier, Bradley would have agreed, whether or not he would have wished to put the matter in those terms. In his view, however, there are no such things as logically proper names. It is not so much that expressions such as 'this' may fail to refer; it is not in dispute that they do refer. It is that in his view expressions such as 'this' are not such that all that there is to their use is their referring function. The difference between logically proper names and ordinary

[5]   See the remarks at the end of the first lecture of 'The philosophy of logical atomism' in R. C. Marsh (ed.), *Logic and Knowledge* (London: Allen and Unwin, 1956).

names is not just what I have said above; it is also that a logically proper name has no function other than to refer, and it is not a name at all if it does not succeed in that. In Bradley's view, however, 'this' has a contrasting function as well – it means *this as opposed to that* and as opposed to other items in a series. Hence its successful use has presuppositions other than that the object referred to exists. On that, if not on other matters, Bradley seems right.

Along with that goes the epistemological point that the subject of a judgment does not pick out anything which could be an object of knowledge by acquaintance. In holding that, however, Bradley does not reject, as he perhaps should have done, the whole notion of knowledge by acquaintance; for, as we have seen, he has to invoke something like that notion for knowledge of the Absolute. William James, who also embraced a notion of knowledge by acquaintance (although opposed in his case to 'knowledge about') said that in his first sensation a baby is acquainted with the universe; although of course the baby knows nothing about it. Bradley would have preferred to use 'reality' rather than 'universe' but otherwise he might have agreed; for it is reality that is given in experience. It does not come, however, already chopped up into bits, as any theory based on sense-data supposes. Russell believed that that was just how it is, and although the early Wittgenstein was more indefinite about the nature of his 'objects', there are grounds for thinking that he had something similar in mind.[6]

At the outset of his lectures on the 'Philosophy of logical atomism' Russell says, 'When I say that my logic is atomistic, I mean that I share the common-sense belief that there are many separate things; I do not regard the apparent multiplicity of the world as consisting merely in phases and unreal divisions of a single indivisible Reality.' It is, however, no part of common sense that reality consists of things which are atomic in any sense, let alone atomic in the sense of being the final and self-subsistent product of a process of analysis. Russell too might have said 'If it were not for my particulars Bradley would be right.'

Russell defines particulars as 'terms of relations in atomic facts',[7] but the account of atomic facts that precedes that definition gives only a relative account of their simplicity. Wittgenstein, at *Tractatus* 4.221, asserts as obvious that analysis must bring us to elementary propositions, and these correspond to elementary or atomic facts. The supposition is, therefore, that atomic facts must exist as a presupposition of the

---

[6] See L. Wittgenstein, 'Notes on logical form', *Proc. Arist. Soc.*, Supp. Vol. 9, 1929, pp. 162–71.

[7] In the second lecture of his 'Philosophy of logical atomism'.

possibility of analysis, and Russell seems to have thought likewise. At 4.211 Wittgenstein says, 'It is a sign of a proposition's being elementary that there can be no elementary proposition contradicting it.' That hardly provides a decision procedure for determining which propositions are elementary, since it presupposes that the other elementary proposition has already been identified. It is nevertheless a feature of elementary propositions and atomic facts that they cannot stand in any logical relations to each other; for that follows from their being the end-products of logical analysis.

It would seem, therefore, that if Russell and Wittgenstein were asked why there must be simples the answer could only be that there must be simples if there is to be logical analysis; for here too the complex presupposes the simple. It is however not obvious at all that there must be simples, since it is not obvious that there is any such thing as logical analysis in the sense presupposed, according to which it is possible to break down what we mean into atomic and basic units of meaning involving absolutely simple, atomic, objects. As far as simplicity is concerned, the situation with regard to logical atomism is exactly similar to that which held good with respect to Leibniz. There is, however, one large point of difference. Leibniz's monads were not only absolutely simple; they had to be capable of reflecting the world from their point of view and so capable of containing a multiplicity in the simple. One might say something similar about Bradley's Absolute. The simples of logical atomism, however, were simple in content also, because they were meant to be the end-product of logical analysis, i.e. analysis in terms of meaning. At least, they would have been that if that was really all that there was to it; but, as we have already seen, they were supposed to be elements of experience also – sense-data. Even so, they could not reflect a world, and the question inevitably arises of how on the basis of such simples it is possible to construct a world at all, since such a world must contain objects with an identity.

The subsequent course of sense-datum philosophy[8] reveals the difficulties in and obstacles to the realization of such a project. But a sensitivity to such difficulties is apparent to some extent in Russell's remark, already referred to more than once, that his particulars are similar in conception to the old notion of substance, except for their lack of the quality of persistence through time, with the addendum that they last only for a very short time indeed. Can something be absolutely simple if it has any kind of persistence through time, however short? Leibniz

---

[8] See my *Sensation and Perception* (London: Routledge and Kegan Paul, 1961), ch. 10.

would not have thought so, and it was his sensitivity to that point that was one of the things that led him to the view that space and time were merely ideal. But then Leibniz's monadism was not, strictly speaking, just a *logical* atomism either.

Even if one ignores the problem of how a theory can involve *logical* atomism and still be about the world, there remains the question of why it should be supposed that experience comes already chopped up into bits, as the reference to sense-data suggests. Bradley's criticisms of his empiricist predecessors, such as J. S. Mill, are powerful in that respect. He does not, however, reject the idea of the 'given' altogether, as we have seen. For anyone who wishes to reject the notion of the 'given' entirely, the appropriate reaction must be something like 'a plague on both your houses'. The same applies to the supposition that reality must basically be simple, at whatever level. The motivation that determines the path followed by both Bradley and his opponents is complex. For anyone who accepts that there is no need for substances to be simple in an absolute sense, and who does not think that ontology has to be determined by epistemology, a good deal of that motivation will seem irrelevant. It is nevertheless important to try to see something of what that motivation consists in; hence the attention that I have given to these thinkers.

Before leaving these matters it may perhaps be useful to give some attention to one further consideration that links them up with other things that I have had to say about substance. The importance given to the notion of a particular in Russell's thinking is obvious. It is at first sight less obvious in Bradley, although it might be said with justice that in his view there is just one particular – the Absolute itself. At the same time there is in Bradley's logical thinking a pull towards the notion of universals too. Although Bradley rejects 'floating ideas', the starting-point, the point of departure for his thinking about reality, and therefore about ontology, is what the human mind brings to bear in the way of ideas in judgment. Ideas are universal in character; hence it is that ordinary substances are concrete universals. There is an obvious premium on the role of universals in all this, and even if the argument concludes with the Absolute as the one big particular it is still the case that it is available to judgment, to discursive thought, only via some maximally coherent system of ideas, to the extent that it is available at all.

Could it therefore be said that emphasis on the notion of the primacy of the particular is missing from Bradley's way of thinking and that we

therefore have here an exception to what was said in Chapter 5 about
that principle? Certainly Bradley does not think that, in the ordinary
sense of these words, what universals exist is dependent on what particulars exist; rather, as far as judgment is concerned, what can be
thought of as a particular depends on what universals can be put
together in a coherent whole. Although that was the issue which I discussed under the heading of the 'primacy of the particular' in Chapter 5,
I also pointed to the fact that the way in which we have to regard ourselves puts an obvious premium on the notion of the particular. There
seems no possibility of our thinking of ourselves as somehow constructed
out of universals. It is only when that point is accepted that we can go on
to ask whether universals have an independent or dependent status in
relation to particulars. The question therefore arises of how Bradley
views the position of the self in his scheme of things.

One answer to that question is that in a literal sense he has no view on
the matter, since these are not his terms of reference. In Bradley's view
the subject of judgment cannot be a term in judgment, and so cannot be
a possible object of a judgment. On the other hand one of the essays in
his *Collected Essays* is entitled 'A defence of phenomenalism in psychology'; its theme is that from the point of view of introspection all
that is detectable is what Hume would have thought of as impressions
and ideas – merely passive states of mind, which nineteenth-century
idealists tended to call 'feelings'. There is, as Hume thought, no self to
be found there, but Bradley draws a different moral from that of Hume.
In his view the 'I' is not a possible subject-matter for psychology; it is
presupposed in judgment and that is the subject-matter of logic, even if
the 'I' cannot be a term in judgment.

In this respect Bradley would agree with the early Wittgenstein's
Schopenhauer-inspired remarks at *Tractatus* 5.631ff., 'There is no such
thing as the subject that thinks or entertains ideas . . . The subject does
not belong to the world; rather, it is a limit of the world.' As far as judgment is concerned, Bradley's point of departure (and in a way that of the
early Wittgenstein too) is the Kantian 'I think'. There are considerable
virtues in that for an understanding of the self and the phenomena of the
human mind generally, as we shall see in Chapter 9; it is not, however,
an adequate point of departure for ontology, as I tried to indicate in
Chapter 3. That is because it is not clear that the conception of an 'I' is
possible without the conception of a 'we', and it is not clear that that is
possible without a shared and public world. If all that is true, then the
suggestions contained in Bradley's thought of particulars having the

status of constructs out of universals are inadequately based, since he has
not worked out satisfactorily an acceptable account of how objective
judgment is itself possible. Without that, the suggestion that what is
universal has in any sense primacy over what is particular simply begs
the question.

7.   Space and time

What are space and time?

To say that the reality which we all share consists of many kinds of things, and that among those things substances have a certain pre-eminence, is to leave out important features of that reality if it is not also emphasized that substances change and persist through time and occupy space. I mentioned these considerations in Chapter 4, but it is important that one should try to arrive at some understanding of them. What in particular are space and time? What sort of things are they? One natural answer is that they comprise continua, three-dimensional in the case of space, one-dimensional in the case of time; that is to say that they consist of continuous manifolds, positions in which can be occupied by substances and events respectively, and which have an existence in their own right. It is in virtue of the occupancy of such positions that events and processes are to be seen as taking place after each other and substances are to be seen in certain spatial relations. That cannot be taken as in any sense a definition of 'time' and 'space', since what I have said about space makes reference to spatial relations, while what I have said about time makes reference to 'after', which must be taken in a temporal sense. Nevertheless, what I have said about continua might well be taken as the natural thing to say.

It would not always have been a natural thing to say, however, and it is arguable that it has become natural only since Newton, whatever modifications to Newton's view have been introduced in modern times. It was not natural to the ancient Greeks to think in that way – they did not think of events taking place before and after other events, of certain events as having happened and other events as being yet to come, or of material things being at places which are related to other places and things that occupy them. It is not to say that they did not have the idea of there being measurable intervals of time and measurable distances between things, but this does not add up to having the idea of space and time as comprising distinct continua in the sense specified above.

The notion of a void which appears in Greek thought as a kind of substitute for the idea of space is simply that of intervals between bodies in which there are no bodies. In general, the Greeks tended to think of the place of a thing in terms of the containing body of that thing, i.e. in terms of the relation between the thing and whatever it is in. This conception receives formal exposition in Aristotle's definition of place as the limit of the first unmoving containing body – a definition which is, unfortunately, circular because 'unmoving' can ultimately mean only 'not changing in place'. Even a void must be contained within a world. In Aristotle's view, there is nothing outside the universe, conceived as the sum total of bodies, and it therefore has no place. Spatial intervals are nevertheless potentially divisible *ad infinitum*.

Temporal intervals, by contrast, were, in Aristotle's view, both potentially divisible *ad infinitum* and potentially extendable *ad infinitum*, since, for him, time is the measure of motion in respect of before and after and there always has been and always will be motion or change. The fact that time is so closely associated with motion or change means that there are at best event-less intervals between events. Even if such intervals can be conceived of as indefinitely smaller and smaller or as indefinitely larger and larger, it does not follow that there was in Aristotle's view a continuum to be called 'time' within which and at moments along which events take place. One might indeed say that for him, and for the Greeks generally, there was nothing to space and time but the possibility of objects occupying places, conceived as I explained above, which are themselves at intervals from each other, and the possibility of events coming before and after other events. Or rather the latter would be all that there was to time but for the fact that Aristotle is rightly conscious of the fact that we regard some events as happening now, some as having happened and some as yet to happen; and he tries to connect up these latter facts with the former ones in such a way as to represent the 'passage' of time. I shall return to such considerations later and to the question why there is no inclination to think in that way with regard to space.

It might be said that all this amounts simply to the relational view of space and time that we find in, for example, Leibniz. For, according to Leibniz,[1] space is 'an order of coexistences, as time is an order of successions'. Space itself is an ideal thing so that 'space out of the world must needs be imaginary'; and similarly for time. Space as we conceive it is simply that which comprehends all places; it is that 'wherein the mind conceives the application of relations'. And once again the situation with regard to time is similar. If there is a difference between this

---

[1]   Leibniz–Clarke correspondence, third letter, in J. J. C. Smart (ed.), *Problems of Space and Time* (New York and London: Collier-Macmillan, 1964), pp. 89ff.

view and that of Aristotle, it is that Aristotle has no concept of space as distinct from places, even if he has some concept of time as distinct from moments or times. In other words, Leibniz admits that we have a conception of space and time in themselves but thinks that the conception should be reduced to something like Aristotle's view. If there is a further difference over space it is that Aristotle would claim that we cannot even imagine anything beyond the universe, since we cannot imagine something more than everything. That however is mere speculation, since Aristotle does not really raise the question.

By complete contrast with all this we find Newton saying in the Scholium to the Definitions of his *Principia*,[2] 'Absolute, true and mathematical time, of itself, and from its own nature, flows equably without relation to anything external, and by another name is called duration . . . Absolute space, in its own nature, without relation to anything external, remains always similar and immovable.' I shall come back to the contrast between absolute and relative space and time directly. What is important for present purposes is that in Newton's view space and time have natures of their own, without any dependence on anything else, and they constitute continua such that one part of either continuum is indistinguishable from any other such part. Any differences that we take to exist are due to the things that occupy places and the events that happen at moments; they are not due to space and time themselves.

Leibniz interprets this as saying that space and time are substances, and makes the objection that if they were as Newton supposed God would have no sufficient reason for putting things at one place or in one order rather than another or for creating things at one time rather than another. That appeal to the principle of sufficient reason is a way of putting the point that where no distinctions exist there is no way of making a distinction; in other words, given what Newton says, there is no sense to be made of speaking of one part of space or time rather than another, since there is no way of determining one place or moment as distinct from others, apart from what occupies those places and times. That is in effect to appeal to a verification principle of meaning in the sense that meaning is restricted to what can be verified.

Newton thought, however, that there was a way of establishing a distinction between absolute space and time and their relative counterparts – which amounts to a distinction between absolute and relative positions, places and times. It is possible to make that distinction if it is poss-

---

[2] Ibid, pp. 81ff.

ible also to make a distinction between absolute and relative motion, since motion is a matter of a body moving from one place to another in a certain time. In the Scholium on the Definitions the distinction is argued for through an appeal to the so-called 'bucket experiment'. It is not quite a 'thought experiment' since Newton refers to what he has experienced; it involves a fairly simple consideration all the same. He considers what happens when a bucket filled with water is suspended and allowed to rotate as a result of the untwisting of the cord that holds it. He says, 'The surface of the water will at first be plain, as before the vessel began to move; but after that, the vessel, by gradually communicating its motion to the water, will make it begin sensibly to revolve, and recede by little and little from the middle, and ascend to the sides of the vessel, forming itself into a concave figure (as I have observed) and the swifter the motion becomes, the higher will the water rise, till at last, performing its revolutions in the same times with the vessel, it becomes relatively at rest in it.'[3] Newton goes on to refer to the 'ascent of the water' as 'its endeavour to recede from the axis of its motion' and says that the 'true and absolute circular motion of the water' becomes known through it. It is presupposed that a merely relative motion would have no such effect.

Subsequent criticisms of this argument, by for example Ernst Mach,[4] have tended to insist that the so-called absolute motion of the water in the bucket may still be motion relative to some other frame of reference, e.g. the fixed stars. Mach indeed asserted that we do not know what would happen if the so-called fixed stars were rotated quickly round a fixed earth, nor what would happen if the sides of the bucket were increased in thickness and mass until they were 'several leagues thick'. If that sort of criticism is right – as it seems to be – the only conclusion to be drawn is that the question of whether there is a single frame of reference, usable in an adequate account of physical motion, is a scientific one, and not one to be answered through any form of *a priori* argument. Newton of course did not, strictly speaking, intend his argument to be an *a priori* one, merely one that can proceed by appeal to a very simply observed case. Nevertheless, the only rational conclusion to be drawn is that the question whether there is such a thing as absolute space (and similarly for time) is not a philosophical issue. The same applies to the question which Richard Swinburne[5] distinguishes as a second issue in this area – whether space and time have properties of their own independent of the objects and events that they contain. Or rather, the

[3] Ibid, p. 85.   [4] Ibid, pp. 126–31.
[5] R. Swinburne, *Space and Time* (London: Macmillan, 1st edn 1968; 2nd edn 1981), ch. 3.

same applies if the properties in question are physical properties, as they seem to be considered to be in Einstein's general theory of relativity.

I make that qualification for the following reasons. The Newtonian argument seeks to establish a distinction between absolute and relative space and time by reference to something that is supposed to show that there are grounds for making that distinction in a particular case. If it were valid it would of course show that space and time cannot be merely a matter of relations between objects and events respectively. On the other hand, if it is invalid, it is not thereby shown that there is nothing to space and time apart from such relations. Leibniz in effect argued that if we think of space, for example, as a big box, there is nothing to determine positions within it apart from the objects which are at them, and if the box is infinitely big there is no hope of determining positions relative to the sides of the box. It might seem to follow from that consideration that such a conception of space must be wrong; but it does not follow directly that there is nothing to space apart from relations between objects.

Leibniz's claim that Newton was saying that space is a substance indicates that he is working with a system of categories which is confined to those of substance and relation. It may be that we ought to look for additional categories. The thought that space and time are merely relations does lead to a problem about what it is that is thereby related. Any extended object is spatial, and its spatiality must, on the relational view of space, consist in relations between elements. But if those elements are themselves spatial the same argument must apply to them; the only way to stop the regress that is generated by that is to suppose that the objects related by spatial relations are themselves non-spatial. As we saw in Chapter 6, Leibniz for a time took seriously the possibility that the elements of reality must consist of 'massy points' – point-like, and therefore unextended, objects which have, all the same, physical properties. The obvious unsatisfactoriness of that notion, and the problem of how one could construct a physical world from such massy points, led him in the end to his doctrine of monads. But that view in turn led to the suggestion that space (and time also) were merely ideal. It is clear enough that the suggestion that space and time consist simply in relations does lead to problems about what is so related. If we say that to speak of space is simply to speak of a kind of relation between ordinary things, it is surely incumbent on us to indicate how those things can themselves be spatial and in what sense.

Similar conclusions emerge from the argument used by Bradley to show, within the terms of reference of his absolute idealism, that space and time are mere appearance because the notions of space and time involve incoherence. He argues for that conclusion by means of a piece of Hegelian dialectic, seeking to show that both thesis and antithesis are unacceptable. In the case of space (and the argument over time is similar) the thesis is that space is not a mere relation. 'For any space must consist of extended parts, and these parts are clearly spaces . . . We should be brought to the proposition that space is nothing but a relation of spaces. And this proposition contradicts itself.'[6] There is, on the other hand, the antithesis, that space is nothing but a relation. Any space must consist of parts which are spaces; but these in turn must consist of parts which are spaces. That is to say that any space must be infinitely divisible, so that at any stage in the division there must be parts spatially related to other parts. 'The terms are essential to the relation, and the terms do not exist. Searching without end, we never find anything more than relations; and we see that we cannot. Space is essentially a relation of what vanishes into relations, which seek in vain for their terms. It is lengths of lengths of – nothing that we can find.'

In the course of the argument Bradley is remarkably free with his use of categories. Of space as a whole he says that it is 'a thing or substance, or quality (call it what you please) . . .' It is clear, however, that the only categories that he seriously contemplates as available are those of substance, quality and relation. Space is evidently not a quality. It is not a substance because it is divisible *ad infinitum* into spaces, and it is not merely a relation, for the reasons given. It is questionable how good the argument is against space being a substance, but it is sufficiently clear that if space is a substance it is not like other substances. There are in any case the Leibnizian arguments against Newton on that score.

What we seem to need at this point is a new category, and that is not altogether surprising since the categories invoked so far apply most obviously to things *in* space and time, to things that presuppose space and time, rather than to space and time themselves. It may be helpful, therefore, to draw attention to Kant's characterization of space and time as forms of intuition. That notion is far from unproblematic, if only because the terms used presuppose the Kantian epistemological apparatus. To speak of a form of intuition is to make reference to the form which perception or objects of perception must take. Kant says that space is the form of outer sense; that is to say the form that ordinary objects of perception must take. Time is the form of both outer and

6   F. H. Bradley, *Appearance and Reality* (London: Sonnenschein, 1893), ch. 4; also in Smart (ed.), ibid., pp. 132ff.

inner sense; that is to say the form which events must take whether they are objects of perception or perceptions themselves. That account says little enough to make clear exactly what space and time are, since it surely presupposes a prior understanding of spatiality and temporality. The use of the term 'form', however, may be illuminating. Although some commentators have suggested that the notion of a form amounts merely to the idea of certain sorts of relations, Kant did not accept the relational view of space and time put forward by Leibniz; he thought that the form could exist without any objects or events to fill it out. On the other hand, he did not accept the Newtonian conception, since he thought that the forms that space and time comprise have an intimate connexion with perception and have no place outside that context.

Kant sometimes says that space and time are not merely forms of intuition; they are themselves *a priori* intuitions. That is a very difficult notion. If we slough off the thought's epistemological skin, however, if we see that the Kantian distinction between intuitions and concepts is the same, once the epistemological presuppositions are removed, as the Fregean distinction between object and concept, it becomes apparent that Kant is saying that space and time are objects, not concepts. To put the matter in another way, to think of space and time is not to think merely of *ways of thinking* about the world; it is to think of how the world actually is. Moreover, space and time are something actual, not merely possibilities, so that, whether or not they have *physical* properties in their own right, they are themselves *something* in their own right. In that case, it is in virtue of space and time being what they are that things and events can stand in the kinds of spatial and temporal relations that they do. Space and time do not consist of either actual or possible relations between things and events; they determine what relations of that kind are possible.

On this view, as we have noted, it is at least logically possible that space and time should have existed without things and events to occupy them. One might put the point in a somewhat picturesque way by saying that God could have created space and time and left it at that, without going on to create anything to occupy them. That is not possible on the Leibnizian view. It *is* possible on the Newtonian view (though Newton's theological conceptions introduce complications in the case of his actual view). The Newtonian view brings with it, however, certain scientific, physical, considerations, and these, however important they are in themselves, need not be of philosophical concern. In Kant, however, we can perhaps find a conception of space and time which is in between these two views; according to it, space and time are something actual, existing in their own right, and it is because they are what they are that spatial and temporal relations between things and events in the world are what they are. The importance of this will emerge also from the consideration of whether space and time are of necessity infinite – something that I shall discuss in the next section.

What then are space and time? It remains very difficult to answer that question, and there is no single category to which one can appeal in answering it. The Kantian notion of a form does something in that connexion, but it would do little enough without further explanation of the context in which it is invoked. Space and time *seem* to constitute the two great continua which give form to the possible relations in which things and events in the world stand. The metrical properties of the spatial continuum can be formalized in terms of geometry, and the role of a geometry is to spell out in metrical terms what is involved in a conception of such a continuum. The possibility of alternative geometries does not make that any the less true. But such geometries would have no application to the world in the context of a physical theory if things in the world did not conform in that respect to what is inherent in such a continuum. However one sums it up, space is such a continuum, and it is because it is as it is that things can stand to each other in relations with certain logical properties – particularly those of asymmetry, irreflexibility, and transitivity. The same applies to time, except that time has one dimension whereas space has three, and except that, as we shall see, we occupy a single position in time – the present – even if what happens at the present is ever-changing; no such thing holds good of space.

Must space and time be infinite?

In the parts of the 'Transcendental Aesthetic' of Kant's first *Critique* which are concerned with what Kant calls the metaphysical expositions of the concepts of space and time Kant propounds four propositions. To be accurate, he sets out four propositions in connexion with space, and five in connexion with time; but one of the latter five does not belong there. The four propositions in connexion with space are: (1) Space is not an empirical concept which has been derived from outer experiences; (2) Space is a necessary *a priori* representation which underlies all outer intuitions; (3) Space is not a discursive or, as we say, general concept of relations of things in general, but a pure intuition; (4) Space is represented as an infinite given manifold. The four relevant propositions about time are similar *mutatis mutandis*. It would not be profitable to go into detail here concerning all these propositions, especially in the terms in which they are expressed. A few general comments, however, may be in order. I shall then fasten on two particular points.

When Kant says that space is not an empirical concept, it is to be presumed that he means that the *concept* of space is not an empirical one. (After all the third proposition mentioned above denies that space is a concept at all.) He is thus opposed to the Lockean claim that we obtain the concept of space by extrapolation from our perception of things standing in spatial relations, and he maintains, quite rightly, that the perception of things standing in spatial relations itself presupposes a concept of space. That is an epistemological point which need not concern us further here, although it raises issues which are important epistemologically.[7] The second proposition maintains – as I said at the end of the previous section – that we cannot have perception of objects without the presupposition that they occupy positions in the continuum of space. To perceive them as standing in spatial relations we must necessarily have a prior representation of the dimension in virtue of which they are seen in those relations. Kant goes on to say, as we might expect from this, that we can never represent to ourselves the absence of space, but we can think of it as empty of objects. Many people boggle at that claim. It seems to me relatively unproblematic to suggest that there may be regions of space in which there are no objects. It is similarly unproblematic to suggest that there might have been a time before there were any events and that there may eventually be a time after which there will be no events. If that is possible it is not a large step to the contemplation of the possibility that there might have been space with no objects – and similarly for time. To think that possible is of course to reject a purely relational view of space and time, but that is a point which we dealt with earlier.

That space is not a concept, not simply a way of thinking about things, seems unproblematic also. It does seem to be the case that spatiality is a property of the world itself and not just a way of thinking about it. That does not prevent the possibility of there being ways, perhaps even alternative ways, of thinking about that feature of the world. We do, that is, have a concept or concepts of space. That, however, does not make space itself a concept. In the course of his observations on this point, however, Kant asserts that we can represent to ourselves only one space (and if space were a concept it might have had a multiplicity of instances). Indeed he insists that space is essentially one. I shall return to that point in the next section. His final point is that space is represented as an

---

[7] For a discussion of the point in connexion with time see my *Theory of Knowledge* (London and Basingstoke: Macmillan, 1971), pp. 196ff.

infinite *given* magnitude. His emphasis upon the word 'given' is presumably meant to indicate that he does not think that space is infinite in the way that Locke conceives it – as the possibility of extrapolation *ad infinitum* from the features of particular spatial relations. The relation of 'being to the right of' has the logical properties of transitivity, asymmetry, and non-reflexiveness, and these make it possible to generate by its means a spatial series that may have no limits. If, in addition, such a spatial series were like the number series, in being determined purely by a relation of this kind and nothing else (as is the case with the relation 'being a successor of' as far as numbers are concerned) it would *necessarily* have no limit. That is how Locke conceives of space and time – as extrapolatable from spatial and temporal relations having these properties, which we perceive as obtaining between things and events.

Kant has already denied that that is how it is when he insists that the concepts of space and time are *a priori*. He claims that any representation of a determinate spatial or temporal interval presupposes a single space or a single time as a whole which is limited to that interval. Since limitation of space and time takes place within experience only in that way, he takes it that space and time must be unlimited and given as such. For that reason, he says, the relation of space to its parts is not thought of as the same as that of a concept to its instances. All the parts of space coexist *ad infinitum*; and similarly for time. So he draws yet again the conclusion that 'the original representation of space is an *a priori* intuition, not a concept'. Space and time are infinite because there is nothing to limit them *as such*; such limitations as occur do so as a result of and within experience.

What in fact follows from this argument is merely that nothing in what we think, nothing in the *concepts* of space and time, puts any limitation on space or time even in relation to possible experience. It is actual experience which provides any limits that there are; but according to Kant such limits are *within* space and time, and so provide no reason for thinking that space and time as such are limited. Yet, even if we accept Kant's terms of reference, the question remains whether space and time themselves do have to be exactly as this way of thinking about them suggests. That is equivalent to the question mentioned above – of whether any spatial series is determined *purely* by a relation having the logical properties of transitivity, asymmetry and non-reflexiveness. There is the further question, from the Kantian point of view, of what sense one can make, in terms of experience, of a limited space and time. That is in some ways a question which has verificationist presuppositions, but it ought perhaps to be faced. One way of considering it is to return to the Aristotelian view according to which the universe, at all events, is certainly finite.

As I said at the beginning of this chapter, Aristotle did not, strictly speaking, have a concept of space. In his view, things have a place in the sense that they are in something that contains them, and the universe – everything – can have no place since there is nothing else for *everything* to be in. For that reason Aristotle takes the universe to be finite (although that conclusion does not perhaps strictly follow). Many critics have thought that the suggestion that there is nothing outside the universe is absurd. Atomists, such as Lucretius, asked what is supposed to happen when one comes to the boundary of the universe. If one attempts to throw a javelin outwards, either it will be stopped by something outside, in which case we are not at the boundary, or it will actually go outwards, in which case there must at least be something outside the universe, some space into which the javelin can move. The Atomists themselves thought that there was a void in which the javelin could move. That was a notion that Aristotle thought absurd for other reasons, but the question of whether there is such a thing as a void outside the total collection of bodies does not seem to be one that can be answered in an *a priori* way, or at any rate not in terms of the considerations so far adduced. Could further considerations be brought to bear by applying the same sort of argument to space itself and not just the universe?[8]

In that case the argument would run roughly as follows: If there were a boundary to space what would happen if we were to try to proceed or throw something further? Either we should be stopped by something beyond, in which case the supposed boundary would not be a boundary, or we should be able to go, or propel something, further, in which case the supposed boundary would, once again, not be a boundary. These suppositions constitute exclusive alternatives. Hence there can be no boundary to space. As Swinburne says,[9] a similar argument could be invoked to show that space is necessarily continuous. He thinks that both arguments are valid, at any rate if taken to show that space is of logical necessity unbounded and continuous. Whether space is infinite as well depends upon additional factors which have to do with how space is best construed in geometrical terms.[10] These arguments seem to

---

[8]   It is not clear that Lucretius, *De Rerum Natura* I. 968ff., meant to do that, but if we import the notion of space into Aristotle's scheme of things the previous argument can be adduced on the assumption that space and the universe are commensurate.

[9]   R. Swinburne, *Space and Time*, 1st edn, p. 31.

[10] Cf. the popular versions of Einstein's thesis – that space is finite but unbounded.

me, however, quite invalid. I shall confine attention to the claim for the unboundedness of space.

A correct formal answer to the question of what happens when we come to the boundary of space is that we can go no further because there is nowhere to go, no further places to occupy. There is nothing that *prevents* further progress, or nothing that *need* prevent it, apart from that; but that is enough to rule out further progress. Such a formal answer may, however, seem unsatisfactory without some account of what then happens. To ask for that is to ask, as I indicated earlier, what sense can be made, from the point of view of experience, of the suggestion that one is at the boundary. The trouble with that request is that it is satisfiable in a number of different possible ways, depending on the fertility of one's imagination. Perhaps, for example, the laws of nature are such that motion slows asymptotically as one comes towards the boundary, so that one never quite reaches it. One is in a sense prevented from going beyond the boundary, but not by something the other side of it. Perhaps the experience one has is like going through a mirror so that one finds oneself coming back into the space that one has apparently just 'left'.[11] Certainly it must be impossible to see or otherwise perceive beyond the boundary, since there is nothing beyond it; once again, however, it is possible to conceive of a number of alternative possibilities as to how things may look – a fog, darkness, an apparent mirror-image – as long as it is not actually the case that one is seeing beyond the boundary.

What Kant says implies that, given our sensibility, no sense can be attached to the suggestion that our experience might be such as to be compatible with the thought that the space occupiable by objects is bounded. It is far from clear that that is so. On the other hand, it is certainly *not* the case that in the imaginary circumstances I have hinted at one is obliged to conclude that space actually is finite or bounded. It is enough, however, for our present purposes, that such a conclusion is a possible one. I do not wish to suggest that space actually is bounded or that it is possible to lay down conditions for its being shown to be so. I do wish to suggest that it is a factual matter, and not an *a priori* one, whether or not space is bounded. Similar considerations apply to time. Whether or not there will be a time after which there will be no further times (no *after*, not just no further events) is a factual matter. Time really could 'have a stop'. It might be added that similar considerations apply to the question of whether space and time are or are not divisible *ad infinitum*. If they were *not* divisible *ad infinitum* that would not necessarily affect

[11] There is a science-fiction story by, I believe, Arthur C. Clarke, called 'A wall round the universe' which attempts to describe such a circumstance.

their status as continua, since it is not necessary to their continuity that between any two parts of space or time, *however small*, there should be other parts, as long as the minimal parts bound each other.[12]

Are space and time infinite, and are they infinitely divisible? I do not know, but there are no grounds for thinking that they must be so logically.

Are space and time essentially one?

The question is not whether space and time form one unified system together. Whether it is useful to think in that way is for science to answer; it is not a strictly philosophical issue. Kant's claim that space and time are essentially one comes, as we noted earlier, in the course of an objection to the suggestion that they might be considered as concepts. He says with regard to space, 'We can represent to ourselves only one space; and if we speak of diverse spaces, we mean thereby only parts of one and the same unique space.' He adds that 'these parts cannot precede the one all-embracing space, as being, as it were, constituents out of which it can be composed; on the contrary, they can be thought only as *in* it'. And he sums the matter up by saying 'Space is essentially one.' *Prima facie* what Kant says amounts to *two* claims: first that we can represent to ourselves only one space, and second that there actually is only one space. In the context of Kant's thesis that space and time are transcendentally ideal but empirically real these two claims collapse into each other. That does not mean that we cannot consider them independently outside that context. We shall have occasion to emphasize this point later.

The question whether there are or could be more than one space is equivalent to the question whether there are or could be sets of places, or of things occupying them, such that within each set the members are spatially related to each other but such that the sets themselves stand in no spatial relations to each other. A similar formula could be produced for time. The answer to the question is that there is no contradiction in the supposition under consideration; *a fortiori*, however, nothing could tell someone occupying positions within one spatial set whether or not there were other such sets. In this case, unlike that concerned with the possible boundedness of space, there is no possible description of experience which is even relevant to the question of whether there are

[12] It is perhaps worth noting that the supposition that they are in fact divisible only *ad finitum* does not raise any Zenonian paradoxes; for Zeno's arguments, to the extent that they are valid and about indivisibles, are so only if those indivisibles are indivisible in principle; they have nothing to say about anything that is merely indivisible in fact.

alternative spaces and times. That has been denied in recent times, but before considering such denials it is as well to be clear what is being asked for.

In the case of the putative boundedness of space what was demanded was a description of experience that was at least compatible with the suggestion that space is bounded (it being assumed that there is no problem over space being unbounded). In a parallel way we need, with reference to the putative possibility of a plurality of spaces, a description of experience which is at least compatible with the suggestion that there is more than one space (it being assumed that there is no problem in there being only one space). The snag is that there is no problem at all about the *compatibility* of experience with the possibility of a plurality of spaces and times. Problems arise only if it is required that the experience provide evidence of such a plurality. I did not claim that this much was demanded in the suggestion that space might be bounded, although I believe that in circumstances such as I described someone might reasonably put forward the hypothesis that space is bounded without being able to provide anything approaching clinching grounds for it. In the case of the suggestion that there may be more than one space and time it is not clear that even as much as that is possible.

Perhaps the first person in recent times to suggest otherwise is Anthony Quinton in a paper entitled 'Spaces and times'.[13] One trouble with Quinton's paper, as others have pointed out,[14] is that it retains a good deal of Kantian terms of reference and epistemological apparatus. This is evident in his closing sentence, 'Our conception of experience is essentially temporal in a way in which it is not essentially spatial.' After all, while our experience seems always to involve time, much of it, as opposed to the *objects* of experience, does not involve space at all. Do we not need, therefore, to distinguish between experience and the objects of experience? Secondly, Quinton seems to think that the distinction between appearance and reality is one that each of us makes and has to make in terms of features of our individual experiences. Thus he says (ibid. p. 144), 'Reality, I am suggesting, then, is that part of our total experience which it is possible and prudent to take seriously', and he uses that idea to eliminate the suggestion that a set of putative experiences which are coherent in themselves but vastly different from our ordinary

[13] A. Quinton, 'Spaces and times', *Philosophy*, Vol. 37, 1962, pp. 130–47. See also his *The Nature of Things* (London: Routledge and Kegan Paul, 1973).
[14] R. Swinburne, 'Times', *Analysis*, Vol. 25, 1965, pp. 185–91; A. Skillen, 'The myth of temporal division', *Analysis*, Vol. 26, 1965, pp. 44–7; M. Hollis, 'Times and spaces', *Mind*, Vol. LXXVI, 1967, pp. 524–36.

ones should be set aside as mere dream experiences. It is far from clear that this is the way in which the question of what is real and what is not is to be decided. Even if these objections are waived we are still left with the problem of whether a set of experiences different from our ordinary ones could ever be so different that the only reasonable suggestion would be that they were experiences of events in a different space and/ or time.

Quinton proceeds by way of what he calls a 'myth', according to which someone living an ordinary life in London finds himself, when going to sleep, waking up in a lakeside village in a quite different culture. Quinton elaborates the myth in an amusing way, and concludes on its basis that it would be gratuitous to suppose that the lakeside life was a dream or that it occurred somewhere else on earth or elsewhere, if no evidence could be discovered of its whereabouts. He says indeed (p. 143), 'There could well be no positive reason whatever, beyond our fondness for the Kantian thesis, for saying that the lake is located somewhere in ordinary physical space and there are, in the circumstances envisaged, good reasons for denying its location there.' I do not think that that is good enough; nor is the suggestion, noted earlier, that it would be unreasonable to set the experiences down as a dream on the grounds that 'beside the lake there is a place for prudence, forethought and accurate recollection' and that that is enough to grant the experiences the status of reality. The contemplated change in experience is not enough to warrant the conclusion sought; the description of the experience is compatible with its being a (surprisingly) coherent dream of an experience of events elsewhere in the universe to which one is (magically) transported when falling asleep. It is not a mere prejudice to cling to the Kantian thesis; for it is within the context of a single spatio-temporal framework that we have learnt to make sense of the world. None of that, of course, is to say that a miracle could not happen so that on going to sleep we are 'transported' (though that cannot be the right word) to another space. It is to say that in the circumstances contemplated there is absolutely no reason to think it the case.

However that may be, Quinton goes on to offer reasons for rejecting even that much in connexion with time. He tries to indicate that analogous myths cannot be produced which would give any kind of coherence to the suggestion that we might be 'transported' to another time. That is because 'if an experience is mine it is memorable and if it is memorable it is temporally connected to my present state' (p. 146), where by 'memorable' is meant merely 'memorable in principle, not in practice'. Hence, if the lakeside events are memorable in principle by the person in London they must have occurred at a previous time and cannot for that reason be located in a different time. Because of the facts that the events *could*, logically at any rate, have occurred in another space but that not even this is possible for time, Quinton comes to the conclusion already noted, that there is an asymmetry between space and time in relation to experience. For reasons that I shall come to in due course, I think that there is such an asymmetry, in the sense that we are in a certain way more imbedded in time than we are in space. But even if that is true, it goes no way to show that we can give definite sense to the supposition that we might lead our lives in a spatially divided way but not a temporally divided way.

I put the matter in those terms advisedly, since that is what Quinton's discussion and subsequent ones by other philosophers in this connexion come to. We are not called upon simply to contemplate the possibility that there is more than one space or time – for that surely remains an obvious formal possibility. The question is whether we can make sense of the idea of lives lived multi-spatially or multi-temporally. Quinton's answers to that question are 'Yes' with regard to space but 'No' with regard to time. In the paper entitled 'Times' in *Analysis* 1965 Richard Swinburne thought that he could justify the answer 'Yes' with regard to time also, and appealed to an alternative myth. His myth consists of a story about two tribes, the Okku and the Bokku, who war against each other continually and are therefore separated into different times by their seer in order to prevent the strife. Subsequently they are reunited for somewhat suspect reasons.[15] It is of course only the seer's say-so in the myth that gives any backing to the thesis that they are made to live their lives in different times, and the subsequent reunion in the one place and time brings with it certain technical problems over changes that one tribe may have made to the geography and physical layout of things that have not been made by the other tribe. Nevertheless, Swinburne believed that considerations of simplicity might lead us to choose a bi-temporal interpretation of the portrayed events.

Subsequently, in his book *Space and Time*,[16] Swinburne changed his mind about that conclusion, on the grounds that the bi-temporal interpretation of the events entails the denial of a logically necessary truth to the effect that 'if it is logically possible for an unconscious material object to have a certain life history, viz. to be at various places for various different periods of time, then it is logically possible for a con-

---

[15]   The seer tells them that as each tribe cannot stop quarrelling amongst themselves they had better have someone else to quarrel with!

[16]   R. Swinburne, *Space and Time*, 1st edn, pp. 205–6.

scious material object to have the same life history'. In the terms of the myth it must be possible for material objects to have a life history in both times; otherwise, according to Swinburne, criteria of identity for the places involved will be missing. Therefore it must be possible for a conscious material being to have a life history in both times. What then happens at the moment of reunion? Swinburne's account of the issue is not altogether clear, but the issue seems to be as follows: The conscious being in question cannot in any way be aware, before the reunion, of what is happening to him in the other time; otherwise, on the Quinton principle, that would connect the times temporally so that they could not be different times. He must therefore have a split life history as a conscious being. The reunion, however, unsplits him so that one part of him becomes for the first time aware of events happening to the other, and *vice versa*. That, Swinburne suggests, is incoherent. (Swinburne actually says something stronger than that, in that he maintains that if a person who has, putatively, had a bi-temporal life becomes aware of the events of one time only at the moment of reunion, he cannot 'of logical necessity' have been experiencing those events in that time. This raises certain considerations about personal identity. Would one say, with reference to a case of split personality in which distinct selves were reunited having previously had no knowledge of each other, that the person could not have had the experiences of one of the selves if he, *qua* the other, came to know of them only at the reunion?)

What all this really shows, in my opinion, is that we can rationally contemplate a person living a temporally divided life only if we are prepared to contemplate his being split without connexion between the selves. Reunion is impossible, not for the precise reasons that Swinburne gives, but for Quintonian reasons – that the reunion would locate the events of both times as having taken place before the moment of reunion because they are in principle memorable at that moment. Although that does not determine what precise temporal relation existed between the two sets of events, it does temporally relate them, which is contrary to the initial hypothesis. While it is true that no such difficulty arises for the possibility of a spatially divided life, so that such a life remains a formal possibility, there could be no good reason for thinking that such a possibility was ever realized. On the other hand, without respect to life histories, it is logically possible that there should be a plurality of spaces and times, in that no contradiction arises from the supposition.

Are space and time, then, essentially one? In relation to possible experience yes, since it seems impossible to conceive of a change of experience which would imply otherwise. Apart from that, is it a necessary truth that there is only one space and only one time? No, since no contradiction arises from supposing otherwise; but it is arguable that that is not a very interesting possibility. At this point, however, I should return to a consideration raised at the beginning of this section, when I pointed out that Kant's remarks about space and time being essentially one involve two separate considerations – the first being concerned with whether we can represent to ourselves more than one space or time, the second being concerned with whether there actually is more than one space or time. The considerations about whether space and time are essentially one in relation to possible experience are really concerned with the first issue, not the second. That is why the questions that I have set out at the beginning of this paragraph receive different answers.

Temporality and temporal becoming

Despite the tentative remarks in the last section about a possible asymmetry between space and time I have so far considered space and time as if they raise no separate issues and can be treated in a parallel way. It is of course true that time has only one dimension while space has three, and that physical events presuppose both space and time while mental events presuppose, directly at any rate, only time. There are, however, other differences between the two. It has generally seemed natural to people to speak of a passage of time; nothing similar seems appropriate to space. To speak of the passage of time in that way is of course to invoke a metaphor, and one that becomes even more explicit when reference is made to the river of time or time's arrow. Whatever may be the case with the metaphor of the river, time's arrow can be conceived as moving in alternate directions according to whether we think of ourselves or possibly events as moving from the past, through the present, into the future or of events as coming towards us from the future and receding behind us into the past. Whichever way it is, the part that *we* play in the image is worth noting. Another way of regarding the matter is to think of events as progressively coming into being, and this has become known as 'temporal becoming'.[17] There has been much dispute whether the phenomenon is objective or subjective in the sense that it is a feature of the mind's view of events rather than of events themselves.

While the metaphors that I have noted presuppose, through the idea of movement, a reference to space, it has sometimes been suggested that the view of time that they convey should be distinguished from that pre-

[17] See, e.g., R. Gale, *The Language of Time* (London: Routledge and Kegan Paul, 1968), chs. 10 and 11.

supposed by physics, where there is a more direct analogy with space. Thus Henri Bergson claimed[18] that the time of physics (*le temps*) involves a direct spatialization of time, in that physics is content to view events simply as related to each other in terms of the relations of before and after. The notions of before and after are not spatial ones in themselves. We can think of things as being spatially before and after others, but there is also a temporal sense of these words, as well as the sense presupposed in a logical ordering; in the series of natural numbers we speak of one number as coming before or after another. But, as Bergson pointed out, the measurement of time is normally carried out via the distance covered by a body moving at constant velocity, relative to the units provided by a constant periodic movement such as the swing of a pendulum or the rotation of the hands of a clock over its dial. Bergson therefore concluded that physics tends to think of time in terms of movement along a line (Newton, it will be remembered, spoke of time as flowing equably). By contrast, the time of consciousness (*la durée*) involves no such constancy, no repetition of events, but a kind of development, an unfolding of events into the future, which Bergson tried to explain by reference to the notion of an *élan vital*.

It is not necessary to go along with everything that Bergson says on this issue to see the force of the contrast between the two ways of thinking about time. (I put the matter in that way deliberately rather than implying, as Bergson does, the existence of two kinds of time.) It is, however, a further implication of Bergson's thinking that the essence of time is to be found in *la durée* rather than in *le temps*, in that the latter, it is claimed, involves a spatialization or rather over-spatialization of time which prevents its real nature from being apparent. That way of thinking has been taken further by other philosophers (as well as novelists such as Proust and Svevo). I have in mind Husserl's *The Phenomenology of Internal Time-Consciousness* and the chapter on 'Temporality' in Merleau-Ponty's *Phenomenology of Perception*, not to speak of Heidegger's *Being and Time*. Merleau-Ponty says that 'when I say that the day before yesterday the glacier produced the water which is passing at this moment, I am tacitly assuming the existence of a witness tied to a certain spot in the world, and I am comparing his successive views'; and he says this to illustrate the thesis that 'the very notion of an event has no place in the objective world'. The chapter in question is in many ways a set of variations on that theme. 'Time is, therefore, not a real process' he says, 'not an actual succession that I am content to record. It arises from *my* re-

18 H. Bergson, *Les Données Immédiates de la Conscience* (Paris: Alcan, 1889; trans. by F. L. Pogson as *Time and Free-will*, London: Allen and Unwin, 1910).

lation to things.'[19] The essential feature of time, on this view, is its thrust towards the future, and this too is a function of human and individual consciousness.

At the end of the chapter Merleau-Ponty tries to meet the obvious objection to this claim for the essential subjectivity of time – that things surely existed and events took place before there were any conscious beings, and the same may well be true after conscious beings have ceased to exist. Like Schopenhauer before him (as we noted in Chapter 2), Merleau-Ponty claims that the only sense to be attached to the idea of things existing before there was consciousness must lie in what verification can be made of that by a conscious being now. Thus he says at the end of the chapter, with reference to the suggestion that the earth may have 'originally issued from a primitive nebula', 'Nothing will ever bring home to my comprehension what a nebula that no one sees could possibly be. Laplace's nebula is not behind us, at our remote beginnings, but in front of us in the cultural world.' There is a great deal of obscurity about this last remark, but Merleau-Ponty's words imply two other theses which he also embraces – that of the primacy of the present (a notion to which I shall return) and that of the primacy of perception (the verificationist thesis that meaning or sense has to be cashed in perceptual terms). It is perhaps the latter notion that looms the larger, and it is present throughout the discussion from the point at which reference is made to the hypothetical observer as a condition of sense being attached to the idea of a succession of events.

If, however, we take seriously Merleau-Ponty's claim that time arises 'from *my* relation to things' we have to recognize in his view a radical subjectivity as far as time is concerned. Time is a function of *my* consciousness. How then do we attain a common perception and understanding of time and its passage? Merleau-Ponty's own answer to that question involves an appeal to something very central in his philosophy – the place of the body in our consciousness and what that makes possible as regards our knowledge and understanding of others. For each of us the present is a living one, and this 'living present' is, because living, one that we can share. It is this fact that, in Ponty's view, mediates and provides a common ground and meeting-place for all our individual pasts and futures which are tied to our individual consciousnesses. Thus, despite the intrinsically subjective nature of temporal becoming, that subjectivity is transcended through the lived present which we can all share and which our bodily existence makes possible.

[19] M. Merleau-Ponty, *The Phenomenology of Perception*, trans. C. Smith (London: Routledge and Kegan Paul, 1962), pp. 411, 412.

This appeal, not only to the primacy of the present, but to the primacy of the lived present, may seem to many an uncomfortable one, since there is an air of magic in the way the lived present is supposed to do the trick of uniting our individual temporal consciousnesses. The notions of past, present and future are surely, at the very least, *intersubjective* notions; they are notions of which we have a common conception, even if each of us, through our individual consciousnesses, fill out that common conception in a distinct way. What seems undeniable in the considerations that lead philosophers such as Merleau-Ponty to a subjective view of time is that there would be no conception of past, present and future if we were not creatures with the kinds of temporal consciousness that we have. To say that is to say that the notions of past, present and future are in a sense anthropocentric.[20] But the anthropocentricity of these notions does nothing to gainsay their objectivity. J. J. C. Smart has in this respect drawn an analogy, correct as far as it goes, between the concepts of past, present and future and colour concepts; each of them is intersubjective while dependent on individual forms of consciousness for their application. It has been common for some philosophers and scientists to maintain that colour is a subjective phenomenon because the attribution of colour to things depends on distinct forms of sensibility. It does not follow from that last fact, however, that colour attribution cannot be intersubjective, and it does not follow that the question what colour a thing has cannot be an objective matter. Similar considerations apply to the notions of past, present and future.

The philosophers whom I have mentioned clearly insist on the indispensability of the notions of past, present and future for a proper conception of time.[21] There are equally philosophers who, while recognizing the part played by these notions in our thinking about time, insist that all there is to time proper is the succession of events construed in terms of the relations of before and after. On this view we come to the notions of past, present and future through the features of our temporal consciousness, but all that is essential to time itself is temporal succession. Moreover, the ideas of the flow of time and of time's arrow have all the foundation that they need in temporal succession itself. It is common indeed among such philosophers to emphasize, rightly enough, the dangers involved in taking the notion of the flow of time

[20] Cf. A. Grünbaum, 'The status of temporal becoming' in R. Gale (ed.), *The Philosophy of Time* (Hassocks: Harvester, 1978), pp. 322ff., and J. J. C. Smart, *Philosophy and Scientific Realism* (London: Routledge and Kegan Paul, 1963).

[21] Cf. also the rather different form of argument of R. Gale, *The Language of Time*, part 1, and the thought of McTaggart to which I shall come in the next section.

too literally, to the extent that the question may arise of how fast it flows, with the consequent implication of times within times.

That way of thinking can be found in, for example, A. J. Ayer's paper 'Statements about the past'.[22] In it Ayer criticizes C. D. Broad's insistence on the importance of the notions of past, present and future for an understanding of what is involved in the flow of time, and his claim that without them time would have to be regarded as, so to speak, static. Ayer maintains that the notions of before and after provide all that is required. The same thesis has been argued for more recently and in a slightly more contemporary dress by Hugh Mellor.[23] Mellor's thesis is too complex to assess in detail, but it relies, basically, on the thought, widely accepted among contemporary philosophers, that meaning has to do with truth conditions. Mellor admits that there is no possibility of the notions of past, present and future being reduced simply to those of before and after. Indeed that point can be extended to cover tense generally (a notion which is, on his usage, much wider than the purely grammatical one, in that it involves anything that is expressible by means of tensed utterances). Tense in that sense is indispensable for the expression of any phenomenon which is backward or forward looking. Nevertheless, he maintains, the truth conditions for tensed sentences and judgments can be stated in tenseless terms.

For that reason he argues against the idea of tensed facts. He points out that their sole function would be to make tensed sentences and judgments true or false; but that role is already performed by tenseless facts, in that these determine the truth or falsity of what he calls 'tensed sentence and judgment tokens' (i.e. the use of sentences or judgments of that type on a particular occasion). So he says (p. 102), 'Provided a token of '*e* is past' is later than *e*, it is true. Nothing else about *e* and it matters a jot.' He goes on to generalize that claim so as to cover all tensed sentences and judgments, saying 'Their tenseless truth conditions leave tensed facts no scope for determining their truth-values. So in reality there are no such facts.'

The conclusion of that argument may seem rather tough. It cannot be denied, however, that '*e* is past' is true if and only if the utterance which constitutes the use of the sentence '*e* is past' is later than, that is to say after, *e*. Hence the truth conditions for the use of that sentence can be stated exclusively in terms of facts about what is after what. Any philosopher who thinks that the meaning of a sentence is given by the

[22] A. J. Ayer, 'Statements about the past', in his *Philosophical Essays* (London: Macmillan, 1954), ch. 7.
[23] H. Mellor, *Real Time* (Cambridge: C.U.P., 1981).

truth conditions for the statement it makes must therefore think that nothing in reality is said by a tensed expression which demands expression in tensed terms. Mellor does not quite say that, because of his claim for the indispensability of tense. His position is rather that even if tensed expressions are indispensable there are no tensed facts; for all the facts required in order to provide necessary and sufficient truth conditions for such expressions are tenseless facts. (He also thinks for reasons connected with McTaggart's argument for the unreality of time, which we shall consider in the next section, that the truth conditions of tensed sentences are either tenseless or contradictory; but that additional thesis is best discussed in the next section.)

Apart from the additional thesis just noted, the argument is parallel to one that says: The truth conditions for the statement that something is of a certain colour are that, for example, the relation between the wavelength of the impressed light and that of the reflected light is such and such, and such facts are all that is required; there is no scope for truth conditions involving reference to colour, and for that reason there are no such facts as facts involving colour; something is of such and such a colour if and only if there are such and such facts about the relation between the wave-lengths of impressed and reflected light. That there is such a parallel should be no surprise, given what I said earlier in relation to the views of J. J. C. Smart. Equally, however, it should be no surprise if I insist, as I did in considering secondary qualities in Chapter 4, that it is an objective fact about something that it is, for example, red; it is, similarly, an objective fact about certain events that they are past. Again, to invoke a different sort of example, something is a triangle if and only if it is trilateral; that does not mean that it is not an objective fact that it is a triangle. In order to rule something out as a fact more is required than that there are other necessary and sufficient conditions for the truth of the statement to which the supposed fact corresponds.

Furthermore, even if it is agreed that the notions of past, present and future, are, like those of colour, in some sense anthropocentric (and that, as we have seen, does not rule out their objectivity), the explanation of why we see events as past, present and future cannot lie entirely in facts about us. It must have something to do with time itself, just as the facts that things have the colour that they do and that we see them as such have as part of their explanation things to do with the wave-length of light that they reflect. Hence, granted that '*e* is past' is true if and only if the utterance which constitutes the use of that sentence is later than *e*, there must also be something about this last fact which explains, at any rate in part, the *possibility* of *e*'s being past, just as something about the wave-length of light reflected from an object explains in part the possibility of that object's being red. In neither case is it *clear* exactly what form the explanation takes, other than that if the one thing were not the case the other would not be the case either; but that does not really affect the issue. There is the structural fact that the past, present and future are related to each other in ways that can be expressed in terms of the relations of before and after; but the relation between the structure of colours and the structure of wave-lengths is more complex. Nevertheless, the important thing for present purposes is that there must be something about time which makes it possible for events to be taken as past, present and future. That fact must not be ignored.

It follows that someone who knew what it was for events to be before or after other events but who knew nothing of what it was for events to be past, present and future would have, if it were possible at all, a grossly inadequate conception of time. It is of course possible to have an understanding of the temporal relationships between events in certain kinds of imaginative fiction without being given any idea of whether those events are represented as past, present or future. The understanding of such temporal representations is, however, parasitical upon our ordinary temporal understanding. Apart from that, indeed, there would be no grounds for thinking that the relationships between the events were temporal at all. If there were no beings with temporal forms of consciousness, there would be no ascriptions of pastness, presentness and futurity; but the possibility of events being construed as such by possible conscious beings would remain. There must be something about time which creates that possibility. It is the fact that that possibility is realized in us which gives us the full conception of time that we have.

McTaggart on the unreality of time

Many of the issues with which I have been concerned emerge clearly from a consideration of J. M. E. McTaggart's well-known (one might almost say 'notorious') proof of the unreality of time.[24] One reason why I have laboured the point that it is essential to time that there should be a past, present and future is that that point plays an important role at one stage of McTaggart's argument, and I think that his own reasons for accepting it are inadequate.

McTaggart takes the notion of an event for granted, and for the pur-

---

[24] J. M. E. McTaggart, *The Nature of Existence* (Cambridge: C.U.P., 1927), ch. 33; also in R. Gale (ed.), *The Philosophy of Time*, pp. 86ff.

poses of his analysis of the concept of time he sees events as terms of three possible series – A, B or C. The B-series is the series of events ordered in terms of the relations of before and after (where those re- lations have a putative temporal sense). The A-series is the series of events ordered in terms of past, present and future. The C-series does not play a material part in the actual argument but it is important for McTaggart's general conception of reality. McTaggart was an Hegelian but he was not a monist in quite Bradley's sense. He thought that reality must be ordered, and the C-series answers to that requirement since it comprises an ordered series of events. The events stand to each other in relations which are transitive and asymmetrical; they can come before or after other items in the series, as numbers in the number series can, without that amounting to a temporal before and after. One might indeed say that the C-series becomes temporal only by being joined to the A-series (so that B = A + C); but that is in a sense something that emerges from McTaggart's argument and is not a premiss of it.

McTaggart says that the B-series is necessary to time but that it is not ultimate or sufficient for time. His reasons for that belief are equally the reasons why he thinks that the A-series is fundamental and such that without it there would be no B-series. His argument rests on the claim that time necessarily involves change and that there is no possibility of change within the B-series alone. He says indeed, 'It would, I suppose, be universally admitted that time involves change.'[25] It is of course true that time as we have it involves change, and without change there would be no possibility of noticing, marking and measuring the passage of time. I have argued earlier, however, following Kant, that there is no contradiction in the idea of a time in which nothing happens, let alone one in which there are changes. A time occupied by a single unchanging process (a continuous unchanging whistle perhaps) seems quite conceiv- able. Hence the most that could validly be claimed is that time involves the *possibility* of change.

Even if one were to waive that objection, it is hardly surprising that there is no room for change within the B-series, since it consists of events alone, and events simply occur; they are not subject to change. As Smart has pointed out,[26] it is substances that change, not events. McTaggart, however, argues that there *is* room for change within the A- series, because an event that is now future will become present, and then past. It has to be said that that is no ordinary change. Peter Geach has

[25] R. Gale (ed.), ibid., p. 89.
[26] J. J. C. Smart, 'The river of time', *Mind* Vol. LVIII, 1949 and in A. G. N. Flew (ed.), *Essays in Conceptual Analysis* (London: Macmillan, 1956).

suggested that it should be called 'Cambridge change' in honour, as he puts it, of McTaggart. Others have called it change *of* time rather than change *in* time. It is the temporal becoming that I mentioned earlier in this chapter – becoming present and then past.

McTaggart's argument can, therefore, be faulted at this stage on three connected grounds: (1) change is not essential to time, (2) change is in any case not appropriate to events, and (3) it is a misconception for the same reason to use the necessity of change to justify the claim for the ultimacy of the A-series. The fact that the argument is invalid does not mean, however, that the conclusion is false. It may remain true that 'without an A-series there is no time'. That is one reason why, in the last section, I laboured the point about the necessity to time of past, present and future. If the arguments there are satisfactory, it will indeed be the case that 'without an A-series there is no time'. Let us go on from that point.

McTaggart's next argument is to the effect that the A-series is impossible. It is incoherent, and, on the idealist principle that the real is rational, anything involving it must be unreal. For that reason reality cannot be characterized in terms of the A-series. Since the B-series presupposes the A-series it will not do either. There is left only the C-series. We need not consider the issues in exactly these terms, and Michael Dummett has written a paper entitled 'A defence of McTaggart's proof of the unreality of time',[27] which says little about the *unreality* of time, but applauds the argument for showing that there is no 'complete description of reality' (i.e., as we shall see later, no complete description of reality which avoids the notion of a point of view, such points of view being multiple). Once again, the conclusion formulated in these terms may be true, whether or not it follows from the argument that McTaggart actually produces.

McTaggart first asks in effect to what category the characteristics of the A-series – past, present and future – belong, and suggests that they must be either relations or qualities. He thinks that the more plausible of these two suggestions is that they are relations, but that in the end it does not make much difference. If the characteristics are relations they must relate their terms to something outside time, since the relations between the terms of the series do not alter. (In effect, in other words, to construe them as relations between the terms of the series would be to reduce past, present and future to 'past relative to . . .' etc., and these relations

---

[27] M. Dummett, 'A defence of McTaggart's proof of the unreality of time', *Philosophical Review*, Vol. LXIX, 1960, pp. 497–505; also in his *Truth and Other Enigmas* (London: Duckworth, 1978).

would amount simply to before, simultaneous with, and after. To say that an event is past is to say more than that it is past relative to some other event.) If the characteristics are to be taken as relating the events of the series to something outside time, what could this possibly be? The same consideration does not arise if the characteristics are taken to be qualities, but apart from the fact that McTaggart does not consider that to be a plausible suggestion anyway, the following argument is taken to deal with both suggestions.

Any one event can have ascribed to it all three characteristics – but they are incompatible. The obvious objection to that criticism is that an event has the three characteristics at different times, so that there is no real incompatibility between them. If it is taking place now, it was future and will be past; it is not present, future and past at the same time. *But*, McTaggart says, to reply in that way is to invoke the A-series yet again. The time at which the event is present, was future and will be past is the present, and this again was future and will be past. To invoke the A-series in order to escape the incompatibility at the first level involves circularity, and this circularity can be exhibited in the form of an infinite regress; every invocation of the A-series to deal with the incompatibility of the characteristics at a given level involves another incompatibility of characteristics at another level and so a further appeal to the A-Series in order to avoid it. This happens for any tensed attribution of a temporal characteristic – not just the ones used in the examples to date. There is, according to McTaggart, no way of avoiding the consequences of using the A-series, and those consequences involve contradiction, or at least incompatibility.

There tend to be two extreme reactions to this. The first is to admit that there is a real incompatibility between the A-series characteristics, and to say that this means that the A-series is contradictory and that 'tensed-ness', as it might be called, is incoherent. Dummett appears to start off in that way in his paper, although as he goes on he softens the conclusion to the one already noted, that no complete description of reality is possible because of the necessity for points of view. Mellor argues in the extreme way throughout. He notes that tensed truth conditions for any tensed sentence are bound to involve an infinite regress, because it will always be necessary to indicate the time at which it is true that the truth conditions hold. To say that '*e* is past' is true if and only if *e* is past sounds unremarkable, but it really needs to be added that what has been said is true if and only if *e* is past now, and that will be so if and only if *e* now now past, and so on. Any attempt to state the truth conditions in a tensed way, but also conclusively, is bound to lead to infinite regress. On the other hand, Mellor says (p. 98), 'To stop and give a definite answer at any stage only produces a contradiction, because if the sentence is true (at some present time) it is also false (at some other).'

Those exemplifying the other extreme reaction may well find an absurdity in this, saying that the trouble only seems to arise because what is being demanded is more than can possibly be provided. What is being required is that there should be *definite* truth conditions for tensed sentences, and in the present context that means truth conditions the statement of which leaves no room for qualification as to when they are supposed to hold. According to Mellor, no tensed sentence can do what is required and the attempt to make it do so involves either infinite regress or contradiction. But, it might be said, this involves a failure to see tensed utterances for what they are. When someone says '*e* is past' there is no indefiniteness in the utterance which needs to be made good by saying *when* it is past, and so on. The use of a tensed utterance is quite clear when the circumstances of its use are taken into account. We understand each other perfectly in this respect, and trouble arises only when the circumstances are obscured in some way, as may be the case when we come across a tensed sentence written down and we have no knowledge of the circumstances in which it was written. Similarly, it might be said that McTaggart simply fails to see his A-series character-istics for what they are and demands that they be what they are not.

One way to express such an objection is to say that there is, as Dummett puts it, 'a blindness to the obvious properties of token-reflexive ex-pressions'.[28] As Dummett defines a token-reflexive expression, it is 'one like "I", "here", "now", whose essential occurrence in a sentence ren-ders that sentence capable of bearing different truth-values according to the circumstances of its utterance – by whom, when, and where it is uttered, to whom it is addressed, with what gestures it is accompanied, and so on'. That account does not explain the words 'token-reflexive' and there is in any case a certain ambiguity in it, in that it does not make clear whether the statement of the circumstances itself involves token-reflexives or not. The notion of a token-reflexive was introduced by Hans Reichenbach, and a token-reflexive was so called because it involved a reference back, reflexively, to its own token utterance; an understanding of such an expression involves an understanding of all that and an ability to identify the utterance in question. What has to be the case for that understanding and ability to be present is an interesting question. In fact, however, we do not have any trouble in understanding

[28] M. Dummett, 'A defence', p. 499.

token-reflexive expressions, although if understanding them involved knowing the implied truth conditions and if *their* statement involved further token-reflexives, there would be real trouble, since we are at the beginning of an infinite regress. Mellor, for one, does seem to use the term 'token-reflexive' in such a way that the circumstances of their utterance do require further token-reflexives in their statement.

Dummett, however, thinks that the objection that McTaggart (and equally his defenders) are blind to the properties of token-reflexives misses the point and involves a 'grave misunderstanding'. This is because there is an asymmetry between temporal token-reflexives and others in an important respect. McTaggart did not think (nor has anyone else) that it is possible to produce a paradox, of the kind suggested for time, in respect of 'here' and 'there' or 'I' and 'you'. Something that is 'here' can easily be regarded as 'there' from a different position, and it is easy to imagine circumstances in which one might say of something that it is 'here', 'there' and so on. Analogously the person who is you (to me) is me (to you). Why is there thought to be a paradox over time but not over space or what these other expressions involve? Dummett claims that a failure to see the difference between these cases is due to a failure to take proper account of the earlier part of McTaggart's argument, when he says that if there were not facts of the kind involving reference to past, present and future there would be no time. There is nothing similar that holds good of space and facts involving reference to 'here' and 'there', etc. Dummett maintains (p. 500) that 'the use of spatially token-reflexive expressions is not essential to the descriptions of objects as being in a space . . . I can describe an arrangement of objects in space although I do not myself have any position in that space.' He goes on to give as an example the space of my visual field.

That example is extremely controversial, and Dummett offers no other example. The whole notion of a visual field raises questions,[29] and it is even more doubtful whether there is anything rightly so called in which there is no here or there. As an analogy in terms of which we are to understand 'a being who could perceive objects in our three-dimensional physical space although he occupied no position in that space' it is very shaky. It has to be admitted that some thinkers have regarded God as being in that position, but they have generally wished to hold the same sort of thing with respect to time, thinking of God as seeing from the point of view of eternity all events laid out in time. I do not want to pass judgment on the intelligibility of these conceptions, but there does not seem to be any asymmetry between them (even if there

---

[29] See my 'The visual field and perception', *Proc. Arist. Soc.*, Supp. Vol. XXXI, 1957, pp. 107–24.

are other problems, for example that concerning the relation between divine knowledge and free-will, which arise in the case of time but not in the case of space). If there is good reason for thinking that the problems over token-reflexives are more acute in connexion with time than elsewhere, we must look to other considerations.

It is certainly true that one cannot say by other means exactly what one says by means of a token-reflexive (or not if it is a token-reflexive through and through). Hence, even in the case of space there will be things that cannot be said if one leaves out token-reflexives, and to that extent a complete description of reality in spatial terms will be impossible. It might be said, however, that that is not worrying, since one can say *all that matters to space* without token-reflexives. That there can be spatial points of view is simply a function of the fact that there are different places, different positions in space. Moreover, one can change one's position in space without any problem, in principle at any rate. That is to say that there is no incoherence whatever in the idea of a change of spatial position. The same is not true of time.[30]

We can change our position in time only by going on living. (There are well-known paradoxes over time-travel which some philosophers think they can resolve. It must be true, however, that my experiences of the events that I witness as a result of the time-travel are after the experiences of the events that I witness before starting. But of course anything is achievable by what is literally magic!) The impossibility of changing our temporal position except by going on living cannot be simply a human limitation; it is due in some way to time itself and our relation to it. If positions in time are not variable in the way that positions in space are, there is an asymmetry between time and space which gives temporal token-reflexives a greater importance in our conception of time than spatial token-reflexives have in our conception of space. If, as seems to be the case, A-series characteristics are essential to time in a way that similar spatial characteristics are not in relation to space, this is not, as McTaggart supposes, because time necessarily involves change and because change is possible only if there are facts involving reference to past, present and future. It is, as I argued in the previous section, because something about time itself determines that we have the temporal point of view that we do, and that temporal point of view is in a sense fixed even if the events seen from that point of view change (a point that Aristotle tried to express by saying that the 'now' was always the same although what is now may change).

[30] It is not true of 'I' and 'you' either, a fact which brings temporality and the notion of the self close together. I shall have more to say about that in Ch. 9.

I shall consider some of the consequences of this asymmetry between time and space in the next section, but it may be as well to emphasize here the kind of asymmetry that it is. There have been attempts to explore the extent to which there are analogies between what can be said about temporal phenomena and what can be said about spatial phenomena. Richard Taylor has argued that there is no asymmetry in that respect, and Richard Gale has attempted to answer him.[31] It might be said that the point that I myself have been making has less to do with disanalogies between spatial and temporal characteristics than with an asymmetry between features of our temporal experience and features of our spatial experience. But, as I have tried to emphasize, it is not just a fact about *our* temporal experience, as opposed to other forms of experience that there might be, that we cannot change our temporal point of view. It is as if we are more firmly embedded in time than we are in space. That is a metaphor and may suggest that the situation is in principle alterable. We can have no conception, however, of what that might amount to. Although Kant did not make much of the notions of past, present and future, he might have said that it is an *a priori* condition of possible experience that there is no way of making what is past or future present. That is how time is for us, and it is because time is what it is that it is as it is for us.

It follows that there is a certain appropriateness to the metaphors that are commonly invoked in connexion with time, even if they depend also on the spatialization of what is essentially temporal. There has been much philosophical discussion about the notion of the direction of time and about the connexion, if any, between that and physical processes. Some philosophers have indeed asked whether there would be anything about time which would merit referring to its direction if there were not a causal ordering and if physical processes were not in some sense and in some cases irreversible.[32] What is clearer is that the future is the future and the past the past. It may not be the case that all there is to the direction of time is to be spelled out in terms of human expectations and human memories. It may nevertheless be the case that our thought of

[31] R. Taylor, 'Spatial and temporal analogies and the concept of identity', in J. J. C. Smart (ed.), *Problems of Space and Time*, pp. 381ff.; R. Gale, ' "Here" and "Now" ', *Monist*, Vol. 53, 1969. See also G. Schlesinger, 'The similarities between space and time', *Mind*, Vol. LXXXIV, 1975, pp. 161–76; B. Mayo, 'Space and time re-assimilated', *Mind*, Vol. LXXXV, 1976, pp. 576–80; G. Schlesinger, 'Comparing space and time once more', *Mind*, Vol. LXXXVII, 1978, pp. 264–6; J. M. Shorter, 'Space and time', *Mind*, Vol. XC, 1981, pp. 61–78. There is an excellent paper emphasizing the importance and uniqueness of A-series characteristics by Gillian Romney, 'Temporal points of view', *Proc. Arist. Soc.*, Vol. LXXVIII, 1977/8, pp. 237–52.

[32] See the paper by A. Grünbaum in J. J. C. Smart (ed.), *Problems of Space and Time*, part 4.

time as having a direction is very much dependent on the fact that we have such expectations and memories. But that those states of consciousness are what they are in being forward and backward looking is due to the fact that time is such that forward and backward looking states of consciousness are possible. An account of time which left out that consideration would be at best impoverished and at worst positively misleading.

Time and human existence

I have already discussed much that is relevant to this subject – for example the anthropocentricity of the notions of past, present and future, and the implications of that for the objectivity of those notions. I have also discussed the question whether those notions are essential to a proper conception of time, and have answered 'Yes'. I wish to underline one further point. We are temporal beings in a more profound sense than that anything which persists through time is a temporal being. A physical object has a past and a future in the sense that it has already existed and will continue to do so. Human beings have a past and a future in the additional sense that certain things are past *for them* and others are future *for them*, if at all (and that 'if at all' sums up the inevitability of death). These facts are a function of the form of consciousness that makes it possible for temporal distinctions to manifest themselves to human beings in the way that they do. The idea of an eternal being with a form of consciousness of things that involves their being, to use Spinoza's words, *sub specie aeternitatis* may or may not make sense, but it is doubtful whether it makes sense at all in relation to ourselves, although some mystics and some philosophers have thought otherwise.

Given the form of temporal consciousness that we have, the time that we occupy is for us a 'lived time', as Merleau-Ponty and others of a similar persuasion have insisted. In this respect it is a truism, and yet more than a truism, that we live in the present. It makes a certain sense to speak of someone living in the past or in the future, but it is a sense which is parasitical upon the more ordinary notion of living in the present. The past and the future are, for consciousness as we know it, secondary to the present. It is this idea to which I referred earlier in this chapter in speaking of the primacy of the present. Merleau-Ponty speaks of the living present opening upon a past which one is no longer living through and on a future which one does not yet live and which one may not live.[33]

[33] M. Merleau-Ponty, *Phenomenology of Perception*, p. 433. In fact he speaks of *my* living present, but that is a product of the subjectivism that I have already criticized. He also has to speak in consequence of one's present opening upon other temporalities – those of others. The problem no longer arises if it is seen that temporal conceptions presuppose intersubjectivity and what Wittgenstein called 'agreement in forms of life'.

He goes on to speak of the thickness (or density) of the pre-objective present, which is a way, a very obscure way, of referring to what a lived present brings with it. That is a point that I must elaborate a little.

There are people suffering from certain forms of brain damage who have lost most of that temporal consciousness. They have no long-term memory, except perhaps that which survives in skills, in knowing-how; they may have little short-term memory and no power of anticipation of the future. Such people may be said literally to be living in the present. As Merleau-Ponty points out, however, a normal life in the present is one that opens upon a past and a future. The life that I have mentioned is at best a very impoverished version of that. It might be said that the life of people of whom we say they 'live in the past' is equally an impoverished version of the normal life. It is, but in a different way. People who live in the past so 'live' in a derivative sense; it is merely that the centre of their consciousness is occupied by things that are in fact past, whether or not they are past for the people in question. The normal case, in relation to which our understanding of time as it is for temporal consciousness is filled out, is the one that Merleau-Ponty describes – the one where it is natural to describe things in terms of the consciousness of a lived present opening upon a past and a future. That is what the primacy of the present comes to, and it is an important notion for an understanding of temporal consciousness.

There is no similar sense in which we could speak of the primacy of the 'here', although we shall see in Chapter 9 that there may be a sense in which one could speak of the primacy of the 'I'. Our bodies of course play an important role in our awareness of the world, and it is arguable that as a matter of psychological fact what is near is most important for most people. That is at best, however, a contingent fact and not the necessary one that the primacy of the present seems to involve. There is a sense in which what is here, rather than there, is a relative matter, just as what is present is. (As J. N. Findlay has emphasized,[34] we speak of present moment, hour, day, year, generation . . .) In a quite different way, however, the present is an absolute, as what is here is not. That is so in the sense previously emphasized – that the content of the present is something that, once we are in it, we can do nothing to alter. As I said earlier, that means we are somehow more embedded in time than we are in space. That a conscious being must be spatial because embodied is a commonplace of much contemporary philosophy, perhaps for a variety of reasons. Less attention has been given by Anglo-Saxon philosophers to the place of temporality in human existence. Some philosophers have

[34] J. N. Findlay, 'Some puzzles about time' in A. G. N. Flew (ed.), *Logic and Language*, Vol. 1 (Oxford: Blackwell, 1951).

thought, as Descartes did, that one can think away the conditions of bodily existence, so that the notion of a disembodied existence can be given some sort of sense; and for that reason a meaning could perhaps be given to the idea of a non-spatial existence. Whether or not that idea ultimately makes any sense, a great many thinkers have thought that it does or have at any rate played with the idea. It needs little argument to reach the conclusion that a non-temporal existence is unintelligible. If that is so there is indeed a sense in which human beings are temporal beings in a more radical way than that in which they are spatial beings.

One concluding remark. Time is one of the richest of philosophical subjects. It is a many-sided topic, and it is also one of the most difficult to treat satisfactorily. I would like to emphasize as a coda that what I have said, whether satisfactory or not, is but a small taste of the riches that are there.

8. Minds

The concept of the mental

I said in Chapter 1 that a discussion of what reality is entails saying something about things, their spatio-temporal framework and the persons or selves for whom they are things. I did not mean to suggest that reality is merely reality *for* some person or persons – that reality is relative to a point of view had by a person or persons – and I took pains in Chapter 2 to emphasize that fact. It is nevertheless a truism that our conception of reality depends upon the concepts that we have, even if reality itself is not necessarily limited by those concepts. Our conception of reality is one that includes persons as well as other things, and an account of reality must therefore make reference to them. The only question is whether it is necessary to give separate treatment to them. Why set human beings or persons (and I shall shelve until later the question whether these are the same) apart from the rest of nature? If materialism were true, that might suggest that there is, in the end, no reason for setting persons apart from the rest of nature, despite the *prima facie* difficulty arising from various facts about human beings, including the fact that we can speak of what reality is *for* them. On the other hand, Hilary Putnam has suggested that the very notion of reference to things, which is involved in the idea of things being reality for us, is something that materialism cannot explain.[1]

To speak of what reality is *for* human beings or persons implies that such beings are conscious which is one reason, therefore, for distinguishing persons from the rest of nature. I shall discuss the notions of a person and personal identity in Chapter 9. It is arguable that the notion of a person should be restricted to beings who are self-conscious as well as conscious, and in that case it might be a matter for argument whether one should include in the class of persons the higher animals such as chimpanzees. But there will be a whole host of animals which are not self-conscious which will not be included in that class, though some of

[1] H. Putnam, *Reason, Truth and History* (Cambridge: C.U.P., 1981), ch. 1, and two articles, 'Why there isn't a ready made world' and 'Why reason can't be naturalized' in *Synthese* 1982, reprinted in his *Realism and Reason: Philosophical Papers, Vol. 3* (Cambridge: C.U.P., 1983).

them, if not all, might well be thought to be conscious. That would be a *prima facie* reason for giving them separate treatment. I shall, however, confine myself in the following by and large to human beings; for they are paradigmatic cases of beings of whom it makes sense to ask what reality is for them.

One way of putting the question underlying what distinguishes persons is to ask about the status of mind or minds. That indeed has been the conventional way of putting the question over the last few centuries, and the question has spawned various theories about the mental and about the relation of the mind to the body. Indeed the currently fashionable materialism can be construed simply as one answer to that question – that what we call mental is just one version of the physical, either because mental items are identical with physical items or perhaps because we can explain everything that has to do with the so-called mental side of a human being in terms of internal systems which have a certain functional role in the economy that makes up that human being, such systems having a purely physical realization.

The first of these theories is known as the identity theory of the mind – that every mental item can be identified with some physical item. There have been various refinements of the thesis, some but not all implying the desirability of eliminating from our ways of thinking the concept of the mental altogether. The second thesis is known as functionalism and has arisen in part from a certain dissatisfaction with some versions of the identity thesis itself and in part from certain ways of thinking that are prevalent within psychology, particularly cognitive psychology. I shall return to some of these issues in the last section of this chapter, although it is impossible in a book of this kind to enter into the kind of detail that a full treatment would entail. A rejection of this whole way of thinking would involve giving separate status to the mental in some way and thus a different theory of the mind–body relation.

Since at any rate the seventeenth century a number of theories about that relation have been put forward, and current forms of materialism constitute variations on just one example of such theories. I say 'since the seventeenth century' because it is not obvious that the problem existed in this form for the ancient Greek philosophers or for the mediaeval philosophers who built upon them. What does exist in the ancient world is a problem about the nature of the *soul* and its relation to the body. The ancient notion of the soul is not, however, the same as that of the mind as it has come to be used in our time. There is a Greek word – *nous* – which is sometimes translated 'mind', but it really signifies intellect or reason. In saying that, I do not wish to deny that those notions of intellect and reason enter into our contemporary conceptions of the mind and the mental. We do speak of 'giving one's mind to something' and of 'mental effort' and those locutions reflect the notions in question. Our more recent conceptions of the mental include more than that however.

Moreover, the earliest and most fundamental conception of *psuche* or soul in ancient Greek thought associates it with life: the soul is what makes something alive. It is in tune with that conception that Aristotle's treatment of the soul in his *De Anima* involves explaining the notion in terms of the capacities for various forms of life that different kinds of living thing possess. Hence plants have souls, if only in the sense that they have a capacity for growth, nourishment and reproduction, these being what life consists in in plants. Animals have in addition sense-perception, and in most cases the capacity for movement. Human beings have in addition to all that reason, and it is the possession of reason which marks off human beings from the rest of nature. In Plato too one can find a tendency to emphasize reason within the soul and on occasion a tendency to identify the two. Plato also tends, as Aristotle does not, to think of the soul as the real self which may survive the body and thus be immortal. Nevertheless, there is no place in the thought of these philosophers for a conception of the soul as the seat of consciousness or a conception of the mind as something *inner* and to be contrasted with the so-called external world. There is no conception of an inner and private mental life.

This last claim has often been disputed; it nevertheless seems to me true. It is important, however, to be clear about what is being claimed. There is no word in Greek that explicitly means 'consciousness' and no word for 'mental' that has a connected connotation. That makes it difficult for a Greek to incorporate such notions in a *theory* about *psuche*. Nevertheless, there are in ordinary Greek usage and the talk of ordinary people, not to speak of that of tragedians and other literary figures, ways of talking about people which *to us* imply their possession of consciousness. Equally a contrast is sometimes made which *we* might put in terms of what is inner and what is outer. Consider for example Euripides' *Hippolytus* (line 612), 'My tongue swore, my mind [*phren* – mind or heart] was unsworn.' Such a saying might well be taken as implying a contrast between the outer, observed behaviour and the inner thought. Nevertheless, that contrast does not appear to be made explicit within the theories of the soul put forward by philosophers, and that fact is very notable in the case of Aristotle. One can speculate about the reasons for this, and one possible thesis is that it required a radical form of scepticism – one which expresses doubt not only about claims to knowledge of things around us but also about claims to knowledge of ourselves – to bring the outer/inner contrast to the surface in philosophical thinking.[2]

However that may be, it is in Descartes that we first find in an explicit form the conception of the mental as that to which we have private and privileged access in a way that does not hold good of anything bodily. Why Descartes came to emphasize the so-called privacy of the mental is a matter for historical speculation; it is not an easy question to answer. But the outcome was the view that we have, as he put it, a clear and distinct idea of our minds in a way that we do not have of our bodies. The idea of our 'closeness' to our minds produced in turn the thesis that we are, essentially, mental, so that to the question 'What am I?' Descartes could answer 'A thinking thing' (indeed a thinking non-extended thing, extension being the essential attribute of bodies, as thought is of minds). That contrast between mind and body is one that has enformed discussion of the so-called mind–body problem ever since. I shall return to it later. It is first necessary, however, to see what kinds of thing a body–mind theory can be and to note certain things about the terms of reference of such theories. I do not claim to have clearly answered as yet the question 'What is the mental?'

Body–mind theories

Descartes' account of the relationship between body and mind is generally said to be a form of interactionism, in that it presupposes a distinction between two substances with distinct essential attributes which nevertheless interact. There are notorious difficulties about how that interaction is to be conceived. Descartes thought that the interaction occurred through the medium of the pineal gland which was therefore the seat of the soul or mind in the body. Such a view does nothing, however, to explain the possibility of interaction between such utterly distinct substances, and on being asked to explain it in correspondence with the Princess Elizabeth of Bohemia he referred to a quasi-substantial union between the soul or mind and the body of which no account could be given; for we have no clear and distinct idea of it, even if the senses tell us of its existence. Such a view has seemed to most commentators obviously unsatisfactory.[3]

[2] See the paper by Myles Burnyeat referred to in Ch. 2, note 3.
[3] But see R. C. Richardson, 'The scandal of Cartesian interactionism', *Mind*, Vol. XCI, 1982, pp. 20–37.

On the other hand, even if one cannot say anything about the nature of the interaction, substances are the kind of thing between which it makes sense to speak of interaction. Indeed, as a mind–body theory, interactionism is paradigmatically a theory about the relation between two substances. It could be conceived of as a theory of the relation between two kinds of process or series of events, but even in that case it is more intelligible if the processes or series of events occur in connexion with distinct substances. Spinoza conceives of the mental and the physical as two aspects of a single substance, but it is difficult to think of the two aspects as *interacting*. There is thus good reason for thinking that the so-called double aspect theory of body and mind is quite a different theory from interactionism and one with quite different terms of reference. Bernard Williams has distinguished between substance dualism and property or attribute dualism;[4] one might want to say that people have two sets of quite distinct properties or attributes, called mental and physical respectively, without wanting to say, as Descartes appears to say, that people are a blend of two quite different substances. But if we think of those attributes interacting it will be in a different way from that in which substances interact.

The thesis that Leibniz puts forward – often called parallelism – that the order of mental events is parallel to that of bodily events, although there are no causal relations between them, is, as it stands, clearly one about events or processes, indeed the order of these, and not obviously about anything that brings in substances. If it was Leibniz' view that in this thesis we are concerned with properties of substances, there is nothing in parallelism *per se* that entails that. The same is true of epiphenomenalism, a view which is sometimes represented as one-way interactionism (the physical produces the mental but not *vice versa*). On the face of it, it is to be construed as affirming a relationship between mental and physical events, processes or states; it says nothing in itself about substances. The same is true of the identity thesis.

Most of the theories, it might be said, have in common a thesis about the relationship between mental and physical events, states or processes. There remains the question of what the states are states of, and with respect to what the events and processes occur. There is no problem over that on Descartes' view, since the states involve two distinct substances; but the very existence of two substances makes it difficult to spell out the relationship. Spinoza's double-aspect view makes it clear that there is a single substance, but it is that very fact which makes it difficult to

[4] B. A. O. Williams, *Descartes: The Project of Pure Enquiry* (Harmondsworth: Penguin, 1978), ch. 10.

think of the states so conceived as standing in a causal relation. It might be argued that there is no need to conceive of them in that way; all that is required is that some theoretical account be forthcoming to explain the relation between the two sets of states in a single substance. Identity might be one possibility, if there is no independent reason for thinking that the difference between the states precludes that; alternatively the relation might conceivably be like that which holds between the macroscopic and microscopic states of a physical substance. It ought at all events to be possible to provide *some* theoretical account of the relation in question. It is in effect part of the thesis of psycho-physical dualism that no such account can be provided, although not necessarily, as with Descartes, because there are distinct substances with distinct essences.

If a theoretical account of the relation between the mental and physical states of a substance were possible it would have to have as a constituent an account of the nature of that substance. One of the advantages of the identity thesis is that it appears to allow of that possibility; if all mental states are identical with physical states there is no problem about a purely physical substance sustaining those states. On the other hand, any thesis which retains a form of dualism is likely to present difficulties in explaining the nature of the substance that makes such duality of states possible. It is perhaps not impossible that there should be a physical substance with both straightforwardly physical states and attributes and others which are in some sense mental. Bernard Williams, as we have seen, seems to contemplate this as a possibility. But there is surely something unsatisfactory about an attribute dualism when no account is forthcoming of the nature of the substance which explains the duality of attributes. An alternative is to suppose that the substance which possesses the two kinds of attribute is neither straightforwardly physical nor straightforwardly mental but something presupposed by both of these. Strawson's concept of a person, which he claims as logically primitive, amounts to that. The question is whether that does enough to make the connexion between the two sets of attributes intelligible. I shall discuss that notion in Chapter 9.

Cartesian dualism

Cartesian dualism is for a variety of reasons the great bête noire and stalking horse of much contemporary philosophy. It is said, for example, that Wittgenstein was passionately opposed to it and showed that it was wrong. Whether that is so or not, it cannot be denied that for most contemporary philosophers Cartesian dualism is obviously wrong; and with that dualism in general is dismissed. I have already indicated the main

aspects of the view and of the consequences that Descartes drew from it
– the existence of two kinds of substance, radically different and with
different essential properties, yet somehow brought together in a quasi-
substantial union of which no account can be given. So far, however, I
have given no account of why Descartes thought that all this must be so,
except in what I said in the first section about privacy. There are three
strands in the story.

There is first the thesis which Descartes inherited from his
philosophical predecessors and which is there even in Aristotle. It is the
thesis which Gilbert Ryle in the *Concept of Mind* calls the official doctrine
and which he describes as treating the mind as a para-mechanical cause.
In Descartes' writings that last thesis is to be found chiefly in the *Passions
de l'âme*; it is there that he speaks clearly of the pineal gland as the seat of
the soul or mind, mediating an interaction between the soul and the
animal spirits in the nerves of the body. Why, however, cannot both
passions and active behaviour be explained purely in terms of what happens in the body and therefore in terms of Cartesian dynamics? Descartes'
answer is in effect that the workings of the intellect and anything that
involves it, including rational behaviour, cannot be explained in terms
of his dynamics; some additional cause is required, which must be external
to that system of dynamics. That is what Ryle calls a para-mechanical
cause. Animal behaviour can be explained without reference to such a
cause, and in that sense animals are machines as human beings are not.
Aristotle too argued that the intellect is an exception to the biological
principles that govern the other faculties of a living human being; and he
drew the conclusion that there is a so-called active intellect which is
separable from the rest of the soul.[5] Descartes inherits the doctrine of
the special status of the intellect and applies it to the human soul in
general. Unless, however, any special considerations can be brought to
bear (as Aristotle indeed appears to suppose) it seems at best an empirical
matter whether rational behaviour, or the movements made in the
course of rational behaviour, can be explained in purely physical
terms.

The second strand is more specifically Descartes' own. It stems from
the 'method of doubt' and the '*Cogito*'. It is argued that I can doubt all
sorts of things, but the one thing that I cannot doubt is that I doubt and
therefore think. '*Cogito* – I think' is therefore an indubitable truth. It is
taken to follow that there must be a thinker – myself. That cannot be a
body, since I can doubt the existence of all bodies, while I cannot doubt
my own existence. I must therefore exist as a thinking thing distinct

[5] See my 'Aristotle's Cartesianism', *Paideia*, Special Aristotle number, 1978, pp. 8–15.

from my body, which as an extended thing does not have the same status as regards indubitability. I shall not discuss this argument here; it has been extensively analysed in many places. It is sometimes suggested that, for Descartes, '*cogitatio*' is a word for any conscious state of mind, and that the argument is therefore designed to show that consciousness has a status distinct from any feature of physical things. I have doubts about the claim concerning the significance of '*cogitatio*', but the argument in any case turns very specifically on a feature of thinking of which doubting is taken to be an instance. The point is that *thinking* must be distinguished from any feature of physical things, because whereas the latter can be conceived not to exist, that is not possible over thinking. Hence the dualism is one between thinking things and non-thinking but extended things. I shall come back to this point directly.

The third strand in the complete story is, however, derived from it. It turns on the difficulty that the account so far given raises for sensation, feeling and perception generally. In the second *Meditation*, when Descartes asks 'What am I?' and answers 'A thinking thing', he says that sensations and the like count as bodily. They are of course dependent on the body, and they do not necessarily involve any thinking; but that is not enough to justify the claim that they are bodily without qualification. They are not, for one thing, extended in any straightforward sense. In the sixth *Meditation*, when Descartes turns to the question of the relationship between mind and body, he gives a different account of sensations. He says that sensations, apparently including even sensations of hunger and thirst, are 'confused modes of thinking'. They are modes in the sense that they cannot be conceived of in separation from what they are modes of – in this case thinking. But they are equally dependent on the body, and so they arise from 'the union and apparent fusion of mind and body'.

Hence, while sensations are dependent on the body they are not just bodily; they would not exist were we not thinking things. If taken literally that thesis is not very plausible, although it would have greater plausibility in the case of most, if not all, emotions, since these involve beliefs, often specific beliefs, about their objects. It appears, however, that Descartes' primary criterion of the mental is the presence of thought. There are nevertheless, in his view, secondary cases of the mental, which depend on the primary ones; these are secondary because they would not exist if there were not a union between the mind and the body. Hence the quasi-substantial union.

The place of thinking in all this is obvious. If, however, we ask why thinking too is not dependent on the body as sensations are, we receive two sorts of answer. First, as was indicated in the first strand of the complete story, thought and its manifestations cannot be explained on the same principles as those which explain the motion of bodies. Second, as was suggested in the second strand, we cannot doubt the existence of thought: we have direct and indubitable access to it. These two considerations are very different from each other, but the great weight of argument, in the *Meditations* at least, is derived from the second. If that is so, it is crucial to Cartesian dualism that it involves an epistemological point about direct, indubitable access to the mental, even if the mental is, in its pure form, restricted to thinking. Much of recent criticism of Cartesian dualism has been directed to that epistemological point. Moreover, it tends to be thought that if the thesis about direct, indubitable access to the mental is demolished so is dualism.

There might, however, be reasons for maintaining a distinction between the mental and the physical, between mental and physical items, without maintaining also the thesis about direct, indubitable access to the mental. Moreover, there might be direct access to at least some mental items without that access being indubitable or incorrigible. Knowledge of our feelings, for example, may be non-inferential and in that sense direct, without it being the case that we cannot be mistaken about those feelings. I shall not go further into these epistemological issues here.[6] They serve to show, however, that there are various aspects of the Cartesian thesis, some of which can be abandoned while still retaining dualism in some form.

Before we can arrive at an assessment of what remains if that is the case it is necessary to be as clear as possible about the notion of the mental; and not enough was achieved in that direction in the first section of this chapter. Most discussions of dualism presume, however, that what is meant by the physical or bodily is clear enough. I am not at all sure that the presumption is fair. It is, of course, encouraged by the success of the physical sciences, but the reduction of, for example, biology to physics remains at best a possibility. Descartes thought that the essential attribute of the physical was extension. That may seem obvious if not very informative; physical bodies must surely be part of a spatio-temporal framework. But the same might be true in some sense of mental items, without this involving any reduction of the mental to the physical. Hence even if extension is a necessary condition of the physical it may not be sufficient as well; or at all events it cannot be presumed to be so without begging the question against dualism. I shall not,

---

[6]   See my *Theory of Knowledge* (London and Basingstoke: Macmillan, 1971), ch. 8.

however, press these points further. I shall presume that we have some intuitive understanding of the physical. What, however, of the mental?

The criteria of the mental

No doubt we have a common-sense, intuitive view also of what sorts of thing count as mental, although Descartes' ambivalence about the status of bodily sensations may be one that many people would admit to sharing if they were pressed on the point. After all, bodily sensations are normally locatable in some part of the body and are for that reason more intimately concerned with the body than are thoughts, for example, even if they too, we believe, are dependent on the brain. At the same time many people would admit that sensations and thoughts have more in common with each other than either of them has with any explicitly physical state, event or process. What is it that they have in common which marks them off as mental? To ask that question is to ask for the criterion of the mental – what characteristic it is that all and only mental items have, such that it serves as a basis for a decision that a given item is mental.

In the *Concept of Mind* Gilbert Ryle maintained that the distinction between the mind and the body was one of category. I have already referred to the thesis that Ryle finds in Descartes, that to invoke the notion of the mind is to invoke that of a para-mechanical cause. To see things in that way is to see reference to mind as a reference to rationality and intelligence and to contemplate the possibility that the explanation of rational and intelligent behaviour lies in a special sort of cause which falls outside the field of ordinary mechanics. Ryle rejects any such explanation, while retaining the terms of reference according to which to speak of mind is to speak of a capacity for rational and intelligent behaviour. In his view, therefore, to explicate the notion of mind is to provide an account of what is involved in the various rational and intelligent capacities and dispositions that human beings possess, and to reject the idea that these entail any appeal to a para-mechanical cause. Ryle says that such an appeal involves a category mistake, by which is meant, roughly, that it looks for the wrong type of thing in rather the same way as, so Ryle represents, someone who at Oxford asks to be shown the university after being shown all the colleges is looking for the wrong type of thing, for he fails to realize that the university is simply the class formed by all the colleges. Whether that example illuminates the idea of a category-mistake generally is open to doubt, but a category-mistake is certainly one that leads to some kind of nonsense through a failure to understand the logic of what is said.

As I said earlier in this chapter, it may be that the conception of the mind as involving reference to intelligence and rationality does correspond to what is reflected in *some* uses of the terms 'mind' and 'mental', and is reflected in *one* strand of Descartes' thinking – the one that he inherited from the tradition going back to Aristotle. It hardly does justice to other uses of those words and to the other strands in Descartes' thinking. Notoriously, Ryle's conception and its theoretical development do not deal satisfactorily with the more passive aspects of the mental life – what John Wisdom once characterized as the flotsam and jetsam that float on the stream of consciousness.[7] They do not adequately deal with sensations, images and other modifications of consciousness.

In using the phrase 'modifications of consciousness' I have made reference to a central aspect of mentality. The two main candidates for the title of the criterion of the mental, which have received considerable attention in recent times, both reflect aspects of consciousness. They are privacy and intentionality.[8] I shall consider them in turn. To say that privacy is the criterion of the mental is to differentiate mental items in terms of the relation that they have to us, whose mental items they are. The notion of the private is of course wider than that of being the object of the direct, indubitable access that Descartes had in mind; for to say that a sensation or thought is private is not necessarily to say that we have indubitable or incorrigible awareness of it. It is to say that we have access to our own mental states in a way that others do not, but it need not imply anything about the epistemological status of that access. To make that point is to begin the task of sorting out the appropriate sense in which mental items can be said to be private. For, as has been pointed out by others,[9] the sense in which pains, for example, are private is not the sense in which my property, my voice or even information that I may possess may be private. Don Locke even specifies a sense of 'private' which he calls 'mentally private', defined by saying that something is mentally private 'if only one person can perceive it'. But he has to go on to say that, while by that criterion pains are mentally private, conscious processes (i.e. such things as perceiving and thinking) are not, since they 'cannot be felt or perceived at all, by anyone'.[10] Moreover, by that criterion certain things may be mentally private for merely contingent reasons, such as that nobody else can get in quite the same pos-

[7]   J. Wisdom, 'The concept of mind' in his *Other Minds* (Oxford: Blackwell, 1952).

[8]   See the opening chapter of Kathleen Wilkes, *Physicalism* (London: Routledge and Kegan Paul, 1978).

[9]   E.g. Don Locke, *Myself and Others* (Oxford: Clarendon Press, 1968), ch. 1, and A. J. Ayer, 'Privacy' in his *The Concept of a Person* (London: Macmillan, 1963).

[10]   D. Locke, *Myself and Others*, p. 10.

ition as I can to perceive the thing in question. One suspects that the definition of 'mentally private' could rule out such contingent impossibilities only by begging the question – only by presupposing a prior notion of the mental.

This is the crux. Intuitively it seems obvious that there is a sense in which mental states and events are private, in that there is a way in which we have access to them which others cannot have. It may indeed be the case that for a large class of such items we are the ultimate authority about them; certainly, if we feel pain it is not up to others to maintain that we do not, although the situation is less clear in the case of more complex mental states. The reason why we have this kind of access to our mental states etc. is that they are ours. A mental state cannot be neutral as far as concerns whose it is. With the ownership of a mental state comes a kind of access to it that is not available to others. It is impossible, however, to define in such terms the sense of 'privacy' in which mental states are private without circularity. For we should in effect be saying that mental states are private in the sense that mental states are, i.e. in the sense that their owners have access to them by reason of that ownership in a way that is not open to others. Hence, while privacy may be a necessary condition of being mental it is not an independent sufficient condition, which enables us to decide simply by its means what is mental and what is not – or not without circularity.

The other proposed criterion of mentality, that of intentionality, suffers from other defects. The criterion stems originally, or does so at least in modern times, from Franz Brentano, who proposed as an account of the mind a classification of mental acts, all of which are or can be related to an object which has, as he put it, 'intentional inexistence'. By that he meant that the object in question is related internally to the act and exists simply in relation to it, whether or not there is anything *in rerum natura* corresponding to it. Every mental act intends, that is to say is directed to, such an object. Thus judgment intends a proposition, whether or not there is a fact to which the proposition corresponds. The proposition has an intentional inexistence in that it exists only in an internal relationship with the judgment. Brentano's own classification of mental acts is somewhat special and arguable, but in more recent times the general doctrine has been resuscitated by, among others, Roderick Chisholm, in order to provide a general criterion of mentality.[11]

Chisholm's account of intentionality tries to make a distinction be-

---

[11] R. Chisholm, 'Sentences about believing', *Proc. Arist. Soc.*, Vol. LVI, 1955/6, pp. 125ff., and *Perceiving* (Ithaca: Cornell U.P., 1957) and many other publications.

tween the intentional and the non-intentional in terms of the form of the propositions used to state the existence of the intentional state in question, e.g. in terms of the form of belief statements. As a consequence there has been an assimilation of the intentional to the intensional and of the non-intentional to the extensional. (A proposition is extensional if its truth depends solely on the truth or falsity of its constituents or possible constituents when these are combined by means of logical connectives definable in truth-functional terms; it is intensional if that is not the case.) There have also been attempts to specify a form of intensional sentence such that it and only it describes a state of affairs that can be characterized as mental. This 'linguistic' formulation of intentionality is unsuccessful if only because it is not sufficient; the criteria fit sentences which have nothing to do with the mental. If, for example, it is claimed that it is a mark of belief that someone can believe p whether or not p is the case, it can be pointed out that exactly the same is true of modal sentences, such as 'It is possible that p'.

It might be said in reply that, whether or not the linguistic criterion of intentionality is valid, it remains true that for a large range of mental states (particularly those that involve belief in some way) the general thesis of intentionality holds good; that is to say that it is possible to be in those states, specified in terms of directedness to an object, without such an object existing *in rerum natura*. There are two objections to that. First, it is not clear that intentional states, so specified, cannot be attributed to physical things or systems[12] (although that could be a crucial objection only if physical things cannot have mental properties, and if property or attribute dualism is a possible thesis they might have them). Second, it is not clear that all the states that we might intuitively think of as mental, e.g. pains and other sensations, are intentional in this way. If they are not, intentionality will not be a necessary condition of the mental, and may not be a sufficient condition either.

The intentionality of consciousness is a thesis which is common among phenomenologists such as Sartre and Merleau-Ponty. One way of interpreting the thesis would be to say that consciousness is always directed to an object as a such and such. Something like that thesis is to be encountered also in a paper by Richard Wollheim[13] under the gloss that all mental phenomena involve a thought (all mental phenomena involve consciousness of an object under the thought that . . .). But he has to admit that the thesis does not hold good of sensations. Thomas

[12] See Berent Enç, 'Intentional states of mechanical devices', *Mind*, Vol. XCI. 1982, pp. 161–82 for one of the latest essays in that direction.
[13] R. Wollheim, 'Thought and passion', *Proc. Arist. Soc.*, Vol. LXVIII, 1967/8, pp. 1–24.

Reid defined a sensation, in contradistinction to perception, as an act of mind that has no object other than itself; it therefore involves no concept of a distinct object.[14] By and large it is true that one cannot have a sensation without being conscious of having it (although even that is disputable for sensations that one is not attending to), but it would surely be misleading, if not downright false, to maintain that one cannot have a pain without having a concept of pain or without having the thought that one is in pain. It is more promising to hold that the form of consciousness involved in sensations like that of pain is, as one might put it, intransitive, as opposed to forms of consciousness that are transitive, where there is a distinct object to which the consciousness is directed. That, however, would go against the thesis that all forms of consciousness are intentional. There seems to be no route to a definition of the mental in terms of intentionality through the notion of consciousness.

Should one infer from the failure of these two criteria of the mental that there is no such thing? Such a conclusion might seem premature unless other candidates are examined, even if no other candidates seem to be in the offing. There are, however, good reasons for accepting the conclusion all the same. The notion of a criterion works perfectly well when one is concerned to specify an item within a given class or genus. (Indeed the traditional idea of definition *per genus et differentiam*, according to which a species is uniquely determined within a genus by a differentia is almost a paradigm of that conception, although it is not to be supposed that it always works in quite that way.) Where, however, there is no wider class or genus the notion of a criterion is not in place.[15] There does not seem to be a relevant wider class under which that of the mental falls, or not at any rate one that is substantive and not merely formal in the sense specified for formal concepts in Chapter 3. If the class of the mental consitutes an ultimate genus there is no hope of finding a criterion of the mental.

How then do we come to have a concept of the mental at all? That is an interesting question, and it is relevant that, if I am right, the Greeks had no such concept. That concept has emerged, as it were inductively, since their time, as a result of the kinds of reflection that Descartes engaged in. The fact that Descartes was wrong in thinking that whatever indubitability attaches to the 'I think' applies to the mental in general does not mean that he was wrong to direct his attention in the way that he did. What has emerged from that, although it may not have been

---

[14] T. Reid, *Essays on the Intellectual Powers* (London: Macmillan, 1941), I.1.

[15] See my *Theory of Knowledge*, p. 71, n. 18 for the same point made in terms of the notion of a category or widest genus.

explicitly there in Descartes himself, is the notion of consciousness, which manifests itself to us in various ways and in various modifications. Since Descartes, our concept of the mental has developed further, so that we can now allow that there can be unconscious mental states, if only in creatures which are in general conscious in a relatively full-blown sense. A creature that was conscious only in the sense of being sensitive might have what Leibniz called 'unconscious perceptions', in the sense that its perceptions involved a low degree of consciousness or attention, but it could not have unconscious mental states as we have come to understand them since at any rate Freud. To give an account of the mental must therefore involve an account of the varying and different ways in which consciousness manifests itself, and it would be wrong to think that the same account holds good over the whole range.

Can dualism be defended?

It is the general contemporary opposition to dualism that makes it desirable to put the question with which I am concerned in this section in the above form. We have seen that Cartesian dualism involves as an essential part a certain epistemological claim – that we have direct, indubitable access to our states of mind, or to, as we must now call them, our states of consciousness (for we surely do not have such access to unconscious mental states). There is no good reason to accept that claim in its generality, although it may hold good in certain special cases. For example, if I am doing something deliberately I can hardly be in doubt or error as to what I am doing, for the special reason that that is what is involved in the notion of deliberate action. Such incorrigible awareness of what one is involved in does not run through the whole gamut of the mental. Nothing that I have said, however, rules out a radical distinction between the bodily and the mental, a distinction that is, as we might put it, ontological and not epistemological in its basis. An ontological dualism need not presuppose an epistemological dualism of the sort that contemporary philosophers who claim to follow Wittgenstein find objectionable in Cartesian dualism (even if materialists find an ontological dualism objectionable too).

There are conscious beings and there are non-conscious beings. That is a dualism of sorts. But of course all the conscious beings that we know of in our everyday lives are also bodily. To say that is not in itself to rule out the possibility of disembodied or non-embodied conscious beings; it is merely to underline the obvious. It can also be argued, along the lines of Wittgenstein's so-called 'private language argument', that, if consciousness did not have expression in a public and therefore presumably bodily form in behaviour, we could have no concept of it. Once again, however, such an argument does not show, and cannot be used to show, that consciousness must always be embodied: all that it shows is that unless consciousness were *normally* embodied we would have no such concept. Exceptions to a norm are always possible, whether or not they actually occur. Strawson has argued, as I shall set out in Chapter 9, that we need the concept of a person as the owner of both states of consciousness and bodily characteristics, and this has led some philosophers to speak of a dualism of persons and bodies (some bodies not being owned in this sense by persons).[16] That amounts to the dualism of conscious beings and non-conscious beings that I mentioned earlier, with the proviso that on this view conscious beings must be persons (and that is certainly a disputable thesis).

I hold no brief for a dualism of minds and bodies as a dualism of substances. Such a dualism would be equivalent to a dualism of soul and body, and that introduces complications, in part theological, into which it would be pointless to enter here. It would in any case raise considerations of a quite different kind from those which have been our concern, e.g. the extent to which sense can be made of the idea of a soul with the individuality to be expected of a person but without the factors which the body normally makes possible – perception and action, for example. It remains true that, with regard to those embodied conscious beings which we meet in our everyday lives and which we exemplify ourselves, we can distinguish two radically different kinds of state that they may possess – conscious states and merely bodily states. The former are not reducible to the latter, to whatever extent they are dependent on them. The question to what extent conscious states *are* dependent on bodily ones seems a question of fact; it depends on whether one can explain all that there is about conscious beings by reference to a theory which invokes bodily occurrences only, or whether it is necessary to bring in mental events and states as well. It would be necessary to do the latter if it turned out that mental or conscious states play a causal role independent of bodily states. Even if that turned out not to be the case, a form of dualism might remain possible however. For the causality could work the other way, as is supposed by epiphenomenalists, even if the only role played by consciousness as a result were that its existence was a conceptually necessary condition of our attributing other things to the being in question. For example, it might be that we could not intelligibly

---

[16] See, e.g., P. Herbst, 'A critique of the materialist identity theory' in C. F. Presley (ed.), *The Identity Theory of Mind* (St Lucia: University of Queensland Press, 1967).

attribute action to something unless it was conscious, even if all the movements that it made could be explained causally in terms of other bodily events, and the consciousness was just a by-product of those.[17]

I have indicated various forms that dualism might take in order to set out the possibilities. Nevertheless, contemporary ideology has it that dualism is false (ludicrously so in many people's opinion). By and large it is not that consciousness and its modifications can be reduced to what is simply physical, but that any mental event or state is in fact a physical event or state. I say *by and large*, because one species of physicalism or materialism is so-called eliminative materialism.[18] On this view a recognition of the identity of the mental with the physical will in due course lead to the further recognition that the concept of the mental is otiose, and that that concept will simply drop out of people's thought. For the most part, however, the thesis put forward is that, despite our ordinary distinction between the mental and the physical, there is in fact only one thing and that is physical. (Note that logically it would have been just as possible to say 'and that is mental'; it might be argued that it is ideology, or what Putnam calls scientism, that dictates otherwise.) Such a thesis may be termed, in contradistinction to dualism, 'psychophysical monism'.

Psychophysical monism

Perhaps the initial stimulus towards psychophysical monism came from a paper by U. T. Place, but the view was taken up by J. J. C. Smart in a paper which has gained a greater notoriety.[19] Smart thought that Rylean 'behaviourism' was satisfactory for an account of most mental concepts, but not for that of sensation. He thought it was satisfactory to analyse most mental concepts, apart from that of sensation, in terms of dispositions to behave in certain ways; belief, for example, might be analysed in terms of a disposition to behave in ways appropriate to the object of the belief. For that reason his initial theory of psychophysical monism was restricted to sensations, which, he said, were identical with brain states (although, strictly speaking, as Smart sometimes recognized, it was the having of sensations that was identical with brain states).

---

[17] See my 'Causality and human behaviour', *Proc. Arist. Soc.*, Supp. Vol. XXXVIII, 1964, pp. 125–42.

[18] See R. Rorty, 'Mind–body identity, privacy and categories', *Review of Metaphysics*, Vol. XIX, 1965, pp. 25–54; also in S. N. Hampshire (ed.), *The Philosophy of Mind* (New York and London: Harper Row, 1966). See also his *Philosophy and the Mirror of Nature* (Oxford: Blackwell, 1980).

[19] J. J. C. Smart, 'Sensations and brain processes', *Philosophical Review*, Vol. LXVIII, 1959, pp. 141–56, but reprinted many times; U. T. Place, 'Is consciousness a brain process?', *Brit. J. Psych.*, Vol. XLVII, 1956, pp. 44–50, also reprinted many times.

Smart's only positive argument for such a thesis was that it led to theoretical economy and removed the need for 'nomological danglers', i.e. things which were exceptions to physical laws. Hence the main bulk of his paper was given up to attempts to meet possible objections, some of which centre on Leibniz's law – that things which, while putatively different, are in fact identical must have all their properties in common. It was in particular necessary to meet the objection that sensations have phenomenal properties, such as intensity, that brain-states do not have. Smart tried to meet that objection by invoking what he called a topic-neutral analysis of the ascription of sensations. He suggested that a sensation could be specified in terms of the idea of something going on in the person which is like what goes on when the person is in a situation itself specifiable in terms of purely physical conditions. For example, the occurrence of an orange after-image might be specified in terms of the idea of something occurring in the person in question which is like what goes on when, in good light etc., one sees an orange.

It was argued by Michael Bradley that the account involved circularity, and it has since been argued by A. J. Ayer that as it stands it is insufficient in any case, since there may be many things going on in me when I see an orange, not by any means all of which are relevant to the specification of an orange after-image.[20] One way to get round this difficulty would be to take seriously a point previously mentioned – that strictly speaking it is the *having* of an after-image or a pain that constitutes the mental event. In that case the so-called phenomenal properties of the after-image or sensation would not be properties of the mental event as such, but of its content. The mental event would be, for example, *having an orange after-image*, and the orangeness, the phenomenal aspect, would be taken into 'the constitutive property of the event', as Jaegwon Kim puts it,[21] so that it is not a property of the event as such, and we do not have to say, because of such phenomenal aspects, that mental events have properties that physical events do not. Having a sensation of a kind to be specified in terms of some phenomenal aspect might be the same event as having some neurological process going on in our bodies.

I say 'might be' because nothing in all this shows that it is so in fact. There are indeed problems about the individuation of events. Davidson has suggested that events are individuated in terms of their causal relations, so that two events are the same if they stand in the same causal

[20] A. J. Ayer, *The Central Questions of Philosophy* (Harmondsworth: Penguin, 1976), p. 128. Michael Bradley's criticism is to be found in his Critical Notice of Smart's *Philosophy and Scientific Realism* in *Aus. J. Phil.*, Vol XLII. 1964, pp. 262–83.

[21] J. Kim, 'Phenomenal properties, psychophysical laws and the identity theory', *Monist*, Vol. 56, 1972, pp. 177ff. esp. p. 183.

relations.[22] It would be a mistake, however, to think that that provides any help in the present case, since it would beg the question to assume that the having of a certain sensation stands in the same causal relations as the having of a certain neurological process going on. If one of these were in fact to cause the other there would be an asymmetry in their causal relations. In any case, as ought to be apparent, there is a good deal of obscurity about the notion of 'having' in the two cases. In any sense of 'having' that seems pertinent it is persons and the like that have these things, and how the notion of a person comes into the picture has not so far been made clear.

Similar points can be made with regard to David Armstrong's generalization of Smart's identity thesis to cover all mental concepts. His *A Materialist Theory of the Mind* is an attempt to bring all mental concepts within the scope of what is claimed by Smart for sensations. He does that by offering a definition of a mental state and then arguing that all mental concepts conform to that definition, because they can be analysed in its terms. Whether or not the analyses are successful is too complex a matter for discussion here. The basic definition of a mental state, however, is that it is a state of a person apt for bringing about certain forms of behaviour. That introduces the same problem about the role of the notion of a person as those which I mentioned above. If one tried to get round that problem by defining a mental state as, say, the state of an *animal* apt for bringing about certain forms of behaviour, the definition would have much in common with so-called functionalist accounts of the mind, as we shall see later. It would, however, also be subject to the same kinds of objection as those which Ayer, as we have seen, makes to Smart's topic-neutral analysis. There are surely states of animals which are apt for bringing about forms of behaviour which are not obviously mental states. If so, the definition is not sufficient.

A further point is that the kinds of theory so far noted do not distinguish between what have been called token identity and type identity. That is to say that it is not clear from these theories whether it is being claimed that every mental state of a given type is identical with a physical state of a certain type, or merely that every token mental state, every particular state, is identical with some token or particular physical state. The second thesis is much weaker than the first, since the first seems to imply the existence of psycho-physical laws connecting a type of mental state with the type of physical state in which it is realized; the second thesis implies nothing of the kind. Putnam, Fodor and others

[22] D. Davidson, 'The individuation of events' in his *Essays on Actions and Events* (Oxford: Clarendon Press, 1980), pp. 163ff.

have argued that it is implausible to suppose that types of mental states each have a single kind of realization;[23] for such mental states are to be found in very different kinds of creature. Hence any given type of mental state or event has a multiple realization, and the best that might be acceptable as an identity thesis is one that confines itself to token identities, i.e. one that says that every particular mental state or event is identical with some particular physical state or event, but not necessarily the same one on each occasion.

The trouble with such a thesis is that its particularity seems to rule out any *general* argument in its favour. Donald Davidson's paper 'Mental events'[24] is important in this respect in that it attempts to provide such a general argument – one that is in effect *a priori*. For that reason alone it deserves consideration. I shall consider only those aspects of it that are immediately relevant. The argument, briefly put, goes as follows. We ordinarily believe that physical events cause mental events (as in perception), and *vice versa* (as in intentional action). When there is causality the events related as cause and effect must fall under strict and universal causal laws. There are no psycho-physical laws. Hence, the events putatively so related must in fact be so under non-psychological, and therefore physical, descriptions. Hence, any event that is mental must have a physical description and must in that way be physical. Hence, every mental event must be identical with some physical event.

Nearly every step in this argument might be subjected to criticism, and there are other papers by Davidson which seek to short-circuit some such criticisms. The most crucial step in the argument, however, is undoubtedly the one that leads to the claim that there are no psycho-physical laws. In order to explain the notion of the mental Davidson invokes that criterion of the mental which appeals to intentionality, while admitting that it may not cover every case. On the other hand, he says that an event may be said to be mental if and only if it has a mental description, and that, as he admits, lets in as mental, even on the criterion mentioned, events that are *prima facie* not mental at all, e.g. a stellar collision to which certain physical predicates apply and which is simultaneous with Jones's noticing that a pencil starts to roll across his desk. For on that account the stellar collision has a mental description – that involved in what is said about Jones noticing something simultaneous with it. *Any* physical event may therefore have a mental

[23] H. Putnam, 'Psychological predicates' and 'Minds and machines' in his *Mind, Language and Reality: Philosophical Papers, Vol. 2* (Cambridge: C.U.P., 1975); J. Fodor and N. Block, 'What psychological states are not', *Philosophical Review*, Vol. LXXXI, 1972, pp. 159–81.
[24] D. Davidson, *Essays on Actions and Events*, pp. 207ff.

description and may for that reason be mental as well, if the account of what it is to be mental is accepted. Davidson seeks to avoid criticism on that score by saying that it is not necessary to exclude what is included only accidentally; what matters is that everything that is mental is included. One may have sneaking doubts about that reply. I mention it only because at a later stage of the argument Davidson relies upon mental 'events' to which the intentionality criterion explicitly applies, to the exclusion of some to which it does not apply. Yet, of course, if *any* event may have a mental description by that criterion of the mental, so have events which are mental by some other criterion. The question that remains is whether they must be mental *only* by the stated criterion if the argument is to work.

What I mean by that is the following. Davidson's argument for the impossibility of psycho-physical laws involves an appeal to another doctrine – that of the holism of the mental. It is claimed that it is impossible to identify beliefs independent of desires that the person in question may have, since in relation to a person's behaviour we can ascribe to him a certain belief only if we know something about his desires – and of course *vice versa*. The interpretation of his behaviour involves reference to a complex of both beliefs and desires, and we cannot distinguish from the person's general mental state the particular state which constitutes his belief, in separation from that which constitutes his wants. It might be argued that that is a problem about the *identification* of beliefs and not about the *nature* of beliefs, and it is perhaps for that reason that Colin McGinn has sought to supplement Davidson's argument by using Putnam's multiple realization thesis to argue for the thesis that mental states, such as beliefs, cannot be terms in natural laws because they do not involve natural kinds.[25]

Even so, as has been pointed out by Jaegwon Kim in the paper already referred to, it is hard to see that what Davidson has to say (and that remains true even when the thesis is supplemented by McGinn, as noted above) applies to all that is mental. It does not, for example, apply to sensations, and they, it might be noted, have the best claim among the candidates so far mentioned to be counted as mental *events*; beliefs are states, not events. Sensations of course have a mental description and count as mental even on the criterion that Davidson puts forward: they can be connected with beliefs and similar epistemic states. They seem, however, to be mental in a more direct way, and even if Davidson's argument about beliefs and the holism of the mental were acceptable it

[25]   C. McGinn, 'Mental states, natural kinds and psychophysical laws', *Proc. Arist. Soc.*, Supp. Vol. LII, 1978, pp. 195–220.

would say nothing for the impossibility of sensations being terms in psycho-physical laws that they may have a description connecting them with beliefs. Hence, Davidson has not shown that sensations cannot be terms in psycho-physical laws, and *a fortiori* he has not shown that causal connexions between sensations and physical states must hold merely under a physical description. With that the claim to have shown the token identity of all mental events with particular physical events collapses also. (It has to be admitted, however, that McGinn has adduced other considerations in order to extend the argument to cover all mental events. The additional considerations presuppose other doctrines which are too complex to enter upon here, but it is clear that the debate continues.)[26]

Davidson calls his position 'anomalous monism'; it is a monism because every mental event is identical with some physical event and there is thus at bottom only one kind of event; it is anomalous because there are no psycho-physical laws connecting types of mental event with types of physical event. He claims that his position differs all the same from materialism in that while he holds that all events are physical he denies that mental phenomena can be given purely physical explanations. Mental phenomena are supervenient upon physical phenomena; psychology has its own principles of explanation even if the mental cannot exist without the physical. If it seems hard to distinguish such a view from epiphenomenalism, according to which mental events are causal products of physical ones,[27] the difference lies in the thesis, which Davidson takes himself to have proved, that such causal relations cannot hold under a mental description. It is a subtle point, but it is a real one given Davidson's views about causality – that for A to cause B there must be a strict causal law under which A and B are to be subsumed *under some description*, although not necessarily under the immediately apparent one. Nevertheless, if I am right, the argument that Davidson himself puts forward for anomalous monism is invalid.

The sensations that are the telling counter-example to Davidson's thesis tell equally against functionalism, which is the currently fashionable thesis among materialists. Functionalism is in effect a form of token identity theory, although some of its ancestors have more to do with behaviourism. That is so, in that, while functionalists do not believe, as behaviourists have done, that mental states can be exhaustively

---

[26]   C. McGinn, ibid., and his 'Philosophical materialism', *Synthese*, Vol. 44, 1980, pp. 173–206. See also his *The Character of Mind* (Oxford: Clarendon Press, 1982), ch. 2.

[27]   Cf. T. Honderich, 'The argument for anomalous monism', *Analysis*, Vol. 42, 1982, pp. 59–64.

explained in terms of, or reduced to, forms of behaviour, they do believe that mental concepts are to be explained in terms of what mediates input and output, where the input is a matter of the stimulation that affects the nervous system and the output is a matter of the behaviour that results. A given mental state, such as a belief, is then supposed to be determined by its precise functional role in the economy which makes possible such links between input and output. Its nature is constituted simply by that functional role. It is what, to use Armstrong's terms again, is apt for bringing about such and such behaviour in such and such environmental circumstances. There are many mental concepts which cannot be construed in this sort of way. Can even belief be thought of simply as something that plays this kind of causal or functional role, particularly if belief presupposes knowledge, and if the input (perception) and the output (action) also involve knowledge in some way? These are, however, questions for the philosophy of mind rather than metaphysics.[28] What has generally been taken to be the strongest objection to functionalism is its inability to deal with sensations and similar aspects of experience.

When Armstrong came to deal with such things within the terms of reference of *his* theory, he did so by construing sensations as impressions of something or other. Pains, for example, were construed by him as impressions of something wrong with the body, although not necessarily under that description. The trouble is that, whatever else may be the case, we seem to be aware of pains as having a certain phenomenal quality and that is not allowed for in saying that pains are impressions of something wrong with the body. The objection that has been made to functionalism in the same context is that it might be possible for there to be the input and output which are characteristic of pain or other qualitative experiences, but with different experiences from the normal ones intervening or perhaps with no experiences at all. This issue has become known as the problem of inverted or absent qualia, where by 'qualia' are meant the qualitative or phenomenal aspects of experience. The suggestion is that the phenomenal character of one person's experiences might be different from that of others; it might indeed be different from that of his own experiences at other times. The notion of inverted qualia stems from that of so-called inverted spectra – the suggestion being that where one person's visual experience is, say, red, another's might come from the other end of the spectrum with all the

---

[28] See my 'Cognitive systems, "folk psychology" and knowledge', *Cognition*, Vol. 10, 1981, pp. 115–18, and some of the papers in my *Perception, Learning and the Self* (London: Routledge and Kegan Paul, 1983).

other spectral relationships between colour experiences inverted, even though the perceptual conditions and behaviour in conformity with those did not differ from case to case. If there were no experiences at all but the same behaviour in the same conditions it would be a case of 'absent qualia'. There may well be objections to putting the issue in these precise terms, but all that we need to note is the possibility of there being differences in the phenomenal character of experiences without there being a corresponding difference in the states postulated as fulfilling the functional role of mediating input and output. If that possibility exists, functionalism is not a sufficient theory of the mind.

Putnam's multiple realization theory provides a natural contrast between mental states defined in functional terms and the variable ways in which such functional states could be realized in physical or other ways. The possibility of inverted and absent qualia has, however, led him in recent times[29] to reject functionalism despite an earlier allegiance to a theory of that kind. There has been a running dispute between Ned Block and Sydney Shoemaker on the issue.[30] The arguments are too complex to make it worthwhile going into detail here, but Shoemaker's conclusion is that, if things are as they are with us, qualia are essential – but that this does not create a special difficulty for functionalism. Qualia are a feature of the realization of those functional states in connexion with which they arise; they play a part in the mental economy, however, by being causally related to states which *are* functionally definable even if they are not functionally definable themselves. Qualia are objects of awareness or belief and it is in that respect that they feature in explanations of behaviour. Pain, for example, is not a neutral experience as far as concerns our attitudes towards it; it involves wanting to get rid of it, not wanting it to persist, and so on, and it is in this respect that it is behaviourally relevant. Similar things may be said about perceptual experiences, including perhaps those of colour.

Shoemaker's gloss on these undoubted facts of the connexion in our mental life between our sensory experiences and our beliefs, awareness and wants is to suggest that that connexion must be causal – as indeed it must be if it is to conform to the spirit of functionalism. Hence an acceptance of his theory of qualia entails also an acceptance of a causal theory

[29] H. Putnam, *Reason, Truth and History*, ch. 4.
[30] J. Fodor and N. Block, 'What psychological states are not'; S. Shoemaker, 'Functionalism and qualia', *Philosophical Studies*, Vol 27, 1975, pp. 281–315; N. Block, 'Are absent qualia impossible?', *Philosophical Review*, Vol. LXXXIX, 1980, pp. 257–74; S. Shoemaker, 'Absent qualia are impossible – a reply to Block', *Philosophical Review*, Vol XC, 1981, pp. 581–99. Some of the papers are to be found in N. Block (ed.), *Readings in Philosophy of Psychology*, Vol. 1 (Cambridge, Mass: Harvard U.P., 1980).

of what it is for something to be an object of belief, awareness and wants. In effect, Shoemaker's theory is that sensations are, as they were for Smart, identical with the physical processes which are their realization, but that they necessarily stand in causal relations to other states, such as those of belief, which are variably realizable and are what they are because of the roles that they play in the general mental economy and not because of their realization. Smart's theory could be characterized as a type identity thesis in respect of sensations together with behaviourism with respect to other mental items. Shoemaker's theory on the other hand could be characterized as a type identity thesis with respect to sensations together with functionalism (and thus a token identity thesis) with respect to everything else, with the proviso that some functional states are causally dependent on sensations taken as mental and not as merely physical items. Whether that is a satisfactory thesis is a matter which must be left to the individual judgment.

None of these arguments, however, sustains psycho-physical monism in a clear form. Without positive arguments in its favour, it must remain a matter of ideology only; that is to say it is in effect a prejudice dictated by what Putnam calls 'scientism'. I do not mean by that to suggest that there are valid *a priori* arguments *against* the thesis. Saul Kripke has put forward an argument in favour of dualism which purports to be just that.[31] It is based upon his thesis that identity statements involving what he calls rigid designators (expressions which designate the same thing in all possible worlds) are necessarily true. He argues that expressions such as 'pain' are rigid designators, and that for this reason if there is an identity between pain and, say, the stimulation of C-fibres it must be a necessary identity. He then argues that there are grounds for thinking that it is nothing of the kind, since it seems that pain could have existed without physical conditions. Hence it cannot be an identity at all. The argument depends, however, on many presuppositions concerning such matters as the thesis about identity and rigid designators, the claim for the status of the expression 'pain', and the question whether the necessity to be attached to the identity if it exists has the same kind of modality as has the possibility of pain existing without physical conditions. Given those complications, the status of Kripke's argument remains uncertain, to say the least. And that is not surprising if, as I suggested earlier in this chapter, the dualism which is at least endemic to common sense is one of a general ontological kind, so that the physical and the mental constitute in fact ultimate but different kinds of thing. It

[31] S. Kripke, *Naming and Necessity* (Oxford: Blackwell, 1980), pp. 144ff.

is no good saying, as Smart once did, 'So much the worse for common sense'. We have to reckon with it as it is if we are to provide a complete account of reality as it presents itself to us.

At the same time it has to be recognized that the mental events and states that I have been talking about are events that take place in relation to people and animals and states that are states of people and animals. As I said earlier in the chapter, the only creatures of these kinds that we know have bodies. In the case of human beings at least, those bodies are the bodies of persons, they are owned by them, and to the extent that the mental states have to do with those bodies, and perhaps anyway, they are owned by persons. The states of merely physical things are not owned by anything in that sense. In the next chapter I shall discuss what persons are, and what their identity consists in, but it must be evident that many of the issues involved must derive from the fact that persons are not mere bodies. Much that I have been concerned with in this chapter is in one way or another prolegomena to the next.

9. Persons and personal identity

Persons and selves

Contemporary philosophical discussions concerning persons centre largely on the criteria of personal identity. Questions about the criteria of identity for Xs are, however, correlative with questions about the kind of concept that the concept of X is. It is the nature of a given thing which determines the sort of circumstances in which it is appropriate to speak of one thing of that kind being identical with what is putatively another. John Locke, who is to all intents and purposes the originator of our modern problems about personal identity raises those problems in the course of a chapter of his *Essay Concerning Human Understanding* (2.27) which is concerned with identity and diversity in general, and there is a sense in which he was quite right to do so. For personal identity does not raise problems distinct from those concerning identity in general unless there is something special about the concept of a person which brings that about.

I say that Locke is to all intents and purposes the originator of our modern problems about personal identity. Mediaeval philosophers were of course concerned with the problem of the principle of individuation, as we saw in Chapter 4, and in confronting the question of what ultimately distinguishes two things or two things of a certain kind they presumed certain answers to questions about the identity of those things. That included questions about human beings and about the soul. Moreover, in theological contexts, particularly in relation to the doctrine of the Trinity, the question was raised whether God, Christ and the Holy Spirit were one *persona* or not. That is sometimes put in terms of whether they constitute one person or not; but the Latin '*persona*', especially in scholastic usage, scarcely corresponds exactly to the term 'person' as used today. Indeed the primary meaning of '*persona*' in Latin is that of a mask, and thereby of a role or character presented. Today, 'person' is in most ways merely the singular of 'people', although there are special circumstances in which the ghost of its etymology still clings to it.

Locke often identifies persons with selves, or at all events draws no real distinction. The notion of a self has none of the suggestions that the etymology of 'person' provides. Nor does it really go with the legal sense of 'person' which Locke, as we shall see, also emphasizes, according to which anything with a legal responsibility and status, such as a company, can count as a person. The fact that the term 'person' can have this usage is one of the things that lead me to say that it is in many respects a term of art, in a way that the term 'self' is not (even if the latter is largely a philosophers' term only). For the term 'self' reflects something about us, as human beings – namely that we are self-conscious and that many aspects of the forms of consciousness we have are reflexive. Thus the question 'What are selves?' may have a greater metaphysical importance and depth than the question 'What are persons?', and there are aspects of the concept of a person which may divert us from the central metaphysical issues.

Even before Locke, Descartes had of course asked the question 'What am I?' in a context which connected thinking with self-consciousness – the context provided by the method of doubt, the '*Cogito*' and the thought that I have a clearer and more distinct idea of my mind or soul than I have of my body. (The identification of oneself with one's soul is of course another echo of mediaeval and Greek answers to the question of what constitutes the identity of people – answers which would make immortality and survival after death conceivable.) The context in which Descartes asked his question indicates that it is something like the notion of the self that he had in mind in asking 'What am I?'. There are clearly a great many possible answers to that question which would not be in point, given that context. If, however, I am right in saying that there is a connexion between questions about identity and questions about the concept of the thing under consideration, it should be clear that the answer to Descartes' question 'What am I?' ought to bring with it answers to the question of the criteria of identity for oneself. Although no detailed view can be abstracted from what Descartes has to say, the identity of a self must have something to do with the continuity of thought.

That consideration clearly concerned Locke too, for he explicitly raised the question of the relationship that exists between identity of man, of substance and of person. He thought it obvious that the identity of man presupposes identity of body, saying 'But yet I think nobody, could he be sure that the soul of Heliogabalus were in one of his hogs, would yet say that hog were a man or Heliogabalus.'[1] In connexion with

---

[1] J. Locke, *Essay Concerning Human Understanding*, II. 27.6; also in J. Perry (ed.), *Personal Identity* (Berkeley and Los Angeles: University of Californian Press, 1975), p. 37. The next reference is to *Essay* II.27.17 (Perry, p. 45).

the question about identity of substance in this context, Locke maintains a certain agnosticism as to what that substance might consist in; hence also an agnosticism on the question of whether only immaterial substances can think and on the question what, if that is so, the nature of a thinking substance can be and what its identity consists in. But Locke is clear that it is consciousness that makes the same person and that 'Self is that conscious thinking thing, whatever substance made up of (whether spiritual or material, simple or compounded, it matters not), which is sensible or conscious of pleasure and pain, capable of happiness or misery, and so is concerned for itself, as far as that consciousness extends.' In section 26 of the same chapter he says that 'Wherever a man finds what he calls himself, there, I think, another may say is the same person.' But he goes on to say immediately 'It [sc. 'person'] is a forensic term, appropriating actions and their merit; and so belongs only to intelligent agents capable of a law, and happiness, and misery.'

The implication of those last words and of what he goes on to say subsequently is that responsibility, rewards and punishments attach to a being only in so far as it can be thought to be a person, and that only in so far as it has consciousness of what it is held responsible for. Indeed one might take Locke as saying that decisions about the identity of a person follow from decisions about what we can hold responsible for what. That might, however, be an uncharitable interpretation. It is clearly an incorrect view in itself. Questions about responsibility must surely arise only when questions about identity have been answered, and not *vice versa*. Locke may nevertheless be right in suggesting that the application of the concept of a person brings with it the applicability of concepts having to do with responsibility and its consequences as regards reward and punishment. We could not have a full understanding of the concept of a person without understanding that. In the light of such a claim however, Locke's answer to the question of the criterion of personal identity seems very odd. For he says that the criterion of personal identity lies in the identity of consciousness, and in so far as we are concerned with the attribution of responsibility, and are therefore looking back to the past, that consciousness amounts simply to memory. His view seems therefore to entail that we can be legitimately held responsible only for what we can remember.

I shall return to the question of the criterion of personal identity later in this chapter. The point to note at the moment is that in Locke's view a person is a self which has self-consciousness at least to the extent that he is conscious of his past as his own. Locke does not, and cannot, say, however, what that self essentially is, except that he allows, like Descartes, that it must at least be a thinking thing, whatever else it is. Locke's willingness to contemplate the possibility that a single person might occupy different bodies indicates, however, that that 'whatever else' does not entail bodily identity. Locke's views met with criticisms from Bishop Joseph Butler, the most well known of which is that 'consciousness of personal identity presupposes, and therefore cannot constitute, personal identity any more than knowledge, in any other case, can constitute truth, which it presupposes'.[2] Butler goes on to emphasize that identity of persons is a strict identity and not the sort of identity which, as he says, we apply to a plant in virtue of the continuity of its life despite changes in its material nature. Identity of persons, he says, 'cannot subsist with diversity of substance'. Thomas Reid similarly insisted that 'The identity of a person is a perfect identity; wherever it is real, it admits of no degrees . . . because a person is a *monad*, and is not divisible into parts.'[3] Both philosophers insist that it is only on the presupposition of such identity in a person that we can go on, as Locke does, to consider what a person may be conscious of.

Whether or not these claims are acceptable they must be taken seriously – and I shall insist on that and emphasize it as I go on. Once again, however, the point has a greater reality in connexion with the self than it does in connexion with persons. In ordinary language we do, after all, say such things as 'He is not the person that he was', and we speak of the development or growth of a person, of becoming a person, and so on. None of these ways of speaking is compatible with what Butler and Reid say about the perfect identity of persons. When, however, one thinks back over one's own past (and, as I shall mention later, similar considerations arise from the contemplation of one's possible future) one inevitably thinks of all the changes that have taken place as changes *in relation to oneself*. Self-consciousness presupposes an identical self, however that is to be analysed. It is that fact which underlies the claims for the perfect identity of the self. It is less than clear that the same is true of the concept of a person, except to the extent that in speaking of a person one is speaking of a self.

Hume was sceptical of much of this. He says, 'There are some philosophers, who imagine we are every moment intimately conscious of what we call our *self*; that we feel its existence and its continuance in existence; and are certain, beyond the evidence of a demonstration, both of its perfect identity and simplicity'.[4] (The identity of a thing constitutes its unity and singleness over time; by 'simplicity' Hume means

---

[2] Perry, p. 100.   [3] Ibid., p. 111.
[4] D. Hume, *Treatise of Human Nature*, I.iv.6 (Perry, p. 161). The subsequent quotations are from the same section.

its unity and singleness at one time.) Hume goes on to say that such philosophers in effect ignore the nature of the experience which they adduce as evidence for their view – or at least they do if their experiences are anything like Hume's. For, he claims, in his own case he can discover no impression of the self, or indeed anything apart from particular impressions or perceptions, each of which may exist separately in such a way that they 'have no need of any thing to support their existence'. 'I never can catch *myself* at any time without a perception, and never can observe any thing but the perception.' There are, therefore, nothing but bundles or collections of perceptions and 'the mind is a kind of theatre, where several perceptions successively make their appearance'. For this reason there is, according to Hume, nothing which merits the application of the notions of simplicity and identity, however much the relations that exist between the perceptions in a bundle – those of constancy, coherence and causality – make us imagine that there is such identity and simplicity. Personal identity is thus a kind of fiction which, because of the imagination, we have a natural propensity to ascribe to ourselves, but to which nothing corresponds in reality; and the same applies to simplicity.

There is a certain oddity in Hume's view, which emerges in its very expression, since he has to use personal pronouns and the like in order to speak of the perceptions and their relationships. (I shall return to that point in the next section in connexion with Strawson.) There can be no doubt, however, that Hume is led to his somewhat eccentric conclusions by the premises of his argument – particularly, as he was to make clear in the Appendix to the *Treatise*, the two principles that he found himself unable to make consistent: that all our distinct perceptions are distinct existences, and that the mind never perceives any real connexion among distinct existences. Neither of these principles is obviously true, to say the least, and the former has the paradoxical consequence, as Hume admits, that a perception can exist by itself apart from any bundle and therefore unowned by any self.

The paradoxical nature of Hume's views on the self does not make the views against which he was reacting right. Nevertheless, Kant was to insist that, as he put it, the 'I think' can accompany all our representations. Every perception or, in Kantian terms, every intuition must be brought under concepts in judgment, and that is an exercise, not only in consciousness, but also in self-consciousness. For in doing this I must be aware, at least in principle, that the representations that I have and the judgments that I make are mine. Representations or perceptions cannot exist unowned or be in any way neutral as to whose they are. Hence, if

Hume could not find an impression of the self, he was not justified in concluding that there was no such thing; he was in effect looking in the wrong place. He assumed that perceptions constituted distinct existences, and did not see that if I am to be aware of any such thing it has to be pre-supposed that it is mine. The 'I' is therefore presupposed in the very having of a perception, so that consciousness with respect to perceptions is *ipso facto* self-consciousness with respect to the 'I'. If one fails to recognize that fact, as in effect Hume did in asserting the distinct exist-ence of every perception, it is not surprising that one finds it impossible to discover the self in experience; for one has blinded oneself to its dis-covery. I shall call this point about the presupposition of the 'I' the 'Kantian point'.[5] It is fundamental to the notion of a self.

The 'Kantian point' does not, however, entail Reid's thesis that the self is a monad and absolutely simple in that way. In the 'Paralogisms' of the *Critique of Pure Reason* Kant rejects the idea that the self can be regarded as a substance and therefore rejects also the idea that it can be thought of as simple in the way that Leibniz's simple substances – monads – were supposed to be. Hence the 'Kantian point' was certainly not regarded by Kant himself as entailing the idea of the self as a simple substance. That is one reason why I said earlier merely that we should take seriously the claims made by Butler and Reid that the identity of persons is a perfect identity (perfect identity going together in this respect with perfect sim-plicity, since what is perfectly simple leaves no room for change). I did not say that we should regard such claims as literally true. The 'Kantian point' seems entirely consistent with the thought that there may be radical changes in the person whose 'I think' it is. It is not, however, consistent with the suggestion that it may be a merely contingent matter whose thoughts and perceptions those which I am aware of may be; they might be someone else's. That suggestion is at least implicit in Hume's account of the issues. It is also worth noting that, although it follows as a truism from the 'Kantian point' that the experiences which are mine are those to which my consciousness can (not necessarily *does*) reach, it does not amount to the Lockean thesis that the identity of a person is commen-surate with the extent to which his consciousness reaches. For the Kantian claim is about *experiences* or *representations* and it is about what *can* be, not what *is*.

In what I have had to say so far, I have continually emphasized that our real concern should be with the self, the 'I'. That implies an essen-tially first-person point of view in our approach to the issues. It is

5   I owe this way of putting it to Ruby Meager.

reasonable to expect, however, that there should be some connexion between this and a third-person view of those issues, and that it will be at this point that the notion of a person will become pertinent again. After all, I am a person and so are other selves (unless we are to allow that animals, which are not persons, are also selves in some cases, and while that is an arguable point it would be foolish to be dogmatic about it, given what chimpanzees, for example, have in common with human beings). In any case we need some account of the framework within which such talk of selves is intelligible. The Strawsonian account of the concept of a person claims to provide that, among other things.

The Strawsonian concept of a person

Strawson is the philosopher who in modern times has perhaps laid the greatest weight on the notion of a person, and in a way that, on his own admission, makes considerations about personal identity secondary. I said earlier that considerations about the criteria of identity for a certain kind of thing and considerations about the concept of that kind of thing go hand in hand. There has, however, been a tendency, even in Locke, to take the concept of a person for granted and to go straight to the question of the criteria of personal identity. I have already suggested that there is a certain artificiality about that procedure, since the term 'person' is, in these contexts, something of a term of art. In his account of persons Strawson does not really present a thesis about what we mean when we talk of people. He says nothing, for example, about something which must surely be essential to the notion of a person as we ordinarily employ it – the idea of personal relations. Rather, he invokes the notion of a person as a largely technical concept, which we need both to invoke and to understand if we are to appreciate issues involved in the mind–body problem and the framework in which we think of ourselves and others.

The reference to the mind–body problem is clear from the fact that Strawson sets out his conception of the matter in conscious opposition to two other points of view – first that of Cartesian dualism and second that of what he calls the 'no ownership theory'. The first view, on his construal of it, maintains that states of consciousness are ascribable only to, and thus owned only by, minds, while bodily characteristics have a similar relation to something different – the body. The second view maintains that states of consciousness do not belong to anything, although they may be causally dependent on the body. We saw something of the first view in Chapter 8; I shall not discuss further whether it really is Descartes' view. Strawson seems to find it difficult to find a definite source for the second view, suggesting that it might have been held by Wittgenstein at one time and by Schlick. In fact, a more plausible candidate is Hume, except that he did not quite put the issue in Strawson's terms.

That is because Strawson associates the two views with certain answers to two questions: (1) Why are one's states of consciousness ascribed to anything at all? and (2) Why are they ascribed to the very same thing as certain corporeal characteristics, a certain physical situation, etc.?[6] These questions in turn are said to arise from a consideration of the ways in which we talk of ourselves. It is clear nevertheless that the two questions are directly related to the two views that I have mentioned, since a rejection of the terms of reference of the first question leads to the 'no ownership theory', and a rejection of the terms of reference of the second leads to Cartesian dualism, considered as a thesis that there are two substances to which quite different characteristics are ascribable.

Strawson's eventual conclusion is that both of these theories are unacceptable. States of consciousness must be ascribed to something, and that something has physical characteristics also. That leads him to the concept of a person as something presupposed by both physical or corporeal states and states of consciousness; it is in that sense 'logically primitive', i.e. not reducible either to something mental or to something physical, since it is presupposed by both. There is, however, a long argument before that conclusion is reached, the first stage of which is to argue that answers to the questions asked are not provided by any account of the unique role played by the person's body in relation to his experience. I shall not discuss that part of the argument; its conclusion can in any case be accepted. The next stage deals with the 'no ownership' view, which, as we have seen, rejects the terms of reference of the first question. Strawson dismisses that view by arguing that it is incoherent.

If I am right in what I said earlier about Hume being a proponent of this view, it should be no surprise that it is claimed that the view is incoherent, since we have already noted the paradoxical conclusion to which Hume's views lead. Strawson's own argument is directed against an interpretation of the 'no ownership theory' which takes the theorist to hold, as is indeed likely, that the states of consciousness or experiences which take place are causally dependent on the states of the body and that that is all there is to the thought that they are had by or owned by anything. I say it is likely that the 'no ownership theorist' will hold that,

6   P. F. Strawson, *Individuals* (London: Methuen, 1959), p. 90.

although it is less than clear that Hume himself did so. He contented himself with the thesis that all that there is to the thought of states of consciousness being owned is their belonging to a bundle of such things. However, questions about the identification of the bundle are bound to arise and it is natural to invoke physical facts to provide that identification, such as its dependence on a given body. For that reason philosophers in more recent times who have wanted to defend something like a Humean point of view (e.g. A. J. Ayer, as we shall see later, and also perhaps Derek Parfit) have generally wanted to say that what we mean by 'having states of consciousness' is that such states belong to a set which is causally dependent on a certain body.

It is in those terms, then, that Strawson construes the thesis in order to criticize it, taking it that what the 'no ownership theorist' wants to say is that by 'having experiences' is meant that such experiences are uniquely dependent on a certain body and that this is a contingent matter. (For exegetical reasons he speaks of that dependence in terms of experiences being had$_1$ by the body, as opposed to the relationship which might be taken to hold between the experiences and an ego and which the 'no ownership theorist' rejects; in that case Strawson speaks of the experiences being had$_2$ by the ego. This is not a point that need cause us much concern.) Strawson says that when the 'no ownership theorist' wants to state the contingent fact of the relationship between experiences and the state of a certain body he has to say something like 'All *my* experiences are had$_1$ by (i.e. uniquely dependent on the state of) body B'.[7] 'Any attempt to eliminate the "*my*" or any expression with similar possessive force, would yield something that was not a contingent fact at all.' It is just false that *all* experiences are causally dependent on the state of a single body. On the other hand, to say that the experiences in question are those that are dependent on body B renders the claim that *those* experiences are dependent on body B analytic and not the expression of a contingent fact at all.

In other words, the identification of experiences depends on the identification of their owner; experiences must be owned. It might be argued that there are two separate points at issue here, one about identification of experiences and the other about the nature of experiences. Strawson indeed goes on to speak of experiences owing their identity as particulars to their owners, and has been taken to task by Don Locke for conflating points about identification and points about identity.[8] The crucial point, however, is about the status of experiences – what I have

[7]   P. F. Strawson, *Individuals*, pp. 96–7.
[8]   D. Locke, *Myself and Others* (Oxford: Clarendon Press, 1968), ch. 7.

already called the 'Kantian point'. It is of course possible to identify experiences in ways other than by reference to their owner, e.g. by reference to some particular quality that they have. In the context, however, that is irrelevant. The question at stake is how one can state the contingent relationship between certain experiences and a certain body in a general way without invoking the owner of the experiences. In that sense Strawson's point is well taken.

It has been claimed by Ayer that it is nothing of the kind and that the apparent validity of Strawson's argument depends simply on the way in which it is formulated.[9] Ayer says, 'The contingent proposition is that if my body is in such and such a state, then an experience of such and such a kind results; the analytic proposition is that if an experience is causally dependent in this way on the state of my body, then the experience is mine. But now it is obvious that these propositions are distinct; so that there is no inconsistency in holding that one is contingent and the other not.' He goes on to say that a person can be identified by his body and the body can be identified by its physical properties and spatio-temporal location, and he adds, 'as a contingent fact there are certain experiences which are causally connected with it; and these particular experiences can then be identified as the experiences of the person whose body it is'.

Whatever may be thought of Ayer's view on the identification of a person, it is certainly true that as a matter of fact there *are* certain experiences causally connected with any given body (those which, in Strawson's terms, are owned by the person whose body it is). But there may well be other experiences (those which, in Strawson's terms, are owned by others) which are also causally connected with that same body. Other people's experiences may be causally connected with the state of my body. It might be replied that if that is so the experiences are not causally connected with my body in the same way as *my* experiences are causally connected with my body. But now the question arises just what that way is, and just what the force of the words 'in this way' is in the first of the passages that I quoted from Ayer. It does seem that if I am to distinguish from among the experiences that are causally dependent on the state of my body those which are mine, there is no way of doing so which does not beg the question as to whose they are. That is what we should expect if experiences cannot be neutral as far as their ownership is concerned. The 'no ownership theory' remains incoherent.[10]

[9] A. J. Ayer, *The Concept of a Person* (London: Macmillan, 1963), p. 116.
[10] Something like these criticisms of Ayer are to be found in G. Madell, *The Identity of the Self* (Edinburgh: Edinburgh U.P., 1981), pp. 61–2; see also his 'Ayer on personal identity', *Philosophy*, Vol. 51, 1976, pp. 47–55.

Strawson's rejection of the Cartesian view is more complicated, and is perhaps made unnecessarily complicated by being introduced as a further comment on the 'no ownership theory'. He first puts forward (p. 99), as a simple but central thought, the proposition that 'it is a necessary condition of one's ascribing states of consciousness, experiences, to oneself, in the way one does, that one should also ascribe them, or be prepared to ascribe them, to others who are not oneself'. This is qualified by a long and crucial footnote, which in effect admits that *being prepared to* ascribe such states of consciousness to others is all that could justifiably be claimed as a necessary condition of the possibility of self-ascription of this kind. This, however, is then qualified in turn by the observation that the distinction between 'the lesser and the larger claim' may well appear idle and possibly senseless given that we are concerned not with a single predicate but with 'the whole of an enormous class of predicates such that the applicability of those predicates or their negations defines a major logical type or category of individuals'.

It is not easy to assess such a qualification. Strawson seems to suggest that it would be otiose to speak of someone being prepared to ascribe a state of consciousness to another if he did not in general ascribe states of consciousness to others. It might well be otiose, but it remains the case that all that the initial argument sustains, strictly speaking, is that if I ascribe states of consciousness to myself it must be logically possible for other-ascriptions to be made. For, as Strawson himself says at the end of his footnote, 'The main point here is a purely logical one: the idea of a predicate is correlative with that of a *range* of distinguishable individuals of which the predicate can be significantly, though not necessarily truly, affirmed.' If, therefore, I ascribe states of consciousness to myself, it must *make sense* to speak of ascribing them to others, but that is all.[11]

What we have covered so far, however, is only part of the argument against the Cartesian. The argument up to this point does not show that states of consciousness cannot be ascribed to Cartesian egos. Strawson gives a brief résumé of the rest of the argument on p. 100, although he adds that it is in fact 'too short'. It reads: 'One can ascribe states of consciousness to oneself only if one can ascribe them to others. One can ascribe them to others only if one can identify other subjects of experience. And one cannot identify others if one can identify them *only*

---

[11] See my *Theory of Knowledge* (London and Basingstoke: Macmillan, 1971), pp. 236ff., and the other references given there. There may be other, 'Wittgensteinian', considerations about the general conditions for the intelligibility of the ascription of states of consciousness which have a bearing on the issue, and it may be that Strawson is hinting at these; but they are not strictly speaking part of his argument.

as subjects of experience, possessors of states of consciousness.' It seems clear that the 'can' in the second and third sentences of this argument-schema must be taken as meaning 'can in fact', and, given what I have already said about the principle stated in the first sentence, the 'can' in that first sentence must mean 'can in principle'. Thus the argument must be invalid because of equivocation.

Suppose we waive that objection. The subsequent filling-out of the final steps of the argument is complicated. It toys, first, with the thought that one might identify others simply as subjects of experience related to identifiable bodies in the way that I am related to mine. Strawson's reply draws attention to the use that 'I' and 'mine' receive in that way of putting things. It is this which leads him directly to the idea that there is, both in our thought about ourselves and in our thought about others, a reference to something which owns both states of consciousness and bodily characteristics, and which thus constitutes a distinct category which Strawson calls by the name 'person'. Moreover, it is a category which is not reducible to those of states of consciousness or of bodies, since it is presupposed by both of these in the course of the argument. It is in that sense (and in that sense alone, it might be added) logically primitive.

This conclusion is subsequently supported by the consideration that if it is a condition of self-ascription that we must be able to ascribe states of consciousness (and anything else that is predicable of persons and only persons – what Strawson calls 'P-predicates') to other persons, then there must be a way of identifying those persons. Since persons are, on this understanding, individuals to which both states of consciousness and corporeal characteristics are ascribable, there must be a way of telling, at least in principle, with respect to such individuals whether they do in fact have such features. It cannot always be the case that the relation between what we observe and the possession of such features is that what we observe is merely a *sign* of the possession by the individual of a state of consciousness. For there would be no basis for thinking that the sign-significate relation holds except in our own case. But according to the argument it was supposed to be a condition of the recognition of it in our own case that we take it to hold good in the case of others. Strawson puts this by saying that there must be logically adequate criteria for the ascription of P-predicates.

I shall not discuss that part of the argument, complex as it is.[12] There is a sense in which the claim that the concept of a person is logically

---

[12] See again my *Theory of Knowledge*, pp. 238ff.

primitive is independent of it, in that such a claim simply reflects the 'Kantian point'. Moreover, much of this part of the argument depends on the earlier stages of it, which we have seen reason to question. While the general argument does not, therefore, provide an adequate refutation of Cartesianism (which is not to say that a refutation cannot be provided), it does reveal that in thinking about ourselves and others we need to have the idea of something that owns both states of consciousness and corporeal characteristics. It is that idea which Strawson refers to as the concept of a person. That usage of 'person' is to some extent technical, and whether it corresponds exactly to the ordinary usage of 'person', if there is such a thing, is arguable. It has been pointed out, by way of criticism, that, according to the criteria offered, animals, or some of them, are persons, and that may offend against the intuitions of some people. It is also arguable whether persons must be embodied, as Strawson claims (though with qualifications). Strawson does allow, in *Individuals*, the possibility of disembodied persons, but only as secondary cases; he also toys with the idea of a dead person – a corpse. There does, however, seem to be a difference between these two cases, secondary or not. To the extent that we can make sense of the idea of a disembodied person, we are surely talking of something that still has or 'owns' states of consciousness; but in the case of a dead person it is difficult to think of anything but the body as having the corporeal characteristics that remain. There is nothing else to 'own' them.

No doubt, on Strawson's concept of a person as well as on others, embodied persons are the norm; otherwise there would not be the public criteria for the ascription of the concept that Wittgenstein insisted on as a condition of the intelligibility of whatever is under consideration. However, in the case which has been so much discussed by, and in connexion with, Wittgenstein – that of pain – the criteria for the concept of pain are constituted by forms of behaviour which are natural expressions of pain. It is important that it is *behaviour* which constitutes the criterion, not just *any* bodily characteristic. Analogously, the criteria for the concept of a person must lie in *behaviour*. Corpses manifest no behaviour; hence if we speak of them as dead persons it is in a recognizably secondary sense of 'person'. Anything that does behave must be either conscious or potentially so. Hence, in a certain sense, the notion of consciousness looms larger in the conception that Strawson is trying to elucidate than does the notion of bodily characteristics as such. It thus begins to look as if the term 'self' is a more suitable term for what he is trying to elucidate than the term 'person'. At all events the precedent for his conception is to be found in the Kantian idea of the 'I think' being able to accompany all our representations, with the possible addition that it is also able to accompany all our behaviour. With that proviso we are back at the 'Kantian point'.[13]

If in the light of all this we return to the two questions with which Strawson began his discussion, the situation seems to be as follows. First, why are one's states of consciousness ascribed to anything at all? The answer is, in effect, because they are *one's*. States of consciousness cannot go unowned, and they are not neutral as regards whose they are. In this respect Strawson's refutation of the 'no ownership' thesis seems cogent and compelling. Second, why are they (*sc.* one's states of consciousness) ascribed to the very same thing as certain corporeal characteristics, a certain physical situation, etc? Well, it is not clear that they must be so ascribable, though I do not mean by that to suggest that it is in any sense necessary that they should be ascribed to different things, as Cartesianism implies. To the extent that they *are* ascribed to the same thing it is because states of consciousness are expressed in behaviour for which a body with corporeal characteristics etc. is necessary. It might indeed be argued, as I have suggested, that that is the normal case which provides the criteria of intelligibility for speaking of states of consciousness at all. That, however, does not imply that it is *necessary* that anything which has states of consciousness must have ascribed to it corporeal characteristics etc., any more than the thesis that the criteria for the intelligibility of talking of pain lie in the fact that pain is naturally and normally expressed in certain forms of behaviour implies that wherever there is pain there must be such expressions.

Hence the answer to Strawson's second question is first to query its terms of reference and then to add that in those cases where states of consciousness *are* ascribed to the very same thing as certain corporeal characteristics etc., the thing that owns the states of consciousness, the self or 'I' in question, may very well be embodied and normally is so. It is in effect the 'Kantian point' which entails the rejection of Cartesianism, since the 'I' which is involved in the 'I think' is not to be identified with the mind or soul. Rather, we ascribe a mind or soul to something to the extent that the 'I think' applies to it. It is a further and questionable step to say that that is what a person is.

[13]   Indeed Strawson admits this to some extent when he says on p. 134 that, by comparison with Hume, Kant – along with Wittgenstein – 'had the better insight' even if his doctrine 'is not as clear as one would wish'. See also Strawson's *The Bounds of Sense* (London: Methuen, 1968).

What are persons?

In the light of what has already been said it may seem either that there is little further to add in answer to this question or that there is no clear and determinate answer to it because of the indeterminacy of the concept. However, 'person' is, as I said earlier, the singular of 'people', and that makes it quite legitimate to ask, for example, what are the implications of speaking of people rather than of, say, human beings. People normally belong to the species *man* and are therefore normally human beings, but to speak of people is to say more than that they have that biological classification. People think, have experiences, engage in many forms of behaviour, stand or are capable of standing in relations to other people (relations which we call 'personal'), and in other relations to other kinds of thing; they may be the objects of ethical judgments and the subjects that make such judgments, they may be held responsible for things and be subject to reward and punishment in consequence, as Locke pointed out, and they make take aesthetic interests in a variety of things – and so on.

To list such factors is not in itself to say what people are, but any account of persons must be consistent with such possibilities. It is also important not to confuse the suggestion which is implicit in what Locke says in explanation of his claim that 'person' is a forensic term (i.e. that the term appropriates 'actions and their merit; and so belongs only to intelligent agents capable of a law, and happiness, and misery') with the suggestion that deciding what counts as a person or which person is identical with which is a matter of deciding who is responsible for what. David Wiggins has spoken eloquently against that latter idea,[14] and rightly. Decisions about who is responsible for what depend upon prior decisions about the identities of persons. Wiggins seems to think, however, that the natural antithesis to the view which he rejects is that 'by *person* we mean a sort of animal'.[15] It is indeed true that all the persons that I know are a sort of animal, but that is simply an autobiographical remark. If God, for example, is a person, Wiggins' proposition is false. But a being for which questions of responsibility do not arise is dubiously a person, to say the very least. In invoking the concept of a person we invoke that kind of consideration too and the one cannot stand without the other.

The title of one of Bernard Williams' papers is 'Are persons

[14] D. Wiggins, 'Locke, Butler and the stream of consciousness: and Men as a natural kind', in Amelie Rorty (ed.), *The Identities of Persons* (Berkeley and Los Angeles: University of California Press, 1976).

[15] Ibid., p. 167.

bodies?'[16] He appears to want to answer 'Yes' to that question and does so by way of criticism of Strawson. It is in many ways a curious question. It is not the same as the question 'Are persons bodily?'. With respect to this latter question I have already had something to say, even if briefly; the answer seems to me to be 'Normally they are bodily, but that is not necessarily universally so'. Williams' own answer is consistent with the thesis of an earlier paper – 'Personal identity and individuation' – which I shall consider in the next section.[17] In that paper he argues for the very strong thesis that bodily identity is a necessary condition of personal identity. If that thesis were sustained it might well seem right to say that persons are bodies since the identity conditions for persons would presuppose those for a certain class of bodies. But the concept of a person is certainly not the same as the concept of a certain kind of body. Indeed, it might be argued that considerations about the body are only marginally relevant to considerations about persons, even in the case of those persons who are certainly embodied. That would be true even if the considerations that *are* relevant could not have any application were there not a body.

All the people we know in everyday life are human beings; they all have bodies. It is not, however, these things which are important for the question of what makes them people, but the sort of things that I mentioned earlier, e.g. the possibility of their standing in certain relations to others. Many of the characteristics which I mentioned in this connexion would have no place if people did not have bodies. Equally, however, they would have no place were the people in question not in some sense selves – conscious, and to some extent self-conscious, beings. It is on these kinds of consideration that the most interesting metaphysical issues in this area turn. Indeed, any view of persons which implies that the factors which we normally take to follow from their being selves (e.g. those about the possibility of personal and other relations) have no relevance to what a person is must be wrong.

But these are cautionary words only. Except in so far as 'person' is the singular of 'people' the term 'person' remains, as I have said, something of a term of art. It is important to be aware of that in going through the issues about personal identity which have preoccupied many philosophers working in this area in recent times.

The criteria of identity for persons

As we have seen, the source of questions concerning the criteria of identity for persons is, as much as anything, Locke's treatment of personal

[16] In B. A. O. Williams, *Problems of the Self* (Cambridge: C.U.P., 1973).
[17] Also in *Problems of the Self*.

identity in his *Essay* (2. 27). He finds the criterion of personal identity in consciousness. Consciousness, he says, makes the same person. 'That with which the consciousness of this present thinking thing can join itself, makes the same person, and is one self with it, and with nothing else.'[18] Since Locke sees the most typical identity question as backward looking in the sense that it asks something of the form 'Is this . . . the same . . . as the one which was . . . ?', the form of consciousness which is directly relevant to personal identity seems to be memory. And so Locke specifies it. (It is perhaps worth noting, however, that it *is* possible to raise forward looking identity questions – 'Shall I in ten years time be the same person as I am now?' or perhaps even 'Am I now the same person as I shall be in ten years time?' – although those questions, as I have formulated them, seem to admit of rather easy answers.)[19]

Criticisms were soon made of Locke's view, construed as saying that if and only if X remembers being Y or having the experiences that Y had X and Y are the same person. I have already mentioned Bishop Butler's point that memory presupposes personal identity and cannot therefore constitute it. He actually says that it is consciousness of personal identity that presupposes personal identity, but it is clear that I cannot properly be said to have remembered having some experience unless it is I who had that experience. I can of course think that I remember having it without that being true; I can have putative memories without my having had the experiences in question. Veridical memory does, however, presuppose personal identity, and in that sense Butler is right (whatever may be said about the parallel that Butler sees with knowledge and truth – 'consciousness of personal identity presupposes, and therefore cannot constitute, personal identity, any more than knowledge, in any other case, can constitute truth, which it presupposes' – a point which Wiggins makes something of).[20]

Reid makes analogous and additional points in Chapter 6 of the third essay in his *Essays on the Intellectual Powers of Man*[21] and argues that Locke confuses personal identity with the evidence that we have of our personal identity. Reid's best-known criticism is that on Locke's view 'a man may be, and at the same time not be, the person that did a particular action'. He argues for this on the basis of an example according to which

[18] Perry, p. 45.
[19] Anglo-Saxon discussions of personal identity have on the whole been backward looking. Heidegger's formula in *Sein und Zeit*, 42, 'das Seiende, dem es in seinem Sein um dieses selbst geht' (usually translated 'a being such that in its being its being is in question') suggests a different preoccupation and perhaps a differently orientated view of the self. But see also Hidé Ishiguro, 'A person's future and the mind-body problem' in W. Mays and S. C. Brown (eds). *Linguistic Analysis and Phenomenology* (London: Macmillan, 1972), pp. 163–78.
[20] D. Wiggins, 'Locke, Butler and the stream of consciousness'.   [21] In Perry, pp. 113ff.

a boy who was flogged at school for stealing apples might become a brave officer who took a standard from the enemy in his first campaign, and then become a general in advanced life. Reid posits that the general can remember taking the standard but not being flogged for stealing apples, but when he took the standard he could remember that. According to Locke's criterion, therefore, the general is the same person as the officer who took the standard, the officer is the same person as the boy who was flogged, but the general is not the same person as the boy. 'Therefore the general is, and at the same time is not, the same person with him who was flogged at school.'[22] The point is well taken, although Reid does not deny that 'The conviction which every man has of his identity, as far back as his memory reaches, needs no aid of philosophy to strengthen it; and no philosophy can weaken it, without first producing some degree of insanity.'[23] That, however, is not a point about the criteria of identity; it is one about our beliefs about our identity, and the grounds for them. Reid in fact thinks that personal identity itself is a perfect identity; it is the identity of a monad and is not further analysable.

Reid admits, however, that this conclusion is derivable solely from a consideration of our own identity. When it comes to the identity of others we proceed on a different basis, and our grounds for judgments of identity are more or less those which we rely on in arriving at judgments concerning the identity of bodies, where the identity, he says, is not perfect. (Hume, as we saw earlier, thought that the last was true of personal identity taken generally.) In this we are presented with a dichotomy between first- and third-person approaches to personal identity, and that distinction will emerge even more sharply as we proceed.

Before going on, however, it will be as well to discuss briefly what is meant by the notion of a criterion in this context. The notion of a criterion has received a great deal of attention in recent times, largely because of some remarks of Wittgenstein – especially his remark that an 'inner process' stands in need of outward criteria. I shall not discuss those issues in particular here,[24] although some discussions of the criteria of personal identity have been affected by Wittgenstein's notion of a criterion. When Locke discusses personal identity it is clear from what I have already said that he is interested in the necessary and sufficient conditions for its being the case that person A and person B at a previous time are the same person. The objections to his account are that

[22] Perry, p. 115.   [23] T. Reid, *Essays on the Intellectual Powers*, 3.4 (Perry, p. 107).
[24] See my *Theory of Knowledge*, pp. 68ff., 222ff.

what he offers is sufficient only because circular and is not necessary at all. If we say that he is concerned with the criteria of personal identity we mean that he is concerned with the necessary and sufficient conditions of being the same person in this way and that he is so concerned because these purported necessary and sufficient conditions follow from something that is a necessary part of the concept of a person. It follows that any claim that the concept of a person is unanalysable is also likely to involve a rejection of the attempt to provide necessary and sufficient conditions for personal identity, at least on that basis, that is on the basis of something about the concept itself. I emphasize the last point, because however we put the question about the conditions of personal identity it is their basis in the concept of a person itself that is the important matter.

Elucidation of a concept need not come via an analysis of it into its constituents. Indeed it is at least arguable that that is never possible because concepts are not isolable entities but abstractions from a web of understanding to which they belong.[25] With respect to any given concept it may be possible to give only the norm for speaking of identity – and that applies to the concept of a person as much as to any other concept. Something might therefore be offered as the criterion of personal identity which is a good deal looser than the necessary and sufficient conditions so far considered. There is also the point which I made at the beginning of the discussion of 'Essentialism' in Chapter 4 about the different forms which questions about identity can take. Some philosophers, in raising questions about personal identity, may be less concerned with the concept of a person than with the conditions of speaking of identity in general. Some of these points will re-emerge as we go on. It may be sufficient to note at present that the meaning of the phrase 'criteria of personal identity' is not something which can be taken for granted. Nevertheless the most important philosophical considerations about the criteria of personal identity are those that do have to do with the concept of a person. If we could provide necessary and sufficient conditions for Xs and so could provide a decision procedure for identifying Xs, that would not have a great deal of philosophical interest if the conditions in question had nothing to do with what it is to be an X; or at least that would be so in the case of an 'X' which is as problematic as 'person' is.

In modern times dissatisfaction with the Lockean account combined perhaps with Wittgensteinian views about the necessity of outward and

<hr>
[25] See my *Theory of Knowledge*, ibid., and p. 272.

observable criteria for psychological processes have led philosophers to emphasize bodily factors as criteria of personal identity. The most extreme view of that kind would be that bodily identity is a necessary and sufficient condition of personal identity. It is hard to find anyone who has argued for just that. Bernard Williams, in the first of his papers on this subject, 'Personal identity and individuation',[26] argued that bodily identity is a necessary condition of personal identity, but not that it is sufficient. He says at the beginning of the paper, 'If I am asked whether the person in front of me is the same person as one uniquely present at place *a* at time *t*, I shall not necessarily be justified in answering 'yes' merely because I am justified in saying that this human body is the same as that present at *a* at *t*. Identity of body is at least not a sufficient condition of personal identity, and other considerations, of personal characteristics and, above all, memory, must be invoked.'

It is not at all clear why Williams thinks that this is so, and he gives no further reasons. One would have thought that normally it *is* the case that *same body* is sufficient for *same person*. To the extent that one is prepared to contemplate the possibility of that not being so, it is likely that one will also be prepared to contemplate the idea of the same body being owned by different persons at different times, as Locke was clearly willing to think; and Williams does not seem to want *that*. The only alternative is to interpret the claim as presupposing a situation in which there is identity of body on two occasions but a person on the first occasion only, so that there is *no* person on the second occasion, as would be the case where the person has died in the interval. In such a case it might even be questioned whether there really is identity of body on the two occasions; but it might be thought too unsympathetic to press that point. In any case, what Williams may have in mind is that the concept of a person does not amount merely to that of a body, but to that plus the other things that he mentions. That, as I suggested earlier, may well be the underlying issue, but it is wrong to state it merely in terms of necessary and/or sufficient conditions.

Hence, while Williams goes on to argue that bodily identity is a necessary condition of personal identity, there is reason for thinking that his real concern is with whether the concept of a person includes that of a body. His subsequent argument is complex, involving, among other things, consideration of the possibility of bodily interchange between persons. His main argument, however, rests on a *reductio ad absurdum* of the thesis that bodily identity is *not* necessary for personal identity; and

---

[26] *Proc. Arist. Soc.* Vol. LVII, 1956/7, pp. 229–52 and *Problems of the Self*.

that depends upon the use of a hypothetical example that has achieved some notoriety. He supposes that a certain person, Charles, wakes up one day with all the memories (or, not to beg the question, all the putative memories) of Guy Fawkes; all his memory claims fit, as far as the evidence goes, the personality and life of Guy Fawkes. Would we say that he had become Guy Fawkes? Williams recognizes the temptation to say just that, but thinks that we are not forced to that conclusion. That conclusion, he suggests, is undermined by the possibility that exactly the same thing might happen also to Charles' brother, Robert. We cannot say that they had both become identical with Guy Fawkes, or we should have to say that they were identical with each other – 'which is absurd' (a suggestion that an unsympathetic critic might think begs the question, since it excludes the possibility that the same person might simultaneously occupy different bodies). Hence, he suggests, since we cannot speak of identity in the reduplicated case we cannot speak of it in the case in which Charles alone is changed. For there is, *ex hypothesi*, no bodily identity.

Williams then goes on to meet an objection to the effect that what clearly applies to the reduplicated case cannot be transferred without further argument to the non-reduplicated one. The argument is tortuous. It depends upon a distinction between identity and exact similarity, a distinction which can evidently be made in the case of physical particulars, where spatio-temporal considerations apply. Williams suggests that we cannot apply the distinction in the case of memories or such things as character. Indeed he casts doubt on the intelligibility of speaking of exactly similar memories (to speak of the same memories would of course imply that we were concerned with the same person, whose memories they were). He does this on the grounds that there is no way of telling whether the memory claims that Charles makes are the same as those made by Guy Fawkes (given that identity of memory *claims* would suggest at least similarity of memories). It might well be objected that this difficulty about verification shows little about the intelligibility or otherwise of speaking of similarity of memories. Indeed Williams surprisingly goes on to allow such a possibility, invoking the idea of 'similarity of one's supposed past'. *But*, he says, the fact that we might say that Charles has the same character and the same supposed past as Guy Fawkes is not to say that they are identical at all, only that they are similar in this respect. A distinction between identity and exact similarity in the case of character and memories has not been made out. So he concludes, 'The only case in which identity and exact similarity could be distinguished, as we have just seen, is that of the body – "same body" and "exactly similar body" really do mark a difference. Thus I should claim that the omission of the body takes away all content from the idea of personal *identity*.'

It is difficult to see how that final conclusion follows at all. What the argument might be taken to show is that we are not *bound* in the Charles case to speak of identity, only at best exact similarity, since all that we have to go on – the memories etc. – can be interpreted only in terms of their exact similarity to those of Fawkes. But Williams needs more than this to show that bodily identity is a necessary condition of personal identity; he needs to show that it is not even *possible* in the Charles case to speak of his identity with Guy Fawkes, and it is hard to see that he has done anything of the kind. (It is only fair to point out that this paper was merely the first of Williams' many writings on personal identity, and in 'The self and the future' which is also included in *Problems of the Self* there are places at which he goes, though uncertainly, in the opposite direction.) Subsequent argument by other philosophers has in any case led to a certain weakening of the accepted position on the relation between bodily and personal identity from the exceptionally tough position maintained by Williams in this paper.

In considering such deviations from the extreme position adopted by Williams the first view to be noted is that of Sydney Shoemaker in his *Self-knowledge and Self-identity*. Shoemaker, following an interpretation of Wittgenstein's notion of a criterion by Albritton, takes a criterion for X to be what provides direct, non-inductive evidence for something's being an X. On this basis he concludes that while bodily identity is *a* criterion for personal identity it is not the only one, and that we sometimes use memory, although only as a secondary criterion – and again only for other persons, since questions of criteria do not arise in relation to oneself. Much weight in the argument is put upon yet another hypothetical case – a science-fiction example, one might say. Shoemaker contemplates a hypothetical future in which brain removal by surgery is possible, enabling surgeons to perform operations on the brain and then to return it to the body. He tells a story of this happening in the case of Brown and Robinson, but where an assistant puts the wrong brains in the wrong bodies. One of the patients then dies (perhaps fortunately for the example) and the other – to be called 'Brownson' – wakes up with all the memories, personality and character of Brown, but with Robinson's body apart from the brain. (It is wise to bear in mind that the apparent personality and character, not to speak of abilities, are likely to be modified by the different body, but we need not dwell on that fact here.)

Shoemaker thinks that in such a case we should be likely to be impressed by the memories of Brown's past life that Brownson manifests, and that this shows that we should take memory as *a* criterion of personal identity. We would do that, however, only in a context in which bodily identity constitutes the norm. Moreover, Shoemaker goes on to argue (in a way too complex to enter upon here) that most memory claims are correct; otherwise it might be suggested that Brownson's memory claims are systematically mistaken. But, of course, the main thing about Shoemaker's example is that while there is not complete bodily identity there is partial bodily identity in the identity of the brain. Hence it might be suggested that we could retain something of the original Williams position but relax it so as to make personal identity dependent on whatever part of the body is responsible for those mental features that go to make up a personality. For this reason David Wiggins suggests in *Identity and Spatio-temporal Continuity* (p. 55) that what we want for personal identity is not bodily identity, nor even for that matter strict identity of some part of the body, but merely the continuance in one organized parcel of whatever is both necessary and sufficient for normal psychological functioning, no part being functionally autonomous (the last clause being inserted to rule out a further contingency that is to be encountered by way of example in the literature – brain dissection or splitting). That organized parcel is of course normally the brain, but that is an empirical point and there is no need to commit oneself to that in setting out a general criterion of personal identity.

In this we are left at least with the claim that if there is to be personal identity there must be spatio-temporal continuity of *something*, and that the criterion of personal identity is provided by the continuity in this way of something fairly specific. It is not in fact clear, however, that spatio-temporal continuity is necessary for identity even in the case of physical objects. In this context appeal is often made, as I mentioned in Chapter 4, to Hobbes' 'ship of Athens', in connexion with which the citizens replaced the wooden parts and built another ship out of the timbers which had been replaced. The question is which of the resulting ships is the original ship – the one that is spatio-temporally continuous with the original ship despite the change of timbers or the one that is made of the original timbers although it has no continuity with the original as a ship. Intuition may tell us that spatio-temporal continuity provides the answer, but it is not absolutely clear that it does. It has been pointed out by Francis Dauer[27] that someone who replaced by stealth all

[27] F. W. Dauer, 'How not to reidentify the Parthenon', *Analysis*, Vol. 33, 1972, pp. 63–4

the stones of a Parthenon with replicas and rebuilt the temple out of the original stones in England could scarcely expect to be declared not-guilty of stealing the temple. A further point against the thesis that spatio-temporal continuity is necessary for identity is that, as was again mentioned in Chapter 4, it is quite possible for certain manufactured articles to be taken to pieces, reassembled into other objects (or even left in pieces), and then be subject to the reverse process. In that case the original object could be said to have a discontinuous existence, and the reassembled object which finally results could be said to be identical to the original despite not existing in the interval (although it has to be admitted that, in *these* cases at least, *something* persists).

The same might be said of human beings on certain versions of the doctrine of the resurrection. Stories of bodily interchange, such as that of the emperor and the peasant which is invoked by Williams in his original paper, imply spatial discontinuity, although not perhaps a temporal one. Robert Herbert[28] offers a particularly telling story of that kind as a reply to Williams (although the story involves what some may find an unbearable sentimentality), in order to indicate that in certain contexts of personal relations a decision of identity may be forced upon one despite everything that spatio-temporal continuity suggests. Perhaps the most conclusive argument in that direction is provided by J. M. Shorter.[29] Once again the argument turns on a fictional example which we are meant to take not only as logically possible but as having implications which are even plausible in certain respects. According to Shorter's story there is a planet Juno in which bodies grow to maturity which are counterparts of bodies of people on Earth. When someone on Earth dies the counterpart body on Juno comes to life, with behaviour, personality, character and memories the same as those of the Earth person. Shorter elaborates the story, complete with philosophical and other doubts on the part of Junonians as to whether their memories are veridical and so on. The question asked is what would happen if communication between Juno and Earth was established. Would it be right for Earth people to treat certain Junonians as relatives who had previously existed on Earth? Shorter argues that it would be right, and emphasizes the point that decisions on personal identity bring with them issues about such things as personal relations, some of which issues may be moral.

[28] R. Herbert, 'Puzzle cases and earthquakes', *Analysis*, Vol. 28, 1968, pp. 78–89.

[29] J. M. Shorter, 'More about bodily continuity and personal identity', *Analysis*, Vol. 22, 1962, pp. 79–85, with something of a sequel in 'Personal identity, personal relationships and criteria', *Proc. Arist. Soc.*, Vol. LXXI, 1970/1, pp. 165–86.

The important point in it all, apart from that, is that in the story there is spatial, if not temporal, discontinuity. (If it were not for the fact that spatial considerations enter the picture Juno might be heaven on some theological conceptions of that!) Hence, if we were to agree that Junonians are the same as their Earth counterparts we should be committed to personal identity with spatial discontinuity, and it would not be difficult to introduce into the story temporal discontinuity as well. Some may think that enough to reject the story.[30] But Shorter insists that it would be wrong to do that, and write off the story as unintelligible, merely on the basis of a general philosophical dogma, and I believe that he is correct in this. There is, of course, no way, *ex hypothesi*, of verifying the claim for identity between Junonians and their Earth counterparts, but one could not, except on the crudest of verificationist principles, take that as ruling out the suggestion that speaking of identity in such cases makes sense.

It might be argued that it makes sense only if the Junonian case is seen against the normal situation in which identity does presuppose spatio-temporal continuity. That seems correct. Things could not always be as they are supposed to be in the Junonian situation, and it is notable that that situation is described generally in terms that presuppose a norm of spatio-temporal continuity. Given what I have said in earlier chapters there seems to be everything to be said for this position. It follows, nevertheless, that spatio-temporal continuity is not a necessary condition of personal identity, although it is the norm against which deviations also can be seen to be intelligible, whether or not such deviations occur. Similar considerations apply to the possibility of disembodied personal existence, although the fact that there are many aspects of persons as we ordinarily understand them which depend essentially on the body, e.g. sense-perception, puts limits upon what we can suppose a disembodied person to be capable of. In the last section of chapter 3 of *Individuals* Strawson allows the possibility of disembodied persons having what is, at all events, a logically secondary existence, but he seems to think that this is conceivable only in connexion with persons who were once embodied. It is difficult to see why that restriction should be imposed once the general possibility of a disembodied existence is admitted, although it might be difficult to think of ways in which intrinsically disembodied persons could be identified in practice. To suppose, however, that that difficulty either limits or removes altogether any

---

[30] See T. Penelhum, *Survival and Disembodied Existence* (London: Routledge and Kegan Paul, 1970) for that verdict in a more theologically orientated context.

possibility of attaching sense to the notion of disembodied persons is simply to embrace verificationism.

It has indeed been claimed by Richard Swinburne[31] that all the theories that I have been discussing (and others too, including that of Parfit which I shall discuss in the next section) are empiricist in seeking for a criterion of personal identity in what can be empirically observed, and are verificationist in consequence. He maintains instead that the concept of a person is simple and unanalysable (a view which is similar in that respect to Reid's). Such a view is, however, implausible with respect to the concept of a *person*, since there surely must be some things which hold good of all and only persons. As has been argued in admirable detail by Geoffrey Madell[32] it is another matter with the concept of the *self* (for with that we return to the 'Kantian point'). He maintains in consequence that what is wrong with much contemporary discussion of these matters is that they concentrate upon the third-person point of view and ignore the first-person point of view. Shoemaker, amongst others, has argued that there is no such thing as a criterion of identity for oneself. The only context in which the question 'Am I the same person as . . . ?' arises is that in which one treats oneself as a third person, as one may do, for example, when looking at old photographs, asking 'Is that me?' That may be so but it does not obviate the necessity of providing an account of the 'I' and of attending to the 'Kantian point' in discussing issues in this area. For, if persons are nothing else, they are beings who can and do have a first-person point of view.

In recent times there has been much discussion in the literature about what would be the case if persons were to split or fuse.[33] The main problems to which such ideas give rise have to do with how, if at all, one would survive in such circumstances; they are less concerned with identity. For, as Parfit points out, identity is a one-one relation and cannot have application where one thing becomes many, or many things become one. It might nevertheless seem important to show that splitting or fusion cannot really happen in respect of persons, and this seems to be one reason, among others, why David Wiggins has wanted to emphasize the connexion between the concept of a person and that of the natural

[31] R. Swinburne, 'Personal Identity', *Proc. Arist. Soc.*, Vol. LXXIV, 1973/4, pp. 231–47.
[32] G. Madell, *The Identity of the Self*.
[33] The issue about splitting was, as we shall see in the next section, raised by Derek Parfit, although the question 'What if we split like an amoeba?' is probably originally due to Antony Flew. It has been taken up by David Lewis and others. D. Parfit, 'Personal identity', *Philosophical Review*, Vol. LXXX, 1971, pp. 3–27 (and in Perry); A. G. N. Flew, 'Locke and the problem of personal identity', *Philosophy*, Vol. XXVI, 1951, pp. 53–68. For David Lewis *et al.* see the first few papers in Amelie Rorty (ed.), *The Identities of Persons*.

kind *man*. For, whatever is the case with amoebae, men do not, and could not as members of the natural kind *man*, split. (Another reason behind his view has to do with his wish to resist the thought that persons could be social constructions – that something is a person to the extent that others so regard it. That is a view which he sees, wrongly in my opinion, in what Shorter has to say.)

In the light of this, Wiggins asks in the last chapter of his *Sameness and Substance* whether a man who had lost all memory (and had perhaps undergone a complete change of personality) after some appalling physical or mental shock, so that there is apparently discontinuity between his present and past selves, is the same person and/or animal as he was. He answers that the common-sense answer, that he is both the same person and the same animal, is right; and he uses this conclusion in order to put weight upon the notion of *animal* in connexion with persons and their identity. I agree with the common-sense answer but with something of a sense of unreality. There are, after all, changes in human beings such that we certainly feel like saying 'That's not the same person'. The man in Wiggins' example might not recognize himself in descriptions of his past. If we insist that it was him all the same, we insist on a formal point akin to the 'Kantian point'. So we should, but does that make it necessary to conclude that *person* goes with *man* and *animal*? There is a sense, after all, in which the original person has not survived. Such is the indeterminateness of the concept of a person, and it reflects what I had in mind in suggesting that the term 'person' is something of a term of art.

Survival

I said in connexion with the Wiggins example that there is a sense in which the original person has not survived. It remains perfectly correct, of course, to say that *he* has survived, and it is reasonable to believe that he would think so too, whatever he might take the content of that suggestion to be. What would he have said if he had known that these changes were to take place? Once again, it would not be unreasonable to suppose that he would think he would survive the changes, however extreme these were. What if he were told (authoritatively, whatever that might mean) that he would cease to exist and be replaced by someone just like him with all the same 'memories', personality, etc? Some philosophers seem to think that there would be no difference as far as he was concerned from what happens in the ordinary way when we go to sleep, for example; there would be no difference between the ordinary case of my waking up and the waking up of someone just like me.

Schopenhauer said that sleep is a constant preparation for death. Is there no difference between, on the one hand, sleeping and waking up and, on the other, dying each night with the creation of someone exactly similar to wake in the morning? Some might say that there is all the difference in the world, because in the one case there is identity and in the other only exact similarity. That difference ought to affect one's view of the future if one *knew* that one or the other was going to obtain in one's own case (though how could one *know*?).

In the paper already referred to, Parfit suggests agreement with this view as far as identity is concerned (although he does not raise the question in quite this form). But on the questions whether one would survive if one were replaced by someone exactly similar and whether one should think that one would survive he gives a different answer (and even suggests at the end of the paper that such considerations might have a bearing on fear of distant death). He thus differentiates between questions about identity and questions about survival – although he sometimes seems to suggest that there might not be much *practical* difference. He is led to this differentiation by a consideration of two sorts of case, of which the first, perhaps, receives greater weight of argument. This is the case of splitting which I mentioned earlier. Since identity is a one-one relation there can be no question of identity if persons can be conceived as splitting like an amoeba.[34] There might nevertheless be questions about survival in these circumstances, and he sees the criteria of survival in the notion of psychological connectedness between mental states provided that this has some basis. The further one gets away from the original person as far as concerns the connectedness of mental states, such as memories, the less one would want to say that the original person had survived. So he says that 'what matters in the continued existence of a person are, for the most part, relations of degree'.[35] (There is an obvious similarity between this view and that of Hume, except that Hume takes the issues to be about identity or beliefs in it, and except that Parfit thinks that mental connectedness must have some basis, normally in the body.)

The second sort of case follows on from this. If degree of survival goes with degree of mental connectedness, then where it seems likely that there will be little mental connectedness, little, for example, in the way of memory of one's past, there is likely to be a low degree of survival. Hence one might say in a case like that of Methuselah that at the end of the very long life the young Methuselah will not have survived.

[34] Although David Lewis, in *The Identities of Persons*, suggests ways in which identity can be reintroduced more indirectly.   [35] Perry, p. 219.

The trouble is that ordinarily one would not say anything of the kind; so that there seems to be a certain degree of conceptual legislation in what Parfit has to say. Wiggins has provided some splendid comment on the whole issue.[36] He considers what someone would think if he were told that tomorrow there would certainly be nobody who was him, but that there would exist someone related to him by Parfit's relation of mental connectedness; and he suggests that whether people would accept that 'offer' is irrelevant to the issues. He points out that the desire to leave traces ('to be remembered by one's pupils or to live on in one's works') can be typical accommodations to the certainty of death. And he adds, 'To me at least it is not clear how much more there would be to the possession of mentally connected descendants than there is in these more etiolated forms of survival. Indeed I think that I myself prefer the more etiolated forms. What I am certain about is that I do not see how the offer of all these things, Parfitian *or* etiolated, can be taken for a proper surrogate (equivalent at the level of imagination, conception and desire) for the continued existence of the one and only person who is me. Unless, of course, I no longer want that continued existence – in which case the etiolated forms of survival are again not equal or tantamount, but simply better.'

I very much agree with those sentiments, although with two qualifications. The first is that the issue is put in terms of what one might desire or take as satisfactory. Feelings about such matters and concern for forms of strictly personal survival vary over cultures. (Consider, for example, such different things as Diotima's reported speech in Plato's *Symposium*, far-eastern feelings about the family and the race, and the Christian belief in a very personal survival after death.) What is undeniable is that my survival, the survival of *me*, is different from the survival of traces of me, whatever form these may take. Secondly, the phrase 'continued existence of the one and only person who is me' seems to me to beg the question in invoking the concept of a person as it does. I might survive as the totally changed person that I discussed in connexion with Wiggins in the previous section. I might not want that if the possibility were offered to me, although I have no doubt that *some* people would opt for survival in any form rather than no survival at all. If that is true, what is it that they want to survive? The only possible answer is 'Them', and it is in one sense a purely formal answer; but it is not the answer given by Wiggins when he invokes the concept of a person.

[36] D. Wiggins, 'The concern to survive', *Midwest Studies in Philosophy*, Vol. 4, 1979, pp. 417–22.

It is in fact the answer implied by the 'Kantian point', which remains crucial throughout these discussions. Questions about the identity of the self, as distinct from questions about the identity of myself or yourself, admit only of a formal answer. The continued existence of a self is the continued existence of whatever has, or owns, a stream of consciousness and, usually but not of logical necessity, a body subject to the changes that bodies normally undergo. When it ceases to exist there may remain a body which is not then 'owned' by anything, and there is no consciousness belonging to whatever had it before. There is, however, no way of breaking down that 'I', that owner of consciousness and body, into the characteristics of what it owns, in such a way as to make it analysable in such terms. To that extent the notion of a self is unanalysable in a way that the notion of a person is not.

'I'

In his *Notebooks* Wittgenstein spoke of two 'god-heads' – I and the world.[37] The thought is in some ways Schopenhauerian and it is a plausible suggestion that Wittgenstein got the idea from Schopenhauer, who owed it, with modifications, to Kant. From the point of view of Kant's transcendental idealism there is the 'I' and the representations that exist for it. There are, of course, things-in-themselves, but as far as concerns the understanding, as is worked out in the so-called 'transcendental deduction', there exist only representations which are united in the unity of consciousness so as to be necessarily mine, necessarily belonging to a subject. This 'Kantian point' remains valid as far as consciousness is concerned. Whereas from a third-person point of view the subject which owns states of consciousness is normally identifiable via the body which that subject also normally has, one's understanding of the same state of affairs from a first-person point of view *presupposes* that subject as the 'I'. There is no question of its identification in the way that there is for others. Wittgenstein puts the point in the *Tractatus* by saying that the 'I' is in a sense outside the world.

These are ways, perhaps groping ways, of putting the claim that reality is such that there is a point of view of it which cannot be expressed in third-person terms. Or, to put the matter in another way, just as that aspect of reality which we call temporal is such that tense is essential to its description and tense is essentially token-reflexive, so something analogous holds for that aspect of reality which involves the self. One would not have given a complete account of all aspects of reality without bringing in what it is for reality to be such for a self. The

---

[37] L. Wittgenstein, *Notebooks, 1914–1916* (Oxford: Blackwell, 1961), 8.7.16, p. 74.

uneliminability of being-for-self parallels the uneliminability of tense. There are indeed good reasons for thinking that these aspects of temporality and being-for-self are connected, as I suggested in Chapter 7.

One way of putting a feature of the thought of the later Wittgenstein is to say that there is a sense in which the 'I' is secondary to the 'we', because the viability of language and what can be expressed in language is dependent upon what Wittgenstein called 'agreement in judgments'. Whatever that means (and it is to some extent a matter of dispute) it suggests that the intelligibility of putting to others what is to be said in first-person terms is dependent on our having certain forms of agreement with others – agreement which Wittgenstein called 'agreement in forms of life'. Nevertheless, even if all that is granted it does not make the first-person point of view any the less a reality, and a complete account of reality must bring in that fact.

Schopenhauer added to that, essentially Kantian, point that the knowing subject, as he called it, must be seen as an agent too. And he saw in that a key to the nature of a further reality which lies behind and beyond representations – to the nature of the thing-in-itself. This is not the place for an examination of that argument, which in any case presupposes an idealist point of view, which, as we saw in Chapter 2, there is no reason to accept.[38] One thing that Schopenhauer does make clear, however, is that any account of the 'I' must involve reference to agency also, particularly agency as it manifests itself in bodily action. The 'I' is not just a spectator in relation to the world; the two 'god-heads' are not related in that way only. The two are *inter*related, so that the world not only affects the subject as it does in sensation and perception, it is also affected by the subject via the agency of the latter and the part that the subject's body plays in it.[39]

Once again it must be said that the fact that the 'I' acts upon the world does not make that world a construction on the part of the 'I'. We are not forced back into a form of idealism by such considerations. It remains true that there are aspects of reality that can be expressed only in personal terms (if that is the right way to put it) and some of those aspects would not hold good were not the 'I' an agent too. Schopenhauer saw this consideration as a key to the insight that ultimate reality consisted in a form of agency itself – the Will. That is not a conclusion to which we are forced either. It nevertheless remains true that something which we might call 'will' is not something that can be left out of any final account of reality in its generality.

---

[38] For the argument see my *Schopenhauer* (London: Routledge and Kegan Paul, 1980), ch. 5.
[39] For a lengthy elaboration of such points see B. O'Shaughnessy, *The Will* (Cambridge: C.U.P., 1980).

The remarks in this section have been to some extent gnomic. The crucial facts are that aspects of the 'I' as subject of experience and agent, and aspects of the ways in which different 'I's form a 'we', so establishing a condition of the intelligibility of expressions of facts about the 'I', together affect what a full account of reality must comprise. Setting out those Kantian, Schopenhauerian and Wittgensteinian insights is a very difficult enterprise, and I make no claim to have carried it out. My remarks are advisedly gnomic. They merely set out the parameters for a complete and successful metaphysics of the kind that this book has been concerned with.

10. Epilogue : Man and nature

The interrelationship between 'I', 'we' and the world that I mentioned at the end of the last chapter, and the kind of metaphysics, construed as a general account of reality, that it gives rise to are not quite the same as the interrelationship between man and nature and the account of things which that consideration gives rise to. To move from self to man and from reality or world to nature is to move to a more concrete and less general level. It follows that the philosophical considerations that such a move results in are different from the ones that arise from the conception of metaphysics that I have been presenting (however consistent I have been in that). The philosophical considerations that I have in mind in so speaking arise mainly from the general question whether and to what extent man is part of nature, and whether nature by itself is self-sufficient in the sense of requiring no rationale outside it.

Kant's account of the metaphysics of his time, specified in terms of subject-matter – its concern with God, freedom and immortality – fits this conception of a philosophical concern with man and nature better than it does metaphysics as I have presented it. Does nature need a rationale in something outside it – in a 'first cause', a God construed in theistic terms as the *ens realissimum* and ultimate explanation of everything else: what Anthony Kenny has called, in the title of one of his books, 'the God of the philosophers'? (So called because, while the being in question is sanctified by being given the name of 'God', its role in the accounts offered is less that of an object of worship than an ultimate explanation or rationale invoked because it is supposed that some such thing is necessary.) Is man necessarily part of nature so that he begins, lives and dies according to natural principles alone, or is there room for an existence, a human existence, outside nature as we ordinarily understand it? Is nature governed throughout by causal principles and is man part of that? If nature in general is subject to determinist principles does that apply to man too? What implications has that, either way, for belief in human free-will?

I have touched on some of these issues, but no more, in what I have had to say, for example on God in Chapter 3 when dealing with Aristotle's view of what primarily exists, on immortality in what I have had to say about the possibility of disembodied existence in Chapter 9, and on materialism in Chapter 8. I have said nothing about free-will and determinism, except in my brief remarks about the importance of agency. As far as determinism is concerned this is in large part due to the fact that I have said little or nothing about causality either. These are all genuine philosophical topics, but I believe that they are best treated under other headings – God and immortality under philosophy of religion, determinism under philosophy of science and methodology, free-will under ethics and philosophy of mind. It might even be argued that it is possible to distinguish a single philosophical subject under which they all fall – philosophy of man (perhaps, though, as a sub-branch of the philosophy of nature, but we need not worry about such complications).

Philosophy of man is not, however, metaphysics as I have construed it, even if some of the issues which I have mentioned as possibly belonging to it can often be found in books on metaphysics. If I am right in what I have said about the relationship between man and nature being more concrete and less general than that between the self or 'I' and reality, it furnishes a justification for not including the philosophy of man under metaphysics. It would, however, be profitless to enter into demarcation disputes in philosophy, and it would be hard and futile to insist upon the exclusion from metaphysics of those topics that I have put under the philosophy of man. What I have said may explain why I have nevertheless not included them. In any case, as I said in Chapter 1, Kant's categorization of the metaphysics of his time as concerned with God, freedom and immortality is, historically, rather idiosyncratic, since those whom he sees as metaphysicians did not have these matters as a central concern.

This sort of historical judgment and the rationale that I have given for separating the issues which seem to me to fall under the philosophy of man from those that fall under metaphysics as I have construed it may or may not be convincing. Things are in any case rarely very tidy in philosophy, and even a casual survey of what philosophers have thought metaphysics to consist in would reveal that there is much else that *might* be considered under that name. I remain nevertheless of the opinion that the issues which I have collected together in this book do constitute a rational whole. If there are other subjects that merit inclusion they are objects for other selves at other places and times.

Bibliography

The following list of books consists in the main of suggestions for further reading as well as works referred to. Other references will be found in the Notes.

Introductory books

W. H. Walsh, *Metaphysics* (London: Hutchinson, 1963)
G. N. Schlesinger, *Metaphysics* (Oxford: Blackwell, 1983)
L. Stevenson, *The Metaphysics of Experience* (Oxford: Clarendon Press, 1982)

Other books which raise metaphysical issues are:
B. Russell, *Problems of Philosophy* (Oxford: O.U.P., 1912)
A. J. Ayer, *The Central Questions of Philosophy* (Harmondsworth: Penguin, 1976)

For connected epistemological issues see:
D. W. Hamlyn, *The Theory of Knowledge* (London and Basingstoke: Macmillan, 1971)

Chapters 1 and 2

P. F. Strawson, *Individuals* (London: Methuen, l959), Introduction

For historical texts see:
Plato, *Republic*, *Sophist*
Aristotle, *Categories*, *Metaphysics*
R. Descartes, *Meditations*
B. Spinoza, *Ethics*
G. Leibniz, *Discourse on Metaphysics*, *Monadology*
J. Locke, *Essay Concerning Human Understanding*
G. Berkeley, *Three Dialogues between Hylas and Philonous, Principles of Human Knowledge*
D. Hume, *A Treatise of Human Nature*
I. Kant, *Critique of Pure Reason* (trans. N. Kemp Smith, London: Macmillan, 1929)
A. Schopenhauer, *The World as Will and Representation* (trans. E. F. J. Payne, New York: Dover, 1969)

G. Hegel, *The Phenomenology of Spirit* (trans. A. V. Miller, Oxford: Clarendon Press, 1967)

F. H. Bradley, *Appearance and Reality* (London: Sonnenschein, 1893)

For recent writings on realism and anti-realism see:

H. Putnam, *Reason, Truth and History* (Cambridge: C.U.P., 1981)

M. Dummett, *Truth and Other Enigmas* (London: Duckworth, 1978)

Chapter 3

Aristotle, *Categories, Metaphysics*, esp. Books 7–9

I. Kant, *Critique of Pure Reason* (trans. N. Kemp Smith, London: Macmillan, 1929)

F. H. Bradley, *Principles of Logic* (Oxford: O.U.P., 1883, 1922)

G. Frege, *Translations* (trans. P. Geach and M. Black, Oxford: Blackwell, 1952), esp. 'Concept and object'

B. Russell, 'The philosophy of logical atomism' in R. C. Marsh (ed.), *Logic and Knowledge* (London: Allen and Unwin, 1956)

A. N. Whitehead, *Process and Reality*, Corrected edition, edited by D. R. Griffin and D. W. Sherburne (New York: Free Press, 1978)

Science and the Modern World (New York: Macmillan Co., 1926)

L. Wittgenstein, *Tractatus Logico-Philosophicus* (London: Routledge and Kegan Paul, 1922), new translation by D. Pears and B. McGuinness (London: Routledge and Kegan Paul, 1961)

Philosophical Investigations (Oxford: Blackwell, 1953)

On Certainty (Oxford: Blackwell, 1969)

P. F. Strawson, *Individuals* (London: Methuen, 1959)

The Bounds of Sense (London: Methuen, 1968)

'Entity and identity' in H. D. Lewis (ed.), *Contemporary British Philosophy*, 4th Series (London: Allen and Unwin, 1976)

M. Dummett, *Frege* (London: Duckworth, 1973)

W. V. Quine, *From a Logical Point of View* (Cambridge, Mass: Harvard U.P., 1953)

Ontological Relativity (New York and London: Columbia U.P., 1962)

D. Davidson, *Essays on Actions and Events* (Oxford: Clarendon Press, 1980)

Chapter 4

Aristotle, *Categories, Metaphysics* 7–9

D. Hume, *A Treatise of Human Nature* (esp. I.iv.5)

G. Leibniz, *Discourse on Metaphysics, Nouveaux Essais*, esp. 23.2)

I. Kant, *Critique of Pure Reason* (trans. N. Kemp Smith, London: Macmillan, 1929)

P. F. Strawson, *Individuals* (London: Methuen, 1959)

A. J. Ayer, *Philosophical Essays* (London: Macmillan, 1954)

M. Black, *Problems of Analysis* (London: Routledge and Kegan Paul, 1954)
D. Wiggins, *Sameness and Substance* (Oxford: Blackwell, 1980)
R. Swinburne, *Space and Time*, 1st edition (London: Macmillan, 1968), ch. 1
A. M. Quinton, *The Nature of Things* (London: Routledge and Kegan Paul, 1973)
S. Kripke, *Naming and Necessity* (Oxford: Blackwell, 1980)
H. Putnam, *Mind, Language and Reality: Philosophical Papers, Vol. 2* (Cambridge; C.U.P., 1975)
J. Bennett, *Locke, Berkeley, Hume: Central Themes* (Oxford: Clarendon Press, 1971), ch. 4

Chapter 5

P. F. Strawson, *Individuals* (London: Methuen, 1959), pt 2
J. Searle, *Speech Acts* (Cambridge: C.U.P., 1970), esp. *c*. p. 120
M. Dummett, *Frege* (London: Duckworth, 1973), chs. 8 and 14
D. M. Armstrong, *Universals and Scientific Realism*, 2 vols. (Cambridge: C.U.P., 1978)
H. H. Price, *Thinking and Experience* (London: Hutchinson, 1953)
D. Pears, 'Universals' in A. G. N. Flew (ed.), *Logic and Language*, Vol. 2 (Oxford: Blackwell, 1953)
M. Loux, *Substance and Attribute* (Dordrecht: Reidel, 1978)

Chapter 6

G. Leibniz, *Monadology*
B. Spinoza, *Ethics*
F. H. Bradley, *Principles of Logic* (Oxford: O.U.P., 1883, 1922)
   Essays on Truth and Reality (Oxford: O.U.P., 1914)
   Appearance and Reality (London: Sonnenschein, 1893)
   Collected Essays (Oxford: O.U.P., 1935)
R. A. Wollheim, *Bradley* (Harmondsworth: Penguin, 1959)
A. R. Manser, *Bradley's Logic* (Oxford: Blackwell, 1983)
B Russell: *Problems of Philosophy* (Oxford: O.U.P., 1912)
   'The philosophy of logical atomism' in R. C. Marsh (ed.), *Logic and Knowledge* (London: Allen and Unwin, 1956)
L. Wittgenstein: *Tractatus Logico-Philosophicus* (London: Routledge and Kegan Paul, 1922), new translation by D. Pears and B. McGuinness (London: Routledge and Kegan Paul, 1961)

Chapter 7

J. J. C. Smart (ed.), *Problems of Space and Time* (New York and London: Collier-Macmillan, 1964)
R. M. Gale (ed.), *The Philosophy of Time* (Hassocks: Harvester, 1978)

I. Kant, *Critique of Pure Reason* (trans. N. Kemp Smith, London: Macmillan, 1929), the 'Transcendental Aesthetic'

H. Bergson, *Time and Free-will* (London: Allen and Unwin, 1911)

E. Husserl, *The Phenomenology of Internal Time-Consciousness* (trans. J. S. Churchill, Bloomington: Indiana U.P., 1964)

M. Heidegger, *Being and Time* (trans. J. Macquarrie and E. Robinson, New York: Harper and Row, 1962)

A. J. Ayer, 'Statements about the past' in his *Philosophical Essays* (London: Macmillan, 1954)

A. M. Quinton, *The Nature of Things* (London: Routledge and Kegan Paul, 1973) ch. 3

M. Merleau-Ponty, *The Phenomenology of Perception*, trans. C. Smith (London: Routledge and Kegan Paul, 1962), pt 3, ch. 2

J. M. E. McTaggart, *The Nature of Existence* (Cambridge: C.U.P., 1927), ch. 33

M. Dummett, *Truth and Other Enigmas* (London: Duckworth, 1978)

H. Mellor, *Real Time* (Cambridge: C.U.P., 1981)

G. Schlesinger, *Aspects of Time* (Indianapolis: Hackett, 1980)

R. M. Gale, *The Language of Time* (London: Routledge and Kegan Paul, 1968)

Chapter 8

R. Descartes, *Meditations, The Passions of the Soul*

B. A. O. Williams, *Descartes: The Project of Pure Enquiry* (Harmondsworth: Penguin, 1978)

G. Ryle, *The Concept of Mind* (London: Hutchinson, 1949)

J. J. C. Smart, *Philosophy and Scientific Realism* (London: Routledge and Kegan Paul, 1963)

D. M. Armstrong, *A Materialist Theory of the Mind* (London: Routledge and Kegan Paul, 1968)

Kathleen Wilkes, *Physicalism* (London: Routledge and Kegan Paul, 1978)

R. Rorty, *Philosophy and the Mirror of Nature* (Oxford: Blackwell, 1980)

R. Chisholm, *Perceiving* (Ithaca: Cornell U.P., 1957)

H. Putnam, *Reason, Truth and History* (Cambridge: C.U.P., 1981)
    Mind, Language and Reality: Philosophical Papers, Vol. 2 (Cambridge: C.U.P., 1975)

D. Davidson, *Essays on Actions and Events* (Oxford: Clarendon Press, 1980)

C. McGinn, *The Character of Mind* (Oxford: Clarendon Press, 1982)

N. Block (ed.), *Readings in the Philosophy of Psychology*, Vol. 1 (Cambridge, Mass: Harvard U.P., 1980)

S. Kripke, *Naming and Necessity* (Oxford: Blackwell, 1980)

Chapter 9

J. Locke, *Essay Concerning Human Understanding* II. 27

D. Hume, *A Treatise of Human Nature*, I.iv.6

T. Reid, *Essays on the Intellectual Powers* 3

J. Perry (ed.), *Personal Identity* (Berkeley and Los Angeles: University of California Press, 1975)

Amelie Rorty (ed.), *The Identities of Persons* (Berkeley and Los Angeles: University of California Press, 1976)

P. F. Strawson, *Individuals* (London: Methuen, 1959), ch. 3

D. Locke, *Myself and Others* (Oxford: Clarendon Press, 1968)

A. J. Ayer, *The Concept of a Person* (London: Macmillan, 1963)

B. A. O. Williams, *Problems of the Self* (Cambridge: C.U.P., 1973

S. Shoemaker, *Self-knowledge and Self-identity* (Ithaca: Cornell U.P., 1963)

D. Wiggins, *Identity and Spatio-temporal Continuity* (Oxford: Blackwell, 1967)

  Sameness and Substance (Oxford: Blackwell, 1980)

T. Penelhum, *Survival and Disembodied Existence* (London: Routledge and Kegan Paul, 1970)

G. Madell, *The Identity of the Self* (Edinburgh: Edinburgh U.P., 1981)

B. O'Shaughnessy, *The Will* (Cambridge: C.U.P., 1980)

T. Nagel, *Mortal Questions* (Cambridge C.U.P., 1979)

C. McGinn, *The Subjective View* (Oxford: Clarendon Press, 1983)

Index

WITHDRAWN
FROM
COLLECTION

FORDHAM
UNIVERSITY
LIBRARIES